KU-211-199

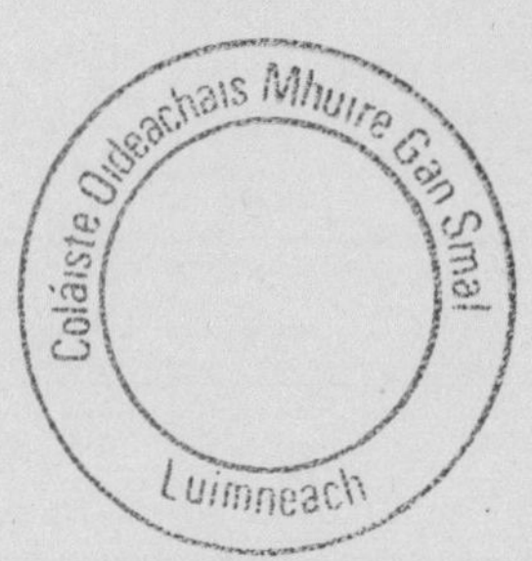
Coláiste Oideachais Mhuire Gan Smal
Luimneach

The School and Moral Development

THE SCHOOL AND MORAL DEVELOPMENT

Barry Sugarman

CROOM HELM LONDON

FIRST PUBLISHED 1973

CROOM HELM LTD
2–10 ST JOHNS ROAD SW11

HARDBACK ISBN 0 85664-061-1
PAPERBACK ISBN 0 85664-048-4

PRINTED IN GREAT BRITAIN
BY EBENEZER BAYLIS & SON LTD
THE TRINITY PRESS, WORCESTER, AND LONDON
BOUND BY G. & J. KITCAT LTD, LONDON

Contents

FOR MY MOTHER

Preface

At any gathering of educators or parents one of the top priority topics of discussion is moral education, usually in the form of specific issues, such as the place of religion in school, boarding vs. day schools, team sports, competitiveness, prefect systems and school councils, school assembly, formality or informality in teacher-pupil relationships, and so forth. What generates the lively interest in these discussions is people's concern to understand how their children (or other people's) are affected by the different ways of running a school and the different aspects of the school experience. Specifically their interest is in how these children will be affected in their outlook and personality—how the school may affect the kind of person they become.

This is an issue of monumental importance and yet the social sciences can at present contribute pitifully little to these discussions, for very few researchers have oriented their work towards such issues. Among psychologists research has very recently begun into altruistic behaviour and into moral judgement; forty years ago there was a major study into honesty and dishonesty in school; there are twenty years or so of serious research into child-rearing practices and their consequences and perhaps forty years of work in general child development. Among sociologists the study of the school as a social organisation has come into existence only in the last few years.

This is the closest one gets to the big issues of moral education and it is not very close, for the question being asked requires a knowledge, firstly, of how schools operate and how they can vary in the ways they operate and, secondly, how these differences affect specific aspects of child development. This book is the first systematic attempt to answer these profoundly important questions, or perhaps we should say rather that it is a survey of what we know that is relevant to answering them, while also taking some bold leaps into the unknown to suggest hypotheses that can be tested some day.

Work on this book began some six years ago at the Farmington Trust Research Unit in Moral Education. It has since been completely revised for publication, thanks to the generosity of my present employer, Jim Germano, Executive Director of Marathon House, Inc., in allowing me to spend this time on the revision.

The Farmington Trust was formed in 1965 with funds provided by the Hon. E. R. H. Wills to advance the cause of moral education. This it chose to do initially by sponsoring the Research Unit in Moral Education, located in Oxford. During the five years or a little more of its existence, the Research Unit produced: *Introduction to Moral Education*, Penguin, 1967, by John Wilson, Norman Williams and Barry Sugarman, two volumes of the journal *Moral Education*, some research reports by Williams and Sugarman and other books by Wilson.

I am no longer connected with the Farmington Trust and they are in no way responsible for the views expressed here. It is my understanding that the Trust is no longer active in the field of research. However, it is my duty and pleasure to make it clear that they supported me and my work during the preparation and writing of this book. I hope it may encourage others to work in this important field and I hope that they will find sponsors no less generous than mine.

PROVIDENCE, RHODE ISLAND, USA

Chapter One

THE SCHOOL AND SOCIETY

SOME SOCIAL FUNCTIONS OF THE SCHOOL

In all the economically developed societies today it is taken for granted that children from the age of five or thereabouts will spend a large part of their waking day away from their families at a place called "school", where they are in the charge of employees called "teachers". At least ten years of each child's life will be spent in this way and the tendency is to extend the period. In less developed societies most children spend these years either working alongside their parents in a junior capacity or apprenticed to an employer. In either of these cases the child is in a situation quite different from that of school. The schoolchild is economically unproductive and earns no money while attending school. He is under many restrictions on his movements and activities, but unlike the working child, these derive from the apparently arbitrary dictates of adults rather than the obvious requirements of work. Whereas the working child works alongside a handful of other siblings or fellow apprentices (roughly, but not exactly, matched in age), the schoolchild finds himself in the company of at least thirty peers, closely matched in age, and one teacher. (In earlier times, this ratio was often far higher.) This fact is in large measure responsible for the extensive rules and restrictions of the school, which in turn play an important part in the over-all effect which the school has on its pupils (Jackson, 1968).

A "school" can be defined as an organisation specialised in providing "education", which can, in turn, be defined in many ways. A school need not necessarily operate by the teachers and pupils meeting together at the same time and place, but this is overwhelmingly the most popular mode of operation—although we may note the existence of a minority of schools which operate through correspondence, radio and television. Our analysis here will concentrate on the school where pupils and teachers meet face-to-face. In most cases, this meeting results from the initiative of the teachers and administrators who create the schools and then solicit customers (if they are private schools), demand attendance by statutory powers (if they are State schools serving those below the age of compulsory attendance) or invite applications (if they are in great demand).

Schools perform a variety of useful functions for the society in which they operate; some, but not all, of these are also useful to the pupil individually. Three functions are valuable from both perspectives: (1) developing the cognitive faculties of the pupils; (2) cultivating socially-approved attitudes and modes of behaviour; and (3) training for particular *vocational* roles. Other functions are important from a societal perspective but not from a pupil's: the main function of this kind served by the school is (4) that of testing and sorting the children into different types (bright and dull, trustworthy and troublesome, etc.) so that they can be "labelled" and treated differently in later life because they will be defined as *prima facie* suitable or not for different social positions.

There is much for children to learn before they can become acceptable full adult members of their society and in economically advanced societies the school plays a significant part in arranging for this learning to take place. Where there is a significantly large immigrant population in a society, this assimilation process is especially clear—for both children and parents. At the same time as they learn the language of their new country, children and parents of the immigrant group are learning the customs and way of life of their adopted society both through explicit teaching and imitation. Their teachers and models are both those who are formally employed as "teachers" and their native-born peers, from whom they learn in the course of normal social interaction in school, at work and at play (see Clark, 1962; Shipman, 1968).

In the following chapter we shall be looking at the different areas of learning which are involved here and at the processes through which they are acquired. For now, however, we shall confine ourselves to comments on three important areas of social learning: impulse control, playing "secondary roles" and acquaintance with the dominant culture.

Impulse Control

Impulse control, also known as the deferred gratification pattern and "future orientation", could be said to be one of the most fundamental elements in the evolution of Western civilisation. The gradual increase in the level of man's rational control over the environment has involved ever-increasing levels of impulse control and planning for the future. Settled agriculture clearly requires much greater patience and planning within a longer time perspective than does the more primitive hunting and gathering culture. Even in the latter, though, the hunters and gatherers who would save some of their food for future needs would be more likely to survive through lean periods than their more greedy and impulsive peers. Not only in economic affairs, but also in interpersonal relationships generally the expression of conflict and hostility has tended to move away from expression in feuding and fighting towards institutionalised methods of resolution (through civil law courts for example) as well as being reduced on account of the increasing tendency of people to restrain impulsive behaviour in response to evolving social norms which proscribe such conduct with increasing strictness.

Impulse control and deferred gratification is highly institutionalised in the school, which therefore plays an important part in further developing these patterns of control in the child on top of the beginning which their families may have made. In school, the pupil is usually required to spend most of his time sitting in one assigned seat, most of the time not allowed to talk or freely interact with his peers, required to wait his turn before joining in a discussion in the lesson, and so on. Intrinsically attractive activities are supposed to be put aside in favour of others whose purpose is hard for the pupil to see, but which are demanded by teachers. The pupil is asked to believe that this will benefit him later and that he will be glad that he did as his teachers demanded. Deferred gratification in the school also involves giving up some leisure time in order to do homework and restraining impulses to attack with words or fists those who anger one in school. Physical aggression is an especially taboo form of impulsiveness in the school. Rudeness or impoliteness comes second, for it, too, is a form of aggression and surrender to impulse.

Readers who are familiar with the most progressive infant and junior schools may well feel that this generalised description does not apply to these schools and, hence, that our point about the central role of gratification deferral is invalidated for such schools. Clearly, it is not so oppressively evident in these schools. But, even so, I believe that the learning of impulse control is still important in these schools—albeit in more subtle ways. True, the activities provided for children to learn from are more intrinsically enjoyable than in the traditional schools. So the distinction between "work" and "play" is less sharply drawn in the minds of pupils and hence less pressure is needed to keep them "working". Still, there remains a need for impulse control and for teachers to insist on it at certain times when it is not spontaneously forthcoming: for example, when two children want to use the same equipment at the same time and one must wait. These kinds of situations, where teachers try to help pupils to learn impulse control and deferral of gratification, exist in both traditional and progressive schools, though in traditional schools there are also more obvious pressures.

Another difference between traditional and progressive schools lies in the extent to which teachers attempt to explain the reasons for the demands placed upon pupils in school. In the more progressive schools, pupils have more opportunity to see that the demands for impulse control are reasonable, in the sense that there is a reason for them—for example, that they should not all talk out at once because no one can hear anything when that happens, that they should not run in the corridor because they might knock over smaller children. These explanations may make the demands easier to accept, but even here there is no getting away from the fact that children in school are learning in various different ways to control their impulses and defer gratification to a greater extent than they did before coming to school.

Prudence is a central feature of the impulse control pattern, applying not only to behaviour in face-to-face relationships where tact is supposed to prevail over the impulse to be rude to those who offend one, but also in making decisions about the allocation of one's resources. Prudence implies thinking of tomorrow and the day after as well as today; it also implies a preference for options which promise moderate gains with low risks of failure over those that carry a small chance of large gains accompanied by the high risk of complete failure. The kind of personality favoured here is the unheroic, reasonable person who is prepared to compromise with an opponent in most cases.

Impulse control also covers the ability to act at a later and more propitious time—when one's initial interest and motivation has cooled off. This other side of impulse control, therefore, involves rekindling motivation to do things which could not profitably be undertaken at the time, when the time is more suitable. The tendency to behave in this way has important bearing on a person's success in several areas of life, not only in the occupational sphere, but also in all areas of his personal relationships where his non-impulsiveness makes it easier to iron out interpersonal conflicts more smoothly and in a reasonable and even-tempered way.

This is not to say by any means that there is a simple linear correlation between the degree of impulse control a person exercises and the satisfactoriness of his personal relationships. Indeed, one can have too much of this quality just as much as one can have too little. The over-inhibited person and the obsessional planner may cause just as much unhappiness to those who are close to him (and to himself) as the impulsive and reckless person (see Hoggart, 1958, on "The Scholarship Boy").

Learning patterns of impulse control is valuable both for the individual and for the society. Hence, the contribution which the school makes to the learning of these patterns is a function it performs both for its pupils as individuals and for the society as a whole. Despite the many other ideological and structural differences between the economically-advanced societies such as the USA, the USSR and the countries of Western Europe, they all have this in common—that the structure of their society depends upon impulse control and future orientation on the part of members. The more important the position of the individual within the social hierarchy, the more crucial is this requirement.

Primary and Secondary Roles and Relationships

A second general requirement of advanced societies which corresponds to one part of the social learning taking place in school, is that members of the society learn to play "secondary roles" as well as "primary" ones. Primary relationships involve two people relating to each other in a wide sense, relating to each other as *people*. Relationships between friends or family members are invariably primary relationships in this sense. Secondary relationships are more limited or "functionally specific" in their focus, such as the relationship between buyer and seller, bus conductor and passenger, and so forth. Relationships of this kind are engaged in, not for the intrinsic satisfactions they give, but for some extrinsic purpose, for example, in order to effect a business transaction. Hence, the parties involved in such a secondary relationship are not concerned with each other as individuals, but only as the occupants of a certain role with a specific function to perform, for example, selling a certain kind of product, issuing tickets on a bus, and so forth. There is neither affection nor animosity between the parties concerned: the relationship is "affectively neutral". In secondary relationships the parties involved are expected to be concerned only with the business at hand and the other person's ability to perform the function needed and not with other aspects of his personality or background. Thus, for example, the bus conductor who might be prejudiced against teenagers with long hair or West Indians is expected to keep his prejudice to himself and not let it affect the way he does his job. That is he must treat his passengers impartially according to the rules of the bus company. He may refuse to allow someone on to the bus, but only when the bus is as full as the rules permit. This is the application of a "universalistic" rule—that the bus may only carry so many passengers. He is not allowed to refuse to admit a passenger merely because he has long hair, when the bus is half empty. That is a "particularistic" decision, based on his own personal prejudice.

The same requirement of universalistic decisions in secondary relationships applies throughout. It applies to bus conductors, to personnel managers hiring workers, to tax inspectors making rulings about tax exemptions, to magistrates passing judgement in court, and so forth. The requirement of "universalism" means impartiality as between individuals who are liked and disliked, intimately related to one, or enemies. Only the rules pertaining to the situation are allowed to decide how the person is treated.

Secondary relationships are specially important in "bureaucratic" organisations in which many people in modern society are employed and with which all of us have many dealings as citizens, as consumers and in our other capacities.

Modern industrial societies could not function without such secondary relationships and bureaucratic organisations. In very small-scale and economically simple societies it is possible for most of the relationships of members to be of a primary kind, with economic production taking place on a family farm or in a family business, with government conducted by a network of hereditary ruling families and so forth. But the existence of industrialised societies with a high standard of living depends entirely on the organisation of the economy and the government on the basis of large-scale bureaucratic organisations, manned by people playing secondary roles in the way we have outlined.

Children can learn to handle primary relationships from their experience in growing up within the family but to learn how to play secondary roles in the way we have outlined they need experience and training of a different kind. They need experience of a social organisation in which they are treated less as individuals than they are in the family; in which they are required to deal with others in this limited fashion, for specific purposes; in which they are required to conform to universalistic rules and set aside personal prejudices in these relationships. The school (especially the secondary school) by contrast with the family, is structured more on the basis of secondary relationships. The degree of this structuring is graduated, so that the pupil is introduced gradually to fully developed secondary relationships (Dreeben, 1968; Parsons, 1961). In the infant and junior schools the rigours of secondary relationships are softened by the system of the class teacher who has a quite personal and diffuse interest in the child compared to the specialist teachers of secondary school. Compared to the mother's interest in the child, however, that of the class teacher dividing her attention among thirty or forty such children represents a considerable step away from the primary relationships of the family.

Cultural Initiation

A third aspect of social learning gives pupils some acquaintance with the dominant culture of the society. Every society has a set of shared symbols, mythology, pantheon of heroes, expressive activities and styles—whether they are mainly in song, legend, drama, dance or some other forms—which is special to that society. In some societies, especially small ones, this heritage is widely shared by the adult population and it can be seen as a common culture. In the other more hierarchical societies there are different cultures for different classes within the society and the culture of the dominant class tends to be viewed by outsiders as the culture of that society. In the most hierarchical societies schools are likely to be the prerogative of the privileged classes only and therefore concerned with teaching the culture of that elite group. As the educational system becomes democratised and gradually thrown open to a wider selection of pupils, this association of the schools with the culture of the elite status group tends to remain, so the schools function to acculturate their pupils to the culture of this dominant group.

In Britain some of the more obvious features of this dominant culture are: the history of Britain and the former overseas empire, learned not only in history lessons but also through the celebration of anniversaries such as Guy Fawkes and Remembrance Day; the monarchy; the rituals and formulae of the established Church, learned through daily religious assemblies, services for special ecclesiastical holidays and through formal religious education lessons; Shakespeare and "good" literature; "classical" music and the works of Gilbert and Sullivan, which though far from "classical" have been long in favour with the British middle class; ideals of fair play; the ethic of queuing. This is clearly a non-systematic and somewhat eccentric selection from the many examples that could be chosen to represent the dominant culture which is transmitted through the school. Let it suffice for now to illustrate the general point that the school performs this function for society and for the individual pupils who successfully learn the lesson and find their social mobility prospects thereby enhanced.

In many small-scale, traditional societies the common culture is transmitted to the new generation by the informal efforts of parents, supplemented perhaps by the elders. In large-scale, economically developed societies such arrangements would probably not be satisfactory. For one reason, the culture becomes far more elaborate with the development of writing and with the emergence of professional culture-producers, such as writers and musicians. For a second reason this culture is not a common culture but the culture of a dominant status group and, in so far as the function of the school is to facilitate the admission of pupils from lower ranking families into higher statuses, they need some means of learning about the dominant culture which their parents cannot give them.

Differentiation and Labelling

The testing, sorting and labelling functions of the schools take place partly within each school but the whole process can only be seen by looking at the educational system as a whole. It is quite apparent that educational systems are stratified, in the sense that differences in prestige are attached to different sections of the educational system: independent, fee-paying schools generally being accorded higher prestige than State-maintained schools, academically selective schools being rated more highly than non-selective ones, and schools to which pupils are assigned as the result of delinquency or disruptive behaviour within other kinds of schools having the lowest prestige of all. To certain segments of the population other kinds of school may carry a degree of negative prestige, too. For example, the non-selective school has this connotation for many ambitious middle-class parents. A certain kind of fee-paying school which lacks the age and status trappings of the more famous and recognised independent schools occupies an ambiguous position in the education stratification system, scorned by some but still preferred to some alternatives, especially the non-selective state-maintained schools.

One of the important social "labels" which a person carries with him is given by the type of school which the person has attended. This is particularly true for young people at the stage of looking for jobs and starting careers. They are labelled as "public school boys" or "secondary modern types" and hence evoke a set of preconceived ideas and prejudices from those who do not know them as individuals. These stereotypes form an initial mental set for face-to-face interaction and also for decisions which are to be made about the suitability of an applicant for a job, membership in a club, or some other social position. Often there is far more information than just former school membership available and often it is seriously considered. The fact remains, however, that in many situations more complete information is not available and that even where it is available and used it still has to overcome the initial mental set created by knowledge of a person's position within the school stratification system.

As well as the stratification of pupils according to the type of school they attended, there is also *within* each school a further process of testing, sorting and labelling of pupils. There is frequent testing of academic learning by formal means of evaluation and constant assessment of pupils' attitudes—at least a constant monitoring by teachers to detect any rebellious or non-conforming behaviour. School reports, usually issued once each term, contain assessments of both work and conduct and on the basis of these assessments there may be a streaming process. There is ample further data on pupils' adjustment to school for those who may wish to make use of it in school records.

The process of labelling pupils on the basis of attitudes as opposed to academic performance is even more highly developed in the school systems of totalitarian societies where there are State-sponsored youth organisations operating in the schools. The enthusiasm with which members utter party propaganda and criticise their peers for ideological shortcomings provides an even better assessment of the level of conformity of each pupil. The most extreme example of this is the Young Pioneers organisation of the USSR, which has almost universal membership among children aged nine to fifteen years. There is an impressive initiation ceremony for new members and the threat of possible exclusion is used as a deterrent to young troublemakers. After the age of fifteen, young Russians may apply for admission to the Komsomol (Communist Party Youth Movement) which is far more selective and includes only about a half of the relevant age group. At this point there is close scrutiny of their past record (Fainsod, 1951).

To return to more familiar environments, in countries like Britain and the USA, it is clear that what many employers wish to know about potential employees is not so much the exact amount of academic learning they have acquired, though they will be concerned with basic literacy and arithmetic, but what most concerns them is whether their new employee will be careful, conscientious, polite; whether he will be able to tolerate difficulties and frustrations without losing his temper and being rude to workmates or clients; whether he will be prepared to work his way up through the more menial levels of the occupation in order to learn eventually all the different aspects of the job; whether he will be able to work with strangers and perhaps some people whom he does not like; whether he can learn to follow the rules of the organisation or profession. In other words, what the employer is most interested in knowing is how far the potential employee has learned impulse control and the ability to cope properly with secondary relationships. He will attempt to discover this in part by examining the pupil's school record and in part by a brief personal interview. Of the two sources of information, that provided by the school will often carry the more weight, the main criteria being how many years of schooling the applicant has completed and some rough measure of his level of achievement.

Thus, although it sometimes seems absurd for many occupations to demand of all applicants that they should possess a certain quantity of examination passes, there is a certain amount of rationality in the practice. The pupil's academic record serves as an indication that he has succeeded in meeting the demands of school to a certain extent—more specifically that he has succeeded in coping with the demands of life in a secondary type of organisation and learned to exercise with some consistency a certain level of impulse control and deferral of gratification.

Pupils who have failed to make good in school may yet succeed in adult occupations as self-employed people or working in small and informal work groups, but the odds would seem to be against their succeeding in large work organisations which resemble the school in their bureaucratic structure and demands for continual self-control—unless they are "late developers" and can prove it. Rough and imprecise though it may be, this process whereby the school system labels pupils performs a useful function for the larger society and especially for employers. Without some such guidance there is no real alternative to the traditional system of recruitment by nepotism, family tradition or chance, all means of selection which are far too inefficient for the requirements of an economically advanced society.

Status Group Solidarity

For the elite status group in society the independent schools which cater especially to their children perform an additional function, by bringing together in one place pupils of similar social background who live scattered across the country. The school functions in this case as an exclusive club during the impressionable years of adolescence. During these years friendships develop which may continue and the experience creates on many people a lasting identification with the school. As an old boy of the school one belongs to an extended social network which may be useful for many years afterwards. Thus the independent fee-paying school contributes greatly to the solidarity of the elite status group and to this extent is functional for this social class or status group. In so far as this group plays an important part in the functioning of society as a whole, then these schools have a wider social function, too (Weinberg, 1967).

SCHOOL AND SOCIETY IN TENSION

The school performs important functions for society but this is not to say by any means that schools as we find them represent the best possible way of performing these functions for society. Historically, schools in most societies have grown up as a result of the efforts of particular interest groups, especially religious ones, to provide ways of bringing to larger sections of the population the benefits of a certain kind of education considered by the leaders of these groups to be good both for their constituents and for the society as a whole (Mitchell, 1964). So, at different times and places religious interest groups have provided elementary education with a strong religious content; trade unions have provided part-time instruction for their members; employers have helped to sponsor instruction of a severely vocational nature and governments have provided full-time and part-time schools for various age and ability levels.

Interacting with these interest groups, however, and often playing a leading part in the development of education have been the professional educators themselves, organised as an interest group in recent times. Here we are thinking mainly of the representatives of teachers in their professional associations, head teachers, principals and other senior executives of educational institutions; and some of those working in universities who have taken an interest in the larger system of education. Because of the crucial part played in the development of schools by the teachers and administrators themselves, both in influencing the development of the larger structure of the educational system and in determining the way things develop *within* the schools, we must look at the kinds of ideologies and value systems prevailing among professional educators.

These ideologies can be seen, for convenience, as polarising around two foci. Some teachers hold as their greatest professional ideal that some of their pupils may come to have a genuine appreciation of the subject which they teach and some interest in intellectual concerns as such. In their own lives such interests and values play an important part. There are other teachers, especially since the advent of the so-called progressive movement in education, whose ideals point in a different direction, that of nurturing and cultivating the individual possibilities of each pupil and trying to develop in them attitudes of kindliness and tolerance towards others. These attitudes they hope to encourage in their pupils by showing such attitudes themselves. The progressive type tends to be found most often in the infant school, the former in academically selective schools. They may, however, sometimes be found together in the same school.

Where teachers of these two kinds are found in the same school there are liable to be conflicts between them since their priorities and values differ. We shall be less concerned with this kind of conflict for the present than with the conflict between *either* of these two kinds of idealistic teacher and important elements in the outside society.

Firstly, we look at the position of the intellectually-oriented teacher, who has great and powerful enemies (metaphorically speaking) in the larger society. Advertising and public relations, two occupations which have a very large total impact on the daily lives of the population through their influence on the mass media, are severely at odds with any vigorous concern for the truth. This is true equally for advertising and public relations on behalf of business interests, government, opposition political parties, trade unions, professional groups, and many ostensibly philanthropic institutions (including educational ones).

The mass media, in so far as they are concerned with truth, tend to restrict themselves to the sensational and superficial rather than attempting to develop a balanced and substantial picture. As for the humanely-oriented teacher, there are many threats in the secular society to his or her values, but perhaps the main one is the widespread attitude among other members of the society that life involves a struggle to attain some degree of material success and security, and that this consideration should prevail over all others in preparing pupils for adulthood. As a corollary, those who take this view feel that pupils should be schooled as rigorously as possible to excel in competitive examinations for admission to higher education and vocational training. This pressure on the schools to give priority to goals of material success explains the fact that the humane teachers have not been able to get a strong foothold in the school system above the infant level.

One result of this value conflict between school and society is that pupils who identify strongly with one or other kind of idealistic teaching and who then become strongly committed to one of these sets of values have difficulty in finding a career where they can hope to practise these values without the need for great compromise—other than in the field of education itself. If they become successful teachers, they will produce other young people like themselves who are, in a sense, misfits in terms of the secular society. Another result of this conflict is that other pupils feel their teachers discredited because the values they espouse are so far from the values held by those adults who are perceived to be successful in the competitive jungle of the adult world. A further aspect of the school-society conflict is that many parents tell their children that such "airy-fairy" ideals as they bring home from school simply cannot be lived up to in the harsh "real" world. This line is more likely to be taken by fathers than by mothers and is more likely to be told to sons than to daughters, because the role of the male is a more competitive one in the world of work.

It seems likely that the number of strongly-committed idealistic teachers of both kinds does not represent the majority of the profession. Their importance for schools, however, is greater than their numerical size would suggest because the official utterances of heads and others who speak on behalf of the schools generally articulate some version of these idealistic values. The strange fact is that, in spite of the gap between the values of the highly-committed teachers and those of most of the adult male population, the school is expected by important interest groups to espouse those idealistic values. In a curious way, many people seem to feel that it is good for their children to be exposed to such ideals when they are young.

Apart from the fairly large (I believe) population who hold this view, what are the interest groups operating to support this definition of the school's functions? One such group is the organised teaching profession. Like all leaders of professional organisations they tend to interpret the objectives of their work in the most idealist (and hence flattering) terms possible. Similarly, heads of schools, directors of education and chairmen of education committees also tend to think in these idealistic terms. Those who actually work in the schools have a further interest in defining the schools' objectives in these terms rather than in terms (say) of ministering to the needs of industry, for the idealistic definition of their social function is also the one which maximises their autonomy.

If the objectives of the school are defined in terms of abstract and idealistic educational goals, the translation of these goals into concrete policies must be a matter of professional judgement. Where, by contrast, the objectives of the school are defined as serving the demands of society, clearly the political representatives of the community are the ones who should interpret those demands and prescribe the policies which they wish the schools to follow. Clearly, the latter situation leaves little autonomy to the professional educators. This represents a powerful motive for the education profession to define its objectives in abstract and idealistic terms.

What is harder to explain than the ideological stance of professional educators is the assent of most politicians on the national and even local levels to this position. One reason is simply the political power of an organised occupational group such as the teachers and the politicians' prudent wish not to antagonise them unnecessarily. A second reason is that the politicians as a result of their own education have in some cases been convinced of one of the idealistic definitions of the school's objectives. This is perhaps more likely in the case of national than local politicians, on account of their generally higher level of education. Yet, a third reason for politicians to acquiesce in the idealistic version of the school's objectives is a pragmatic one, namely that to define the school's objectives in more concrete terms is to set specific goals and targets and so to set up highly visible criteria of success and failure. This, as every politician knows, is a dangerous thing to do whether in the area of education or target figures for new houses or in any other field, for unpredicted problems (such as economic recessions) are liable to arise and force a diversion of resources, resulting in all-too-obvious failure.

For these various reasons the objectives of the school for official purposes tend to be defined in such abstract and idealistic ways, whether emphasising more the values of intellectual enquiry or those of humane concern.

The attempt to *implement* such values in the school can hardly be expected to show much success. The schools are beset by a further problem resulting from their idealistic definition of objectives, namely the practical difficulties and frequent failures in attempting to devise organisational procedures and teaching methods which will permit these values to be expressed and realised on a large scale.

Intellectual curiosity is a value upheld in schools; but it must be stopped promptly when the bell rings for the end of a lesson and switched to the subject of the following lesson. Tolerance, concern and kindliness are principles supposedly upheld in the schools; but what becomes of these ideals when children are exposed to a succession of short-stay, inexperienced teachers who change six times a day and who can only maintain in a classroom either a situation of rigid order based on fear or one of chaos?

Although we emphasise here the great difficulty of fulfilling high, idealistic aspirations in education and the inevitability of at least occasional failure, even in the most propitious conditions, it is nevertheless true that some teachers and some schools are successful. It is unclear whether we should regard these successful examples as surprisingly numerous relative to the difficulty of what they have attempted and successfully accomplished, or whether we should regard them as few in number relative to the many who have not achieved what they have achieved. What is clear is that the minority of schools which have been successful in terms of either of our two versions of idealistic goals have a great significance for the teaching profession. They are an inspiration to many teachers who struggle to realise their own idealistic conception of education in a working situation where they lack any strong, direct support from colleagues and superiors. In analysing the consequences of failure to achieve idealistic goals in education, we do not mean to imply that failure is universal—by no means. It is, however, common enough to be a significant feature of the education system and the consequence of this failure are an important feature of the system.

The fact that schools do often have explicitly stated ideals which are not adhered to has both a benign and malign effect. The benign effect is to encourage those who note the discrepancy between ideals and practice, either teachers or pupils on their respective level, to challenge the anomaly which this represents. Teachers may bring this to the attention of their heads and senior colleagues; pupils may bring it to the attention of any of their teachers or directly to the head, or through the medium of a school council. These comments may be welcomed or not; they may be openly discussed or not; they may lead to ameliorative action or not. Where these attempts to bring about reform fail or where those who notice such discrepancies do not bother to bring them to anyone's attention because they fear the consequences or simply do not expect anything to be done about it the malignant effect sets in. Alienation from the school develops (either on the part of teachers or of pupils in such a situation) and the feeling develops that those who control the school are not only repressive, but hypocritical.

Teachers who feel this way soon leave the school and perhaps the profession, according to an educational Gresham's Law that bad staff (when entrenched in a position of power) drive out the good ones. Pupils cannot vote with their feet in quite the same way—but they will tend to be rebellious. If they fear to make open protests, their wish to preserve some kind of integrity of personality in the face of such a hostile environment may lead them to deviant behaviour of a more secretive kind, such as drug-taking, sexual acting-out or writing bitter, alienated manuscripts, rather than breaking windows or causing disturbances in school.

Believing that the young as they grow up construct a world-view based on generalising their early experiences, the impressions that young people form from their schools are likely to be second only to the effects of family on their picture of the nature of their society. Hence, a pupil who finds in his school fine words talked about intellectual enquiry and "the truth" while lessons never permit a dissenting view to be discussed or questions on fundamental issues to be asked; or the pupils who hear uplifting sermons in assembly about the importance of kindliness to others and respect for other people's points of view and consistently finds that teachers do not want to hear his point of view when it differs from their own and have no time to listen to his explanation of what happened when he is in trouble—these pupils, unless they see powerful examples to the contrary are likely to conclude that hypocrisy is a general phenomenon among adults. They will similarly conclude that supposedly universalistic rules which they have encountered in the school do not possess, contrary to what they were told, any quality of inherent moral rightness but rather they are merely patterns of behaviour foisted by those who have power on those who have not. Hence, as soon as they are free from the power of the school, they are fully justified in violating those rules. This view has a compelling logic: if the authority figures who impose rules cannot act consistently with their own declared ideals that can only mean that they have no inherent validity. And if that is so there is nothing wrong with queue-jumping, littering, stealing, lying, and so forth when you can get away with it without punishment. It is as serious as that. Where the school allows a radical gap between its ideals and its practice, it risks undermining all efforts to teach pupils the meaning of universalistic rules.

CONCLUSION

Clearly we are assuming that the school does make *some* difference to the development of its pupils: that going to school at all makes a child different from the way he or she would have been had she or he not gone to school; and that going to one kind of school makes pupils develop rather differently from the way they would have developed attending a different kind of school. The first assumption would appear to be untestable for all practical purposes but the second one, alleging the differences between schools of different kinds, is testable and has already accumulated a certain amount of research tending to support it. (Appendix One.)

There are studies comparing schools with different types of formal structure: streamed *versus* unstreamed primary schools and comprehensive *versus* selective secondary schools; there are others comparing schools with similar structure but different "atmospheres". There are also studies which sought only to show that different schools appear to have different influences on their pupils, without pinning it down to any specific feature of the school. Such "school effects" have been shown for delinquency rates and for altruism. Among the variables which have been found to differentiate pupils at schools with different atmospheres and which were assessed concurrently (that is, while pupils were still attending school) were: truancy; leisure interests; listening and remembering, neatness, ingenuity; emotional stability, assuming responsibility, self-expression, tolerance. Among other variable differentiating pupils after they had left their schools were: academic performance in university, intellectual curiosity and objectivity, resourcefulness; and feeling competent to play a part in the governmental process.

There are studies of different teaching styles and their consequences, sometimes in conjunction with other variables. A recent large-scale study of primary schools looked simultaneously at the effects of formal streaming and teachers' attitudes on a strict-tolerant scale, finding that *neither* made any significant difference to academic learning while *both* had an effect on attitudes towards school and self. Studies concerned only with teacher-differences have found pupils taught by different teachers to differ in cheating; amount of minor classroom delinquency; cooperativeness, involvement, activity, achievement and abstract thought development.

It must be emphasised that the variables mentioned above have generally been found in only *one* study each to differentiate between pupils subject to different regimes of either school or teaching. A fuller account of this research may be found in Appendix One, where the full references are given, together with some discussion of the methodological problems that bedevil research in this most difficult area. This corpus of research would perhaps not entitle one to assert very confidently that any one *particular* effect could be attributed to differences between schools, but I believe that we are entitled to the conclusion that there is a definite *prima facie* case for accepting the general proposition that it may make some difference to pupils' development which school they attend.

CHAPTER 1 REFERENCES

Burton R. Clark, *Educating the Expert Society*, Chandler, San Francisco, 1962.

Robert Dreeben, *On What is Learned in School*, Addison Wesley, Reading, Mass., 1968.

Merle Fainsod, "The Komsomol: Youth Under Dictatorship", in Alex Inkeles and Kent Geiger (eds.), *Soviet Society: A Book of Readings*, Houghton Mifflin, Boston, 1961, pp. 147–63.

Richard Hoggart, *The Uses of Literacy*, Penguin, Harmondsworth, 1958.

Philip W. Jackson, *Life in Classrooms*, Holt, Rinehart and Winston, New York, 1968.

G. Duncan Mitchell, "Education, Ideology, and Social Change in England", in George K. Zollschan and W. Hirsch (eds.), *Exploration in Social Change*, Houghton Mifflin, New York, 1964, pp. 778–97.

Talcott Parsons, "The School Class as a Social System: Some of the Functions in American Society", in A. H. Halsey *et. al.* (eds.), *Education, Economy and Society*, Free Press, New York, 1961, pp. 434–55.

M. D. Shipman, *The Sociology of the School*, Longmans, London, 1968.

Ian Weinberg, *The English Public Schools: The Sociology of Elite Education*, Atherton Press, New York, 1967.

Chapter Two

SOCIALISATION AND MORAL EDUCATION

SOCIALISATION

One of the four major functions which we attributed to the school in Chapter One was "cultivating socially approved attitudes and modes of behaviour" or "learning to be an acceptable member of the society". And it was under this general heading that we discussed the two themes of the learning of impulse control and learning to play secondary roles and relationships. This kind of learning is most often discussed in the literature as "socialisation". This concept has played a central part in the development of anthropology, social psychology and sociology (Danziger, 1971). Even political scientists have now a recognised sub-field known as "political socialisation", concerned with discovering how the child learns about the political system, develops attitudes towards it and learns how to participate in it. Socialisation has been used by anthropologists, to cover all the learning which takes place as the children in a particular society learn the culture or way of life of that society and so learn to be fully accepted adult members (see, for example, Beals and Hoijer, Chapter Eight). However, there are a number of important points to be taken into account.

We may look at socialisation on several different levels. Firstly, socialisation into *any* society: on this level, impulse control is essential though more economically advanced societies require higher orders of impulse control than less developed ones. Secondly, socialisation for *certain kinds* of society: learning to handle secondary relationships is an essential part of socialisation for advanced societies but not so much for others. Thirdly, socialisation for a *specific* society or sub-culture (a distinct religious group, locality group or social class) within a specific society: here we might study the question of what has to be learned in becoming (for example) an upper class, English gentleman—a certain accent and other habits of speech, the rules of etiquette surrounding debutante parties, the accepted attitudes to team games, girls, the State, trade unions, and so forth—and *how* these things are learned—to a significant extent through the institution of the independent boarding school.

The major problem with the concept of socialisation is its built-in assumption that it is one of cultural repetition and continuity. Developed first by anthropologists studying small-scale, technologically simple and apparently unchanging societies, it assumes that what is basically involved is small boys learning to become like their fathers and small girls learning to become like their mothers. While this may be a good way to view socialisation of early childhood in the family, it will not suffice for looking at socialisation in the school.

For a start, there would be no need for schools if the aim of socialisation were to make children like their parents, for the obvious and best way to achieve this end would be to leave it to the parents themselves. Schools exist because those who run them and those who were responsible for setting them up believe that socialisation is inadequate. They believe that the continuance and prosperity of the society requires that all children should be educated to *higher* levels of attainment than their parents not only in academic terms but also in terms of social, emotional, and moral development, as a basic right of the individual, aside from the consideration of societal welfare.

Yet even this formulation oversimplifies the issue, for socialisation in modern society is concerned with a *different kind* of education. For example, it is argued that modern education places far more weight than formerly on creativity and flexibility, giving pupils the skills and self-confidence to adapt their responses to new situations, and should *decrease* the emphasis on traditional ways of doing things—whether procedures for handling data (such as computing long division sums) or patterns of social relationships. As Margaret Mead expressed this view over twenty-five years ago:

> "We must concentrate upon teaching our children to walk so steadily that we need not hew too straight and narrow paths for them but can trust them to make new paths through difficulties we never encountered to a future of which we have no inkling today." (M. Mead, 1943, p. 320)

Recent thinking argues that society is changing at an ever-accelerating rate and therefore any given set of response patterns which a pupil learns in school would become inappropriate and maladaptive in terms of his ability to adjust to changing technologies and patterns of work arrangements (such as automation in its many guises) and changing patterns of private lives (such as the redefinition of male and female roles in marriage, the changing expectations of children, the effects of rehousing and so forth). In the context of constant change and an unknown future *flexibility* is seen as the only insurance, both for the individual and society.

Apart from these functionalist arguments there is the ethical view that human beings should have the chance of the greatest possible choice in their lives, which depends on the alternatives open to them. The number of alternatives depends on several factors, both situational and personality ones. Other things being equal, the person with more flexibility and therefore the possibility of functioning effectively in a wider variety of situations has more alternatives open to him.

The concept of flexibility, however, is also insufficiently well-defined to provide a substitute for that of socialisation. As we have used it so far, flexibility refers to a number of separate attributes, such as having a flexible cognitive structure as opposed to a rigid and stereotyped one, or having a wide repertoire of social skills. Because of the complexities of this concept, the most satisfactory approach is to look at the various dimensions of development, and then try to put together a suitable conceptual model with which to analyse this complex process of learning to be an acceptable and competent member of society.

DIMENSIONS OF DEVELOPMENT

The process of growing up entails learning of many different kinds or development along different dimensions. Since our purpose is to analyse some of the contributions made by the school to this process of learning and maturation, and since we have shown why the "received" concept of socialisation is unacceptable as a short-cut, global concept, we must examine the main dimensions of "social development"—that is, the process through which the individual comes to terms with his society. Having broken this down into its major elements, we can set about constructing a new conceptual model to replace socialisation. The one we shall put forward here is that of "the morally-educated person", though the reader is free to construct other models that may please him better.

(1) *Skills.* Very many different kinds of skills may be learned. We shall here divide them into three main categories: psycho-motor skills, intellectual skills and communication skills. Psycho-motor skills cover such things as learning to walk, write, paint, swim, dress oneself, ride a bicycle and operate more complex machines, such as the typewriter or abacus.

Intellectual skills are essentially skills of mental data-processing and problem-solving. They can be measured very imperfectly by a variety of intelligence tests. Although there is a large (and hotly debated) element of genetic determination or limitation in the extent to which these skills may be learned by any individual, differences in the environmental learning situation and opportunities between children account for a significant amount of the individual differences found in this respect.

Communication skills overlap to a great extent with what are also called "social skills". Here we are concerned with the ability to express oneself and comprehend the meaning of others through speech, the written word and non-verbal media. The language ability that is involved here is also very much involved in the other intellectual skills to which we referred.

The child will presumably have learned to talk before coming to school—though the immigrant child may still have to learn to talk in the language of the majority—but all children at the age of school entrance will have a long way to go in the development of advanced language skills. The significance of specifically linguistic development for a range of other aspects of the child's development has been explored by Bernstein and we shall discuss his ideas in Chapter Five when looking at home background and its effects on response to school.

Social skills refer to various abilities which are to a high degree learned or learnable and which affect one's effectiveness in dealing with other people (Argyle, 1969). On one level we may observe that the content of social skills is culturally variable. The behaviour expected of a friend, neighbour, son or lover is different in each case and each one may be different in one society compared to another society.

On another level we may note that different social skills are required in playing secondary roles from those required for primary ones. In secondary relationships it is necessary to get on with the job in hand, keeping irrelevant considerations (such as liking or disliking the other person) out of play; one accepts that the other person in a secondary relationship is required to play a role, governed by a set of precise rules, which may require him to act in a way that is out of keeping with the primary relationship which exists between these two at other times.

On yet another level we may observe that, cultural variations notwithstanding, there are certain basic criteria of social skill which apply to any situation. The following comprise a minimum list:

(1) Knowing the cultural expectations and the consequences of non-conformity.

(2) Ability to read accurately the signals sent out by other people (both verbal and non-verbal) and to interpret them accurately, hence to have some insight into their feelings and their probable reactions to any action by oneself.

(3) The ability to send out signals that are intelligible to others and hence to make one's feelings and opinions known.

(4) The ability to gain social acceptance as a role partner, which depends in good measure on conformity to the wide range of customs of the group (as well as the most specific role expectations) as well as the ability to present oneself as an acceptable person.

(5) The ability to present one's views persuasively when others are not in agreement and would tend to ignore them.

In relation to all social skills one may hypothesise the existence of a "social distance" effect. That is to say that however good a person is in a social skill with members of some group "close" to him (e.g. family, friends), he will be less good with people from other groups with whom he interacts less frequently (e.g. members of same town, age group, caste, social class).

The growth of social skills is a cumulative process, since experience of social interaction is essential for their growth, and access to this experience tends to be related to the individual's previous level of social skill. Those who are slow in developing social skills will not only find their social relationships less rewarding (and hence tend to withdraw from them) but also will be less welcome as friends than the more socially skilled ones. Tending to get less social experience in general and especially less experience of those more advanced in social skills, they become further retarded.

In school, however, this "free market" can be set aside to some extent by teachers who are skilful in planning group work and group activities—so that pupils who are generally excluded and retarded in social skill development may have more chance of social experience. The use of actual role-playing exercises in the classroom may also be applied to the problem of developing pupils' social skills more effectively.

(2) *Knowledge*. This is the area of learning where the impact of the school is most obvious. However, the area of knowledge which may be affected by the school is a lot wider than commonly realised, for it goes well beyond the area of conscious teaching. Perhaps this will be clearer if we drop the term "knowledge" and replace it by the term "cognitive assumptions". This has the further advantage of making room for learning of superstition and inaccurate "knowledge" which may have just as significant an influence on the child's view of the world, and hence, on his behaviour, as any more reputable cognitive assumptions.

From his earliest years, the child has learned to make cognitive discrimination between objects—those that are good to eat and those that are not, those that are to play with but not to eat, those that are to look at but not to touch. This cognitive discrimination is the very basis of all learning. Having discriminated between objects it is then possible to learn about their individual attributes and their relationships to one another. This is the basis for all learning about the structure of the world around one. The child learns about the principle of gravity by hard experience and how to cope with it by trial and error; he acquires a set of working assumptions about the social order in a similar way. He learns the expectations which those who surround him hold, what they will do when he violates them, how far he can go before the sanctions are applied and what combination of charm, temper, threats and low cunning is most effective in getting him what he wants. In these crude processes of testing the environment and forming conclusions about how to operate within it, the child acts as a neophyte physicist, psychologist and sociologist.

The child's cognitive assumptions about these two realms

(physical and social) will have the greatest importance in understanding and predicting his behaviour. The learning of these assumptions will be well advanced before he begins school. Parents, friends, teachers and anyone the child observes can contribute to it. Explicit teaching will play a part but discovering things for himself is probably the most important way of learning about the social order. A number of important social norms are rarely stated explicitly—for example, the one about telling "white lies" in preference to passing unfavourable criticism to someone's face, even when one is asked directly by the person in question for one's candid [*sic*] opinion. Only by discovering that the unstated norms carry more weight than the verbal pseudo-request can one come through such encounters unscathed.

(3) *Attitudes*. At the same time as the child is acquiring a knowledge of these various things we have mentioned, he is also acquiring attitudes towards them. But although the two learning processes take place simultaneously, it is helpful to discuss them separately, since their operation is in many important respects different. We have mentioned that one area of cognitive learning concerns the structure of the physical world. As he learns more or less about this, the child may acquire different attitudes towards the "facts" he is learning: he may find it fascinating, boring, or frightening. As he learns about the structure of the social order and (for example) the existence of authority positions and status differences, he may develop an attitude of respect for those who occupy these positions, he may resent them, or he may accept their existence as something unalterable.

In school, attitudes are being developed towards teachers, towards authority, towards adults in general. Attitudes towards his peers, which had certainly been developing before he ever came near a school and which continued to develop to some extent independently of school, are also affected by the pupil's experience with fellow-pupils here. And in so far as these experiences are conditioned or affected by the way the school is organised and the kind of population that it brings together, we can consider this part of the impact of "the school" on the pupil. Most important of all, perhaps, attitudes towards himself are being moulded in the pupil by his early experiences, including those he meets in school. These attitudes concerning his likeability, competence and basic worth will be of the greatest importance in his long-term development (Coopersmith, 1968).

(4) *Values and Moral Principles.* Implied beneath the attitudes discussed in the previous section, we may infer "values" or generalised criteria in terms of which many different objects and people may be compared or evaluated. Thus we speak of "attitudes" to (for example) crossword puzzles, politicians, motorways, books, the opposite sex, etc. But we speak of "values" (for example) of preferring activity to idleness (or *vice versa*), benevolence to exploitation (or *vice versa*), urban to rural life (or *vice versa*), and so forth. The difference is that "values" are more abstract and general.

Moral principles are based on values but involve a different sort of proposition. Whereas a value indicates that A is preferred to B, a moral principle indicates that one *ought* to strive for A, that this is an obligation on one who claims to accept this moral principle and that blame properly attaches to him if he fails to do so (allowing for extenuating circumstances).

In the development of the individual child values emerge only slowly and relatively late. A definitive part of the process of growing to maturity may be considered to consist of taking stock of one's attitudes to all significant objects and to integrating them in terms of a few central values. The process of trying to do this accounts for some of the difficulties of the adolescent period.

The sense of moral obligations (or "conscience") is being instilled in the child from early times—at first attached rather indiscriminately to the parents' expectations of very different kinds: including together perhaps such disparate prohibitions as not spilling food on the floor, not reading in bed after "lights out", not telling lies, and not setting fire to the house. A moral *principle* involves this feeling of moral obligation attached to a *class* of actions defined in terms of *universalistic* categories. Thus a person may feel a moral obligation not to tell lies to parents but a moral principle would involve not telling lies to anyone, or to anyone except those who clearly are treating one as an object of exploitation and not a person with equal rights, e.g. the agents of countries at war with one's own or dishonest salesmen.

Schools and churches are especially given to expounding universal moral principles; some families are also. This seems to be a characteristic of certain kinds of societies to expound their normative expectations in terms of *universalistic* moral principles. In the past, it was the case in most societies that the nature of the moral obligation of the young could be adequately stated as to live like their elders and to follow the tradition of the society in all particulars. There would be no reference here to general moral principles expected to apply impartially to all.

In our own society, in practice, these moral principles represent ideals that are contradicted all the time by our behaviour, which is often socially condoned. Thus the moral principle of truth-telling is abrogated in situations defined as giving compliments or "telling white lies" or "putting the best face on it" in presenting oneself or one's work to others whom we wish to impress favourably. At the same time, therefore, as the child is learning from his own observations about the reality of the society in which he lives, he is learning from the explicit preaching and pronouncements of school teachers and headmasters, supplemented by parents, ministers of religion and politicians, about the moral principles that are supposed to operate. Coping with the perceived contradictions between these is one of the greatest sources of difficulty and distress to the young person growing up in our society—and to some older ones, too.

(5) *Personality Variables*. Some of the dimensions of development which we have already discussed may be considered as personality variables (values, attitudes and moral principles) but there are other personality attributes which have not yet been covered and which are important—attributes such as intraversion-extraversion, dominance-submissiveness, emotional stability-instability, strength of conscience and the ability to control impulsive urges. Heredity and family environment seem likely to be the most important determinants of these attributes, though the school may play a part, too—especially when its influence is in the same direction as that of the family.

(6) *Behavioural Habits*. This is something of a residual category. In addition to acquiring skills of various kinds, cognitive assumptions, attitudes, values, moral principles and other personality attributes, children acquire a variety of more superficial behavioural features such as speech habits, styles of dressing,

mannerisms of gait, posture and gesture. In so far as they carry connotations of membership in a particular social group they make the individual more or less acceptable among different social groups. The boy with public-school mannerisms tends to be more welcome than most others at the hunt ball but less welcome than most at the local dance hall.

Interconnections

The six areas of individual development with their various subdivisions adumbrated above represent a useful approach to the problem of analysing the impact of the school on the development of the individual pupil. In reality, of course, they are not as separate as presented here. To understand the process of individual development in the school, we must take into account the interactions of these aspects one with another.

We have noted already that the holding of cognitive assumptions presupposes the intellectual ability to discriminate the events or objects in question from others. Holding an attitude or a moral preference makes the same presupposition and holding a moral *principle* presupposes a certain level of intellectual skill in abstract thinking. Kohlberg has shown that children develop through a definite series of stages in moral thinking, of which thinking in terms of moral principles is the last stage to be reached. Before arriving at that stage children typically go through earlier stages of expedient orientation to moral choices, conventional conformity responses (the "good boy orientation") followed by the stage of respecting authority and "doing one's duty" before reaching the penultimate stage of "contractual legalism" and finally an orientation to moral principles of a universalistic kind with conscience providing the motivation. The same researcher also demonstrates that intelligence is a factor that affects the development of moral thinking in these terms (Kohlberg, 1966).

Members of different societies vary greatly in the psycho-motor skills which they develop most fully and these correlate with variations in the cultural value system. In most advanced Western societies the skill of writing is very highly developed; in various non-literate societies other motor skills may be developed by the average member to a degree unknown in our society, for example, wood-carving, spear-throwing and tree-climbing. The point here is that those skill areas which are held in high regard throughout a certain group will tend to be cultivated most assiduously by the young.

Attitudes and cognitive assumptions are closely linked in practice. Assumptions may lead to attitudes: if one believes that most people in good jobs get them not through merit, but nepotism, this is likely to affect one's attitudes to those people and the privileges they claim. Conversely, people with strong vested interests in certain attitudes develop rationalisations or cognitive beliefs which (if they were true) would justify such attitudes. Thus people who are prejudiced against members of alien groups are easily persuaded to believe any allegation that reflects unfavourably on them (Berelson and Steiner).

Closely related to intellectual skills is the matter of "cognitive style" or the way in which a person organises his information about the world outside. People vary according to the complexity or simplicity of their organisation and the extent to which they attend to subtle differences, rather than polarising things into oversimplified categories. O. J. Harvey has labelled these cognitive styles as "concrete" and "abstract" and has shown how they can predict many other attitudinal and behavioural tendencies, including empathic ability or ability to take the role of the other person and see things from his point of view (abstract thinkers perform better), the tendency to stereotype people and form sweeping judgements from little data (concrete thinkers do this) and resourcefulness in changed situations (abstracts do better). The abstract cognitive style clearly must be an essential feature of the flexible person, able to readjust readily to unfamiliar situations; and it seems likely that the same cognitive style is also required for thinking in terms of universalistic moral principles (Harvey, Hunt and Schroeder, 1961).

In his earliest learning or interaction with his environment, the child is not only acquiring a set of working assumptions about the environment but also ways of dealing with it and ways of learning about it (cognitive and conceptual styles). These are all closely interrelated. If the child learns to see it as basically orderly and predictable, he is likely to feel that it can be manipulated to achieve his objectives (or some of them). If, however, the child's early experiences with the environment suggest that it is capricious and unpredictable, an attitude of fatalism is more likely and a lack of motivation to learn about the environment—except perhaps from an aesthetic and/or religious perspective. The role of parents or other early guardians in mediating the child's experiences of the environment (as well as being themselves the most important part of his environment) is absolutely crucial. Hence differences between children are more likely to be due to differences in the way parents have treated them and programmed or structured their experiences of the rest of the environment as they are to be due to actual differences in the physical environment itself.

An attitude favouring (say) courage may lead one to commitment to a moral principle that one should act courageously, but it need not. Excuses can be found to excuse or rationalise one's cowardice (cognitive assumption) without necessarily undermining the favourable attitudes to courage. One area of individual development interacts with another, influencing it under certain circumstances but not invariably, so that it is necessary to treat them as separate areas of development in order to be able to analyse these interconnections.

The Morally-Educated Person

No one can deny the complexity of social development, the process of growing up and coming to terms with the requirements of social life. Each one of the seven areas of development or learning presents formidable complexities of analysis. Is there any way in which this monumental task can be reduced to more manageable proportions?

One approach would be to select one area of learning or one sub-area as the subject of investigation and to explore the conditions under which more or less effective learning of this kind took place. Thus one might investigate what kinds of experiences in school tended to produce the best results in (say) altruism or tolerance (attitudes in specific areas), or in social skills of specific kinds, say in making friends with peers, or dealing with strangers in formal organisations.

Another approach would be to set up conceptual models of character types such as the "morally-educated person", the "upper-class English gentleman", the "flexible but loyal worker" or any such personality constellation as one wished. Having chosen such a model, it would be defined in terms of the dimensions defined above: certain kinds of skills being more salient than others, certain cognitive assumptions being required, certain attitudes, values and perhaps moral principles. Our task would then be to consider and investigate what conditions were conducive to the acquisition of each of these attributes.

The former approach (single, specific attributes) has the advantage of being more manageable in scale but the disadvantage that there are not many single attributes which stand out as being intrinsically interesting or outstandingly important in themselves. This is the main advantage of the character-type approach—that one can specify a collection of attributes which represent a cultural ideal either in the society under analysis or in the minds of a smaller group of people who are one's clients or in one's own personal value system.

The model of the morally-educated person (MEP, for short) is believed to represent the values common to a number of societies within the cultural tradition of Judeo-Christian humanism and liberal democracy. It also incorporates the attributes of the flexible person needed by modern economies and less vulnerable to the insecurities of life in modern society. The MEP, defined by John Wilson, thus represents in the opinion of this writer (though not necessarily in that of Wilson) not so much a morally absolute standard but rather one which represents the most central moral values of our society and a number of others in the same cultural tradition, as well as being a functional requirement of these societies in economic and political terms (Wilson, Williams and Sugarman, 1968).

A fundamental characteristic of the MEP lies in the area of attitudes to other people: he has concern for other people, feels impelled to help them when they are in need and disinclined to exploit or take unfair advantage of them for his own benefit. On the level of moral principles, he would maintain that other people's needs and wishes should count and be considered alongside his own. Cognitively, he is aware of their wishes and feelings; emotionally he is inclined to meet them half-way. We can assess people for their degree of concern for others in two ways: in terms of *how much* personal sacrifice they are prepared to make in order to help members of a specified group of familiars (or strangers) or by taking specific levels of sacrifice (e.g. lending money, tolerating eccentricities, running an errand) and seeing how wide a circle of other people he would be prepared to make that kind of sacrifice for. The former definition might be called the "intensity" of concern and the latter the "extensity" of concern. How the two dimensions of concern correlate with each other is a subject still to be investigated.

If the individual is to carry out successfully a policy of consideration for others and not to bungle it, he will need social skills of many and varied kinds. He may, for example, have decided that his friend is worried about something and that he ought to help him, but if he is lacking in tact (or other social skills) he may end up hurting his friend's feelings instead.

Concern for others and a tendency to be accommodating calls for a sensitivity and perceptiveness to the other people with whom our subject comes into contact. This quality is a skill rather than an attitude like concern, and is learned by practice and (where available) training.

Sensitivity is just one aspect of the social skills or role-playing skills which are necessary in order to be able to maintain the kind of social relationships with others which a concern for their feelings and interests indicates. The kinds of skills which are most important will, on one level, vary greatly between cultures. In middle-class British culture, for example, there is a great emphasis on tactfulness and politeness, whereas in certain lower class and teenage cultures, the emphasis is on more aggressive and extreme forthrightness. Acceptance is contingent on expressing oneself in ways defined as appropriate within the culture of the group in question.

One further difficulty may stand between a person's good intentions, based on concern for others, and for their successful accomplishment—a need for a number of psychological qualities if all these good intentions are to be brought into play. On the positive side, he needs the guts or moral courage to go ahead and do what he feels he should do, risking possible rebuff, or failure. On the negative side, he needs to be free from prejudice or dogmatic thinking which would prevent him from appraising the situation objectively and free from phobias or obsessions which would sidetrack him from his plan of action.

So far we have considered factors that affect a person's behaviour, but we have not considered his reasons or motives for acting the way he does. Intuitively one feels that someone who gives money to a beggar mainly to impress his companion is masquerading as a morally-educated person while not really being one. The same applies to someone whose motive is fear of being rebuked by his father, the wish to avoid uncomfortable guilt feelings or the desire to acquire good points for the Day of Judgement. This consideration, therefore, unlike the previous five, concerns not whether our subject does "the right thing" but whether he does it for an acceptable *reason*. It is not suggested that people should always stop and think before doing anything, but that they should be alert to those situations which are out of the ordinary and would involve serious consequences for a wrong decision.

In view of what we said above about the importance of concern for others, in defining the MEP, some kinds of reasons are preferred to others. Reasons of the kind, "I gave him money because he needed it, and people should help others in misfortune", indicate a morally-educated person. Reasons that get "low marks" include, for example, "I just feel it is right", "My father always told me to do it", "The Bible says you should", and "Everybody else does it".

We are concerned here with two closely-related points: (1) thinking in terms of general (or universalistic) moral principles and (2) considering other people's interests. Each point requires some clarification.

Universalistic moral principles are prescriptions that apply to *all* people or to *all* in a defined situation. For example, "thou shalt not commit adultery" refers to all married people and "love thy neighbour" refers to everyone. Children and the insane are generally not held liable to these imperatives but that means that they are not considered as "people". These principles serve both as criteria for judging whether actions already past are good or bad and also as criteria for deciding whether one should or should not proceed with a certain course of action which is contemplated.

One commonly passes private judgement on things that other people have done, saying "well done" or "he should never have done that". One also passes judgement on oneself, though usually more leniently. These judgements are mostly private thoughts which are kept to oneself or perhaps shared with a trusted third party, but our judgements of another person's conduct are not often conveyed directly to them. The situation of telling another person what one thinks of his conduct is experienced by most people as one in which there is a felt pressure to flatter the other person or at least to soften adverse judgements.

This pressure is not just a subjective phenomenon, for there is a social expectation of loyalty to friends which is found very widely in many societies and sub-cultures. What we mean by calling it a "social" expectation is that not only the person whose conduct is under criticism will complain against the friend who condemns it, but so too will other members of the group. "That is not how a friend should act"; "He let his friend down"; "He shouldn't have said that". This is the ethic of *particularistic loyalty*—that one stands by one's kinsmen and friends, also one's co-religionists, ethnic fellows and countrymen, or fellow-members of any in-group.

In conflict with this ethic is the rival ethic of *universalistic integrity*, that one makes objective judgements on the merits of the case, judging the conduct of one's kinsman or friend and total stranger by the same standard. Thus, for example, personnel managers in charge of hiring staff for good jobs, administrators of welfare funds and adjudicators for merit awards are all supposed to exercise strict impartiality in assessing claims of strangers and intimates for jobs, welfare benefits and merit awards.

Their employers and a certain body of public opinion expects them to act with such universalistic integrity. Their needy or greedy friends and kinsmen, however, expect them to follow the ethic of particularistic loyalty and there is a body of public opinion in their support, too.

The ethic of universalism and the ethic of particularism clash in another way besides the one we have just outlined. The attitude of concern for other people which was the first defining characteristic of the MEP to be mentioned and which is also the first to develop in the individual, depends on seeing and responding to other people as *individuals* and on being able to empathise with them. In this sense it is like the particularistic attitude. The ethic of universalism, however, requires the application of *impersonal* criteria—and hence requires one to see the person objectively while making the judgement. The personnel manager in our example is fond of his incompetent brother and appreciates his good qualities as a husband and father to his family; but if he is to do his job according to universalistic normative standards, he must put aside his particularistic feelings and consider only the man's suitability for the job.

Concern for other people's interests thus commits the MEP to taking into account *all* the major consequences of his actions, not just their consequences for those who are actually present in person—the general requirement is for the MEP to *consider the consequences* of his proposed action *for all* those involved. Sometimes, indeed, it is right to help the person who asks even though this involves distressing others or breaking the law—as, for example, did those brave folk living in Nazi-occupied Europe who concealed Jews and others being persecuted by the Nazis.

The MEP is not invariably a law-abiding person—that depends upon the nature of the laws in question; in some societies he will be on the whole law-abiding, while in others he can only be an outlaw or a revolutionary. There is no way to short-cut the complexities of this kind of analysis using some such model as that of the MEP. We can no longer make do with the convenient formula that equates conforming to the law with morality—Eichmann *et al.* have made sure of that.

We have discussed the MEP and the dimensions of his personality so far without taking any account of the *other* person for whom we are asking him to show concern. How does *he* behave towards the person who is our main focus of interest? What is the past record of their relationship? Suppose that this other person has consistently treated our subject with disrespect or cruelty? Are we still to insist that, in order to be considered as an MEP, he must show concern for his tormenter and try to help him? Are we suggesting that he should "turn the other cheek"?

Assume, firstly, that we have a situation where our subject experiences extreme abuse from only one other person and not in the rest of his relationships. In such circumstances, to show a given level of concern would have to be considered as meriting a much higher "score" on this dimension than showing a similar level of concern under more friendly circumstances. However, to avoid this person could hardly merit a negative score under the circumstances, though to act in a hostile manner would. Now assume a situation when our subject is frequently the victim of such abusive or hurtful behaviour, as for example in the case of members of an oppressed minority group: in these circumstances the consequences for "turning the other cheek" are likely to be more serious for the individual's mental health.

So we are obliged to face the issue of the possible *conflict* between concern for others and concern for oneself. We refer not to the more familiar conflict between altruism and "selfishness" but to another conflict—that between concern for others and concern for one's own basic requirements of mental and physical health. Is a healthy personality destroyed by failure to stand up for one's rights under certain circumstances? Is a healthy personality (including self-respect) necessary to be the kind of person who spontaneously feels concern for others and wants to show it? Is it necessary in order to be a good parent and a good partner to show the specially-important kinds of concern required in those roles? The answer to all these questions, I believe, is "yes". Therefore, an MEP does not always turn the other cheek—not when he is subjected to a barrage of abuse and disrespect which threatens his self-respect.

Is the conclusion from this discussion of moral principles that the MEP has to learn to think and behave in terms of universalistic standards at all times and to eschew always the particularistic response to people as individuals? Not so, for the concern for other people which began our definition of the MEP, is inseparable from the ability to see other people as *people*, as individuals with unique and incommensurable value. Only when we engage in intimate relationships in this way—with spouses, children, close friends—then and only then can we meet their emotional needs for human concern, love and respect. If we cannot do this we are failing our moral obligations in a big way, and no amount of generosity in giving help to strangers can compensate for failure here. The emotional needs of one's close friends and family cannot be met by just anyone, so one's obligations are proportional to one's irreplaceability. And the only way to meet them is by being particularistic, by seeing and responding to these people as unique individuals who are valued because of our special relationship with them.

Furthermore, it is only when we allow ourselves to know other people in this fashion that we can put ourselves imaginatively into their shoes and empathise with them. Only in this way does one come to understand other people and, as one extends one's range of experience of people, to acquire any delicacy in handling human relationships.

So it is necessary for the MEP to grow up with the habit of responding to other people in this particularistic and holistic way and it is necessary for him to set aside this mode of response sometimes. The point we are now making is how *both* modes of response are required for the MEP, along with the ability to set one aside and change to the other. This requirement to balance the two sometimes makes for excruciatingly painful choices.

More people are capable of thinking in universalistic terms than are capable of both thinking and acting this way. To act in terms of universalistic principles is often to disappoint those making particularistic claims on one, so it requires a good deal of moral courage. One of the earliest ways of discovering this is by being made a prefect at school, a position in which teachers expect universalistic rules to be enforced impartially on other pupils, including one's friends. There are institutional arrangements for facilitating this shift of loyalties, such as the fostering social distance between prefects and other pupils by giving them a "prefects' room" and other privileges which reduce the amount of informal interaction with non-prefects, while attempting to reduce social distance between teachers and prefects, by entertaining them socially, consulting them about some matters of school administration, in order to increase the amount of identification by prefects with teachers' values. While this may help to ease somewhat the pains of laying aside familiar particularistic loyalties, it can never be easy even under optimum conditions. And in practice conditions are usually less than optimal.

Let us summarise this definition of the morally-educated person. He or she is someone who has concern for other people such that their feelings, wants and interests count with one and are not lightly overridden for the sake of one's own goals; the MEP is competent at social skills, good at knowing other people's feelings and good at knowing and expressing their own; knowledgeable about the physical and social worlds; the MEP is objective and unprejudiced in sizing up situations and unafraid to proceed with the plan of action intended; lastly the MEP, when thinking about what to do in an unfamiliar situation or in passing judgement on action already taken, thinks in terms of universalistic moral principles based on concern for the rights of other people as well as himself.

KOHLBERG'S THEORY OF MORAL DEVELOPMENT

Our model of the MEP corresponds closely to certain of the character types defined by various psychological studies as the most mature, autonomous, or developmentally advanced (Wright, 1971). Outstanding among all of this research is the work of Lawrence Kohlberg (1966, 1969), though it focusses only on the dimension of moral judgement and not on the whole seven dimensions in terms of which we have defined the MEP. However, he shows how some of these other dimensions relate to the one which he has studied with great care, namely the manner in which people make moral judgements and the criteria they employ to justify or explain their decisions or judgements. The focus of his research has been on the *reasons* people employ in making these moral judgements or decisions, rather than the conclusions to which they come.

Kohlberg's research indicates the existence of six stages in the development of moral judgement, hierarchically related, in the sense that for a person to reach any given stage, he must proceed through the prior stages in sequence. Thus to facilitate the development of children into MEP's the aim of the moral educator should be to accelerate their progress through the sequence, rather than trying to push them directly into Stage Six from a much earlier one.

A *Stage Six* person on Kohlberg's scale makes moral judgements on the basis of general moral principles which he has chosen to be his moral pole stars and his incentive for sticking to these principles lies in not wanting to endure the self-reproach which he must suffer if he fails. These principles may sometimes lead him to flout social conventions and disobey laws. It is not clear, however, whether these principles must (in this theory) be altruistic in nature and, if so, why. A *Stage Five* person takes a social contractual or legalistic view of moral obligations. They are binding because of an implied social contract among the members of society, which is necessary for social order. Thus, in the view of such a person, unusual circumstances may make a particular law unreasonable in a particular case and hence mitigate the blame incurred by the law-breaker, though this cannot condone or excuse the violation as such. Although laws are regarded as somewhat arbitrary at bottom, obedience to them is regarded as a necessary principle of society.

The *Stage Four* person also has a legalistic outlook but without the more sophisticated qualifications recognised in Stage Five. In Stage Four acts are regarded as being categorically right or wrong, regardless of motives or circumstances. At this stage there is a strong orientation to "doing one's duty", showing respect for authority and maintaining the given social order for the sake of maintaining it.

Stage Three is labelled as the "good boy" orientation. At this stage, a person evaluates acts mainly according to the intention of the actor, assumed if necessary on the basis of naive stereotyping. If the intention was benevolent, or if it seems like the kind of thing a "nice" person would do, then it is judged good and *vice versa.* The main motivation of a *Stage Three* person is to avoid the disapproval of the other people he comes into contact with. By way of comparison, the Stage Four person is also attuned to the avoidance of disapproval—but on a more formal or institutionalised level, for example, bad ratings in his file.

Stages One and Two Kohlberg regards as "pre-moral". Guilt feelings do not play any significant part. At *Stage One* a person is guided by a "trouble-avoiding set", following the guideline that one should obey those who have the power to punish you, in order not to get punished. In evaluating the seriousness of acts, the Stage One person responds only to the external, physical nature of the act, for example the child who broke ten cups while helping his mother is considered naughtier than the child who broke two cups while playing a prank and disobeying his mother. At *Stage Two* there is more of an orientation towards seeking rewards (as opposed to just avoiding punishments as in Stage One) and hence approving acts which meet an instrumental need for oneself (or occasionally for someone else). Provided that an action meets such a need, it will be approved by the Stage Two person, regardless of the fact that it may be against the law and regardless of its other physical consequences. Shifting from Stage Two to Stage Three (the "good boy" orientation) involves adopting the guideline "what would the people I deal with think about it?"

It should be reiterated that many moral dilemmas may be decided either way by respondents at each of these stages. Although certain kinds of actions are inherently less likely to be approved of at some stages of moral thought development, what Kohlberg is essentially describing is a sequence of changes in the way people define and evaluate moral alternatives. Of course, it is likely that other aspects of human development will tend to correlate with these stages of moral thought and indeed, some have already slipped into even this very brief summary—such as the absence of guilt feelings (an affective element) in Stages One and Two.

Having shown the existence of this general developmental sequence in moral thought, Kohlberg shows, secondly, that the sequence is not just found in Euro-American cultures but in widely different ones such as Mexico and China (Taiwan). On the basis of this, he claims that this developmental sequence is a universal feature of human development, transcending cultural differences. Thirdly, in this summary of Kohlberg's main findings, he shows that there is a significant degree of consistency for each individual in his level of response on the Kohlberg moral thought scale as between different questions presenting different situations.

This conclusion radically revises the earlier findings of Hartshorne and May (1930), long regarded as definitive, based on their monumental experimental research, and the interpretations placed upon them by later workers. They had concluded that cheating was unpredictable from one situation to another and that any general factor involved was rather weak. That research, it must be remembered, was done with young school children (under fourteen years), presumably at earlier stages in terms of the Six-Stage scale. Kohlberg's US study found that thirteen-year-old boys most often gave responses associated with Stage Three, followed by Stage Four and Stage Two (in that order) next in order of frequency. Kohlberg argues that in this age-range moral judgement is indeed developing and incorporating values unfavourable to aggression and to theft, but not to cheating yet. Whereas theft and aggression have obvious harmful consequences for others, cheating does not and requires a more advanced stage of moral thought to appreciate it as a moral imperative—probably Stage Four or above. Thus, among the age group studied by Hartshorne and May, resistance to cheating is determined by situational and expediency factors. At later developmental stages cheating decreases, Kohlberg finds, producing a correlation between amount of cheating and stage of moral thought.

Although it is not completely clear whether Kohlberg's Stage Six person corresponds exactly to our MEP, it is clear that our MEP has to have the moral judgement of the Stage Six person. Kohlberg's stages of development reflect a process of increasing universalisation of judgements. Stages One and Two are totally egocentric; Stage Three is perhaps a little less; Stages Four and Five are based on a respect for laws and other general categories of socially-defined norms; Stage Six is based on universal, abstractly defined general principles, not tied to any one society or societies. Of course, this theory has far more to it than this. Kohlberg insists that the stages do represent qualitatively different modes of moral thinking, which are not reflected in a one-dimensional scale of universalism.

For our purposes in this book, though, we are interested in the one character type of the MEP and its prerequisites. And the MEP, we must reiterate, is not to be identified with the Kohlberg Stage Six person. Rather he is a special sub-type of that class, defined additionally by his concern for other people, his adept social skills and competence in functioning in his environment, his fair-mindedness and strength of character—all of this in addition to the universalistic quality of his moral thought.

CHAPTER 2 REFERENCES

Michael Argyle, *Social Interaction*, Methuen, London, 1969.

Ralph L. Beals and Harry Hoijer, *An Introduction to Anthropology*, Macmillan, New York, 1959.

Bernard Berelson and G. Steiner, *Human Behaviour: An Inventory of Scientific Findings*, Harcourt, Brace and World, New York, 1964.

Stanley Coopersmith, "Studies in Self Esteem", *Scientific American*, February, 1968.

Kurt Danziger, *Socialization*, Penguin, Harmondsworth, 1971.

Hugh Hartshorne and M. A. May, *Studies in Deceit*, 3 vols., Macmillan, New York, 1930.

O. J. Harvey, D. E. Hunt and H. M. Schroder, *Conceptual Systems and Personality Organizations*, Wiley, New York, 1961.

Lawrence Kohlberg, "Moral Education in the Schools: A Developmental View", *School Review*, Spring, 1966, pp. 1–30.

Lawrence Kohlberg, "Stage and Sequence: The Cognitive-Developmental Approach to Socialization", in David A. Goslin (ed.), *Handbook of Socialization Theory and Practice*, Rand McNally, Chicago, 1969.

Margaret Mead, "Our Educational Emphasis in Primitive Perspective", *American Sociological Review*, 1943, reprinted in George D. Spindler (ed.), *Education and Culture*, Holt, Rinehart and Winston, New York, 1963, pp. 309–20.

John Wilson, N. Williams and B. Sugarman, *Introduction to Moral Education*, Penguin, Harmondsworth, 1968.

Derek Wright, *The Psychology of Moral Behaviour*, Penguin, Harmondsworth, 1971.

Chapter Three

THE SCHOOL AS A SOCIAL SYSTEM

This chapter views the school as a system of patterned social relationships, within which the various kinds of learning we have enumerated take place. The relationship between social context and nature of learning is an intimate one. Some aspects of learning take place "in" the school, for example, the learning of English grammar, wood-working skills and reading music. Other and quite vital aspects of learning occur not merely "in" the school but "through" the school, that is, "through" the patterns of social relationships which are permitted and required by the structure of the school. For example, as a result of spending five or more years in a school governed by a head who made unexplained decisions about new rules with no prior consultation of pupils or staff, pupils would be likely to develop certain images or cognitive assumptions about the nature of authority (not only in the school but wherever it is found) and certain attitudes towards such authority.

Let us assume that these pupils experience similar kinds of parental authority at home. We may compare them with another sample of pupils attending a different school, where reasons are given for the existence of the main rules and those who make the rules consult those who will be expected to obey them; these pupils also find a similar kind of authority at home. It is likely that pupils at this second school will develop different images of authority and attitudes towards it compared to those at the former school.

We shall emphasise learning *through* the school far more than learning *in* the school, for the latter is relatively obvious and has been the traditional focus of discussion among educationalists. Through this approach the social scientist can make his most useful contribution to a better understanding of the school's part in moral development.

In recent years a considerable amount of research has been done in schools, using the conveniently captive population of children as guinea-pigs on whom to try out tests of ability, measures of attitudes and methods of teaching. Yet in all this research *in* schools there has been relatively little research *on* schools, that is research focusing on (for example) social interaction in the classroom; variations in the formal structure of the school and their consequences for teachers and pupils; the roles of heads, teacher, counsellor, house-tutor, deputy head and so forth; the authority system of the school and how it is buttressed by rules and rituals.

This lack is surprising, for the sociology and social psychology of the school got off to an exceptionally promising start with Willard Waller's *The Sociology of Teaching* published in 1932. Despite its now archaic psychology and its complete lack of "hard" data, this book is an impressive example of what can be achieved by sophisticated analysis allied to a real understanding of how the situations under analysis look to the people involved —both teachers and pupils.

The next published work of any importance came thirty years later. Recently, however, there has been an upsurge of interest in the school, producing case studies of single schools, studies covering several schools of the same type, studies covering several types of school and, most recent of all, detailed studies of a single classroom. A more detailed review of the literature will be found in Appendix Two which contains references to thirty-five studies. In addition there are various published attempts which apply theoretical concepts of sociology or psychology to the school, of which the most valuable is that by Bidwell (1965).

This quantity of literature does not, however, basically contradict our original statement about the paucity of research on the school as such. In relation to the complexity of the issues and the ground to be covered, the empirical studies cover it like a scanty fig-leaf and the theoretical discussions with few exceptions are less helpful than two theoretical discussions of social systems or organisations which make no special reference to schools at all (see Parsons, 1965 and Katz and Kahn, 1966).

Only when one tries to put together a synoptic view encompassing the social structure of the classroom and of the school as a whole, the pupil's informal social system and that of the staff-room, on each level taking account of communication, division of tasks, power and authority—let alone the effects of participation on the individuals—does one realise how sketchy and incomplete are the ideas of knowledge and how vast the areas of ignorance. And the problem is not just a lack of knowledge as to what goes on in all these aspects of the school's functioning but, for great areas, no one has so far any idea even how to state what we need to know. It is this lack of a conceptual framework, through which we can define the problems clearly, even more than the lack of exact knowledge, which indicates the parlous state of the sociology and social psychology of the school.

One may think of the school as being a kind of limited small community. From this view-point it is seen as an organisation having a rather comprehensive set of customs and routines, distinct from those of other groups or organisations in the society and tending to constitute a sub-culture which looms very large in the lives of its members. The appropriateness of such a view-point is fairly obvious in the case of boarding schools; for other schools it may or may not be so appropriate. Whether it is appropriate is a matter of fact: how closely the individual school does conform to the assumptions of the model of the school as a community. To decide this, one has to look at several aspects of the schools in question, such as how large a part they do play in the lives of their members, how distinct are the customs and routines of the school from outside society and how high are the boundaries between school and outside.

Since this model fits some schools well and others poorly it seems, therefore, that we should seek another model which will not take these characteristics as given or constant but will treat them as variables and so enable us to analyse their relationships to other variables in the social organisation of the school. For this reason we choose to employ the model of the school as a social system.

BOUNDARY, INPUTS, OUTPUTS

We now begin to look at the school as a unit in its own right. As such we may conceive of a *boundary* dividing the school from the environment or the larger social system. This boundary may be a physical one, like the high wall or fence around a Borstal. More often it takes the purely symbolic form of notices to outside visitors and rules restricting pupils from wandering abroad during school time. This boundary should not be seen as simply spatial or territorial. It is rather a matter of "social space". Pupils who are on a field trip or an organised school holiday are considered to be still under school jurisdiction and expected to obey teachers, who are held responsible by the general public for their conduct. The same children on holiday with their parents are considered beyond the boundary of the school. In intermediate situations, however, such as the time when pupils are travelling between school and home consensus often breaks down. Schools often try to control pupils' behaviour at this time but are not always effective, partly because pupils and parents do not always accept it but more because of the practical difficulties of detection. Grammar schools have often tried to control pupils' activities during their evenings and weekends, even though pupils lived at home, by forbidding them to take part-time jobs or join voluntary organisations. The heads of these schools defined their pupils' leisure time as falling, to some extent, within the boundary of the school. This is most sharply illustrated by the institution of homework.

The boundary also enables us to conceptualise the degree of control which the school attempts to exercise over what pupils may bring into the school with them. School rules may attempt to regulate the kind of clothes the pupils may wear, forbid the importation or consumption by pupils of tobacco or other drugs, pornography, pets and many other possessions which the pupils may legitimately keep at home.

The notion of a boundary further enables us to conceptualise the flow of inputs and outputs between the school and the larger society. Into the school across the boundary flow various *inputs*, notably three kinds: resources (money and supplies), personnel, (pupils and teachers), and expectations or demands concerning how the school will run and what it will achieve. The demands that matter are those endorsed by the governing body or controlling agency of the school.

The governing body and controlling agency may be one and the same body, as in the case of the US local school board or the governors/trustees of independent schools in either country. Or they may be two separate bodies, as in the case of state-maintained schools in England. Where we find both, the main issue is the balance of power between them. In the case of state-maintained schools in England the managers (governing body) have negligible power; the local education authority (LEA), a branch of county-level government, has considerable power over certain defined areas (such as the arrangements for assigning pupils to different schools); the national government, acting through the Department of Education and Science has the legal right to impose any requirements on schools, either directly or through the LEAs, but very rarely does so, although they do determine the length of compulsory attendance and the broad nature of religious worship and teaching. Through their control of school finances both levels of government have great power over the whole state school system.

The governing body may be visualised as located at the boundary between schools and outside society; the controlling agency may be viewed as part of the outside society with special relevance for the school. Where there is no governing body, the head simply deals directly with the controlling agency. The latter is rarely absent, whether it is the LEA, national ministry of education, some other government ministry, or a professional or trade association for inspecting and licensing specialised vocational training schools.

The governing body, located at the boundary, functions in several ways: it receives resources from outside sources and channels them into the school; it recruits staff and pupils, in some cases selecting from an excess of applicants and in others beating the bushes for suitable personnel; and it responds to pressures seeking to influence school policies, formulating its own official policy, taking the former into account as much as it feels necessary.

The *outputs* of the schools flow out across the boundary to the larger society. They consist of all the changes which the school has produced or made possible in its pupils: all the learning of skills, knowledge, attitudes and behaviour, as well as the analogous changes in staff, especially in the form of "professional development". These outputs are, in theory, open to comparison with the expectations handed down by the "controlling agency" which has the power in law to dismiss staff who fail to meet their standards, to withhold funds or to close down the school in the event of their extreme displeasure.

The controlling agencies themselves may be in different kinds of relationship with their own constituencies. The autonomous local school boards found in the USA have to fear the reactions of the local voters who directly elect them. The private trust which controls an independent school is less hamstrung. Though free from institutional dependence, it is inevitably constrained by the views of the parents on whom it is financially dependent for fees and by those of the old boys on whom they depend for gifts and legacies.

The governing body exists *at* the boundary and by its behaviour can determine in part the nature of the boundary itself. This body may operate so as to protect the school from pressure groups and opinionated members of the public, or it may side with them and demand full responsiveness to every complaint and demand. The governors of an independent school may secure a great increase in autonomy for their school by cultivating more diverse and plentiful sources of funds so as to decrease dependence on particular sources, or by improving the image of the school so that recruitment of both pupils and staff is facilitated. In this sort of way the governing body can influence the boundary relations between the school and the larger society.

Equally important from the head's point of view is his relationship with the governing body or controlling agency itself and the degree of autonomy permitted to him in running the internal affairs of the school. Schools in England appear to enjoy a degree of autonomy in this respect considerably greater than those in most other countries. They are very much freer from governmental interference than the schools of France or the Soviet Union, and also more free from the interference of organised parents' groups than the schools of the USA. On the other hand, the power of the organised teachers' associations is relatively great in England, which may impose some restraint on heads' freedom of action (Baron and Tropp, 1961). It can also happen that the head and the main teachers' union in his school are lined up together in a struggle to get the LEA to accept a certain change of policy. This is more common in primary schools, where the head is commonly a member of the same union as his staff and may indeed be a leader in union affairs.

The effectiveness of the school in producing its outputs is affected by the inputs available to it, including the kind of home backgrounds from which pupils come, the quality of teachers and the generosity with which resources are provided, which will affect (amongst other things) pupil–teacher ratios. In addition to these input factors, though, it is likely that some ways of organising the school are more or less effective than others in terms of producing specific outputs.

INTERNAL ORGANISATION

Certain organisational approaches may be precluded in schools with certain input conditions, but across the broad range of variation, organisation may be regarded as independent of input conditions. That is, a wide range of organisational alternatives exists in any school and which combination is adopted will affect both the school's effectiveness in terms of producing its output and the kinds of operational problems which are met in running it.

Within each school there is generally an *official structure* which describes the allocation of duties and responsibilities among staff. This usually includes a scheme for dividing pupils into teaching groups, a timetable dividing up the work day and a plan for assigning teachers to particular groups of pupils at specific times. Aside from academic work, the official structure commonly covers "pastoral" duties and extra-curricular activities. Each school has a chief executive or head, appointed by its governing body. One of his main responsibilities is to ensure the operation of the official structures established in the school and to make such modifications to them as seem to him necessary, subject to the approval of the governing body and controlling agency. The head who takes over an established school inherits the official structures set up by his predecessors, of course, and his scope for modification is limited by what he can persuade the governing body and staff to accept—not forgetting the parents, pupils and even the organised former pupils, who are influential in some schools.

We find a big difference in the power exercised by the heads of independent and maintained schools. The newly-appointed head of an independent school is likely to be confronted by a long-established group of senior staff, especially house-masters, who are well-connected with members of the governing body and well-known to parents. These staff are virtually irremovable and are a powerful and conservative obstacle to the reforming head. The head of a maintained school is likely to have a higher rate of staff turnover, hence a smaller core of established senior staff. On the other hand, he may have difficulty in recruiting qualified staff and will therefore be unwilling to squeeze out senior staff who oppose his policies. Provided that he can engage the support of a significant part of his staff, there are few policies that the head of a maintained school cannot put into effect. For some policies, such as starting a school council or introducing a prefect system, the support of pupils is also necessary to its success. Even without securing this support there is nothing to stop the head of a maintained school from going ahead with his innovating—nothing except good sense.

Staff and pupils enter a school with preconceptions of their roles which are modified by their experiences in the school. They find that certain ways of behaviour are established as normative among their peers. There is a process of informal socialisation which affects both new pupils and the less experienced teachers and bends their preconceived notions in the direction of those practices established among their peers. Older teachers would be an exception to this. Younger teachers and especially those straight from training are very susceptible to the influence of the established staff and the general atmosphere of the common-room. In addition to these more subtle influences, there is the fact that the new recruit's first year of teaching is done on probation and he or she will get no teaching certificate without the recommendations of head and departmental supervisor. This implies a great weight of conservatism or tradition in the school. Big changes within a relatively short space of time are not generally possible, except when the head can ruthlessly purge and replace his staff and uses very great tactical skill. Even the head who is starting a new school is constrained to some extent by the preconceptions of the staff and pupils whom he recruits. So, unless he can afford to be very choosy, he will find it hard to set up in his school structures and procedures that deviate widely from those which are conventionally accepted as normal in the educational world.

In the course of day-to-day events the behaviour of pupils and teachers will not conform perfectly to that laid down in the official blueprint. The strains of responding to situations that were not foreseen in the plan and the strains of reconciling previous habits with new expectations will lead to the innovation of new practices, some of them not anticipated, others anticipated and forbidden.

Within any school there are certain elements of the structure which function as *social control* mechanisms. "Social control" refers to the provisions made within the school for detecting deviance and imposing sanctions, as well as (to a lesser extent) noting excellent performance and rewarding it. Since the teaching staff have been trained, tested and screened before appointment it can be assumed that they can be trusted to conform to a far higher degree than can pupils. Hence the investment of time and other resources spent by staff in checking up on pupils is vastly greater than that spent by the head and senior staff in checking up on other staff. It should not be forgotten though that, at some level, social control is done *to* the staff as well as being done *by* them.

Staff are sometimes assisted in matters of pupil discipline by some specially appointed pupils in the role of "prefects" or "monitors" and this work is often supervised by a senior member of staff appointed to this job of chief disciplinarian by the head, who remains ultimately responsible. "Corrective action" in response to deviance by pupils may take different forms. A private reprimand may suffice or a general warning to all may be necessary as well. Suspension or even expulsion may take place for a severe offence, while a lesser one will merely put the offender in the head's "bad books". Certain kinds of deviance indicate, to the head who is willing to see it, a short-coming in the official structures. This may lead to corrective action on the system level, removing the causes of the deviant behaviour.

Pupils whose conduct is revealed as praiseworthy will be praised and rewarded in various ways—with privileges, prizes, good testimonials, positions of privilege and so forth. But approval and disapproval expressed by teachers remains the most pervasive of all sanctions in the school. The effectiveness of the system of social control is crucial to the smooth functioning of the school and the form which this control takes is likely to have a significant effect on the attitudes to authority developed by pupils.

Another set of mechanisms exists within the school whose function is to build up the *motivations* of members so that they will strive to conform to the official norms. These mechanisms also function to remove psychological obstacles to conformity which may exist, a function which can be called "*tension management*". The difference between these mechanisms and social controls lies in the fact that social controls come into play *after* the event, whereas motivation and tension management operate *beforehand*. Given a perfectly effective system of tension management, there would be no need for social control. It is, however, not easy to find an example of such a situation.

Those mechanisms of social control and motivation which support the official norms of the school are not the only ones operating within those boundaries. Pupils in general, and certain categories of pupils in particular, may develop their own social system in which roles and norms are defined in ways that differ from those officially approved; they may also elaborate these roles and norms in ways extending far beyond the definitions, though not necessarily in conflict with them; and they may have their own system of social controls operating mainly in informal (but powerful) ways. Teachers in general and certain categories of them in particular may do exactly the same. In such cases one has a three-way confrontation between (1) the officially prescribed structures, (2) the deviant social system operating among pupils and (3) that of the teachers—though not necessarily including *all* pupils or *all* teachers.

There is no aspect of the school whose functioning is not affected by the efficiency of *communication*, since this is a fundamental element in all social relationships. In a complex organisation, such as the school, the problem is not just to get A and B to talk clearly and listen carefully to each other. The head must be able to get messages to all staff and all pupils, or to any particular set of them, such that they are accurately received and understood; he must be able to get accurate feedback on how well staff and pupils are complying with the expectations of the official blueprint; staff must have access to him with information on the difficulties involved in attempting to fulfil certain expectations; there must be ready interchange of information among staff, especially pertaining to the behaviour and unfolding personalities of pupils; the latter themselves must be able to get adequate information as to what is expected of them, what choices are open to them and what are the probable consequences of non-compliance: equally pupils must have access to staff when they have grievances or personal problems.

On the other hand, it is possible for the communication system to be overloaded with messages, with the result that production of outputs is hampered. In most schools, though, there are formal rules prescribing who may communicate with whom, when and in what manner. In other words, communication is restricted to "proper channels" with a consequent loss of information.

Every school will have a number of rules indicating categories of prohibited and prescribed conduct, though there will be much variation between schools in the actual content, extensiveness, explicitness and formality of the rules. They play an important part in relation to social control and tension management.

In addition to the school-wide rules each teacher will add his or her own rules for each of the classes they teach. As the years go by, pupils are exposed to more specialist teachers in any given year (or week) and exposed to them for shorter lengths of time. As pupils find that there are common denominators among the rules set up by their different teachers, as well as rules which are idiosyncratic to certain individual teachers, they tend to learn that some rules can have an existence and validity independently of the individuals who enforce them.

In the school one can, in principle, discern some allocation pattern of rewards and punishments, whether or not anyone consciously intends it to be so. This analysis implies firstly, making some kind of catalogue of the various rewards that are utilised: such as school reports, prizes, "points", praise from teachers, testimonials, privileges and so forth. Having defined the rewards, one then has to see who gets them: whether it is, for example, the outstanding scholars, the star sportsmen, or the most morally-educated pupils, or some other group. What kind of excellence is most highly rewarded in each school? We might hypothesise that the more heavily any particular line of excellence is rewarded, the more intensely it will be pursued by members of that school, other things being equal.

However, it should be appreciated that the school where certain awards are made annually or termly with great ceremony is probably rewarding this area of behaviour less effectively than the school where less dramatic rewards and reinforcements are given weekly or daily by staff who show by their own examples that they are truly committed to that set of values and behaviour.

There is a second aspect of reward systems in schools that must also be considered. This involves looking beyond the question of what kind of achievement is most highly rewarded to establish to what extent any *one* kind of excellence monopolises the rewards allocated in the school. In other words, we are concerned with the degree of pluralism or multi-dimensionality in the reward system of schools. The more uni-dimensional is the reward system of a school, the more pupils it tends to exclude from a feeling of success; and hence the less favourable will be the aggregate of pupils' attitudes to school, with obvious implications for social control.

The social control system of the school, based on positive and negative sanctions (rewards and deprivations) operates in different ways in different sectors of the school. In the area of academic work sanctions operate automatically and independently of the school, in so far as pupils will have to compete for future social positions in a merit-based competition. If they do not conform, they are likely to fail their exams. We are assuming here that teachers know better than pupils what is required to pass the exams and that their demands on pupils correspond closely to those requirements.

In so far as pupils are indifferent to future success, are aiming at success in fields not governed by scholastic entry criteria, or have privileged entry to desired future positions, these sanctions will not apply. These are all atypical situations, of course. For most pupils their chances in the labour markets are predetermined by their performance in school, and to the extent to which they are aware of this, the problem of social control within the school is simplified. It is simplified because the reward system internal to the school is supplemented by a vastly greater universe of anticipated rewards in the occupational system. To a great extent this accounts for the greater docility of middle-class pupils in the school compared to working-class pupils (though it is also due of course, to the differential socialisation experiences of these two groups of pupils). This also suggests why we would expect far fewer problems of social control within schools in totalitarian societies, where the monolithic labour market is so highly controlled by the state, than we find in schools in the West. Thirdly, one would predict on the basis of this principle that pupils who expect to work in their own family businesses will be worse risks from the point of view of school discipline than pupils of similar social class who expect to seek jobs in the open labour market.

In other sectors of school life where rules exist and pupils' conformity is expected the sanctions are multiple and less obvious. To the extent that those who play the dominant roles in these areas (e.g. house-masters, prefects) are liked and respected by pupils, the latter will tend to emulate them and their standards. The sanction involved is partly the pupils' desire for approval from the admired superior and partly his "identification" with the other.

Even aside from the above, the existence of a hierarchy of privileged and status-bearing positions open to pupils serves as an incentive. Promotion to monitor, house prefect, head boy, etc., presumably depends upon the pupil's convincing the appropriate superiors that he conforms to a satisfactory degree to the norms and expectations of the school. For pupils who lack any "identification" with school authority figures that would by itself motivate them to conform to these standards, the desire for the prestige and privileges accruing to a prefect may provide sufficient incentive.

A pupil's reputation with his teachers and head can have important consequences for his future career, constituting a further set of sanctions. It gives the teacher a considerable power over his pupils which is none the less effective if it is unstated on the teacher's side and subconscious on that of the pupil.

Social control in the recreational area, by contrast with the previous two, is in the hands of pupils to a relatively great extent. Schools will vary in the extent to which there are formal structures for activities of this kind, such as clubs, societies, fraternities, but in all cases we may expect to find an informal process among pupils whereby they vary the warmth of their feelings and behaviour towards their fellows or the respect they accord them.

Among pupils there are sometimes found individuals who have a stable position of influence over the others, perhaps because they have earned the regard of the general body of pupils over a period of time, or because they are bullies with loyal henchmen. In that case the operation of this sanction system is more highly structured, and woe betide the teacher who finds such an individual in his class and makes an enemy of him.

COHESIVENESS, RITUAL AND AUTHORITY

To what extent can the school be viewed as a cohesive unit? The degree of its cohesiveness is a fundamental factor in determining the effectiveness with which pattern maintenance in the school is achieved and also in determining the impact of the school upon the values and attitudes of those who go through it, both pupils and staff.

Cohesiveness is a difficult concept to define but for our purposes here we will regard cohesiveness as the property of a group in which the members feel themselves to be closely bound together, with a strong loyalty to each other, to the group and to the norms and values which exist among them as a group. This is the kind of property one associates with a well-run sports team, military squad, friendship group. Note that the examples which come most readily to mind are small groups in which the members have a common activity. Within the school, cohesiveness will often be a property of cliques of pupils, of classrooms, the staffroom, extra-curricular groups, sports teams and so forth. The question here, however, refers to the school as a whole.

A primary school at assembly, with all present singing enthusiastically together or listening attentively to the head, clearly represents a high degree of cohesiveness. Similarly, a whole school out on the sports field cheering for the school team represents this. Note, however, that both our examples refer to occasions that are quite short-lived in the life of the school where they happen. After the assembly or the sports event, they all return to their separate classes and lessons. Then the level of apparent cohesiveness drops sharply, as there is no visible focus for it and it remains at best a latent property of the school, ready to be called forth by some appropriate event.

Ritual and ceremony both play important parts in the social system of the school, especially in relation to cohesiveness. "Ritual" refers to certain forms of social behaviour which are highly stereotyped, indicating the formal relationship existing between individuals and the formal definition of the social situation in question. Between teachers and pupils in the school, especially in certain types of school, ritual plays an important part in defining, reinforcing and stabilising teacher-pupil relations in the officially approved form (Waller, 1932, ch. 10). That is to say, the function performed by such rituals as the teacher insisting that pupils stand when he enters the classroom is to symbolise and impress upon all concerned the status difference between teachers and pupils as well as the formality of their relationships. The wearing of academic gowns by teachers makes the same point again. Since many rituals in the school serve to underline status differences between teachers and pupils, it might seem that the effect of rituals would be to diminish rather than increase cohesiveness. This, I suggest, is not so though the situation is complex and a little paradoxical.

Rituals of the sort mentioned have the effect of emphasising the similarity among pupils in their social position, at the same time as they emphasise their distinction from teachers. Cohesiveness among the pupils as a large peer group is thus enhanced—but is this at the expense of the cohesiveness of the school as a whole (both pupils and staff)?

There are or were schools (examples spring more readily from the past than the present) which appeared to achieve a certain kind of cohesion on the basis of a highly ritualised system. The old-fashioned elementary school, sometimes in quite tough areas, which operated a ritualised, regimented but smoothly operating regime represents one answer to this problem. This system does not depend upon similarity of background and attitudes between pupils and teachers, but upon a highly ritualised system of routines regulating behaviour. These can be readily understood and learned by all pupils. Their very repetitiveness gives them a compelling force, which makes conformity relatively easy. I think it is not at all unreasonable to suppose that many pupils in such schools felt a measure of pride and identification with the school, if not pleasure in their participation. The possible long-term effects on pupils of such a regime will be discussed later.

"Ceremony" refers to a special class of rituals in which a relatively large number of participants are involved and their attention centred on a common object or activity. The principal examples would be the school assembly and the school gathered to cheer their representative team in contest.

The distinguishing feature of ceremony, which differentiates it from ordinary rituals, is its ability to generate strong emotional responses from the participants. The staging of the ceremony in itself has a dramatic power, based on the effect of the massed bodies, the music, the lighting, the focusing of all eyes on one object, frequently a symbol of the group which is solemnly paraded into place (flag, mascots, and so forth). Whereas the effect of ritual in general appears to be ambivalent, on the one hand increasing cohesion but, on the other hand, emphasising divisions within the body, ceremony appears to have a more unequivocal effect in increasing cohesiveness in the group.

The functions of both ritual and ceremony lie in the area of pattern maintenance. Ritual in general reinforces the officially prescribed pattern of social relations on a habit level. It reinforces these definitions, not explicitly by spelling out the rights, duties and expectations, but by the opposite approach of creating unreflecting habits through sheer repetition and drill. Ceremony operates on a more affective or emotional level, tending to create sentiments of identification with the group as a whole and a feeling of loyalty to it.

In the US high school the most important ceremonies are the graduation and prize-giving and the inter-school sports matches. In English schools there is the daily assembly though this is not as highly ceremonialised as the assemblies for the end of term and other special occasions. The inter-school sports match takes place within a competitive context which casts the team as the champions of the whole school who appear in great numbers to cheer them on; it is helped by the dramatic staging, with music, chanting, cheer leaders, and so forth, to produce a very powerful effect. Powerful though it is, however, it tends to unify the members of the school in terms of a set of values unrelated to the official academic or moral objectives of the school. The assembly or graduation ceremony, though it may be less powerful, does permit the head to articulate the official values and ideology of the school. The emotional power of the inter-school contest derives to an important extent from the conflict or competition in which "the school" is a competitor. This is a situation analogous to that of warfare on the national level or a strike on the level of industrial relations. In all of these situations cohesiveness is increased for the group which finds itself involved as a major party to a conflict, in which gains or losses will accrue to all group members more-or-less equally. The school assembly, graduation ceremony or speech day lacks the emotive power which the conflict situation bestows. On the other hand, these occasions do give the platform to the head, who has a relatively suggestible audience to hear him articulate the official values and ideology of the school.

It should be noted that ceremonies will not necessarily involve the whole school as a unit. They may also involve smaller units, such as the house or the year group; they may involve smaller units still, such as the form or tutor group, extra-curricular clubs or fraternities. It is likely, however, that school authorities will discourage or forbid ceremonies by smaller units within the school if they seem to reach a level of intensity that may threaten their members' loyalty to the larger school collectivity.

Compared with the family, the authority patterns of the school are far more formal and impersonal. Whereas in the family the child associates authority with two particular people (its parents), in the school authority is vested in a much larger number of adults, whose social position is formally designated and formally defined. In the school authority is thus associated with a certain social position rather than with certain persons. The ritualisation of teacher-pupil relations in the school helps to underline this distinction up to a point. There are, however, two distinct types of positional authority and the distinction is a crucial one. One is based upon custom and tradition; the other is based upon a formal body of rules and regulations. In practice, of course, these two principles overlap and many schools fall in between and combine both principles.

Individual schools will vary greatly in the way they combine these two principles of authority. In schools which are most highly ritualised, rules will be implicit and a customary or traditional authority system implied. At the other extreme are schools where rules are explicitly stated and where reasons are often given for having these rules. At one end of this scale teachers are likely to justify their authority by claims of "I'm the teacher and I say so" or "That's the way we do things in this school" and at the other end by reference to the formal rules and the justifications attached to them.

Though the amount of emphasis placed upon ritual in the school may vary greatly from school to school, it is not suggested that any school could be entirely without ritual. Even a school with the most highly rationalised authority system is unlikely to be operating without a good deal of custom and ritual. The test of a rationalised authority system is what happens on the rather rare occasions when someone questions one of the rules. The person who is challenged attempts to show that the rule was formulated in the approved or legitimate fashion and, on being pressed further, how it is necessitated by one or more of the generally agreed values of the systems, such as the requirements of safety, getting pupils through exams, smooth administration, etc. Experience of this kind of authority system plays a crucial part in pupils' learning to think in terms of universalistic moral values and principles. Since, as we have argued earlier, this kind of thinking is part of being a morally-educated person, schools cannot produce such people unless they incorporate at some stage or on some level a rationalised authority system.

THE HEAD

The role of the head or principal in the school is an important one, not as the key to the whole puzzle but rather as the leading actor on a crowded stage. We have tried not to give the misleading picture of the school as a tightly regulated bureaucracy but rather as a somewhat fluid system in which a variety of actors with differing interests and resources work out their relationships within the framework of an official structure backed up by a variety of sanctions, many of which are in the control of the head.

In general, the head is chief executive, responsible for recruitment, planning, evaluating the performances of staff and allocating sanctions, as well as modifying the structure; he is also the foreign minister of his school and responsible for receiving official visitors, representing its interests *vis à vis* outside bodies, especially the local education authority or other controlling agency; he performs the ritual function of symbolic "head of state" on ceremonial school occasions (such as assembly, speech day, etc.); he is the leader of his staff, leading them in the direction of the objectives he articulates for the school, seeking out and maximising the areas of common agreement among them, helping them to work together more effectively by smoothing out areas of conflict, arbitrating where necessary, and planning policy and structural modifications to facilitate the effective working of the staff together in the light of needs which emerge; and finally he may serve as the judge of final appeal as well as the public executioner for difficult cases of pupil discipline.

Some heads in fact spend a portion of their time in teaching but we shall, for the purpose of this discussion, regard such activities as lying outside the role of head proper. We shall view such situations as one person playing two roles—that of head proper and that of teacher. Similarly, one *might* find schools where the head helped to tend the gardens, clean the corridors or serve the lunches—whether due to emergency staff shortages or to his holding atypical views about the virtue of physical labour—but it would not seem helpful to regard these tasks as an integral part of the role of head.

It will be helpful to keep in mind two distinctions. The first distinction concerns the different *channels and recipients of* the head's influence: there is his *direct* influence on a few selected individual pupils; his *direct* influence on individual staff members considered in its own right and his influence on pupils *through* his influence on staff. The second distinction refers to the *medium* through which the head's influence is exerted. He has, by virtue of the legal authority delegated to him by the controlling agency (LEA or governing body), control over the allocation of various material resources within the school and the authority to modify the official structures of the school. Thus he controls the allocation not only of material resources but also of physical space and timetable time among the various subjects that are taught and activities which are engaged in at school and as between any set of categories of pupils that may be imagined—such as those of different ages, sex, ability level. The other main medium through which the head exercises his influence in the school is that of personal persuasion. This he exercises on an individual level with individual pupils and staff as well as on a collective level in staff meetings and school assemblies. On the level of personal persuasion and influence the head can appeal for compliance on the basis of the common commitments that he and his teaching staff have as professional educators and the common goals implied, to their personal liking for him and wish to oblige, to their motives of self-interest which may suggest to them that gaining his approval will lead to preferment, or by "charismatic leadership", radiating inspiration.

In practice the head is most influential when he operates

through both media simultaneously: using both his powers of personal persuasion and his control of resources and structure. The importance of his control of resources and structure is not only that it matters to a particular teacher how much time he is given with his pupils and how much in the way of resources are allowed to him, but this factor also serves as a concrete demonstration of the sincerity of the head's support for his work. This is especially important where a head is introducing a new policy. A "new policy" usually means, not a shift from depreciating a certain line of emphasis in the school to emphasising it, but a change from merely paying lip service to it to really supporting it in more concrete terms. In the very important area of attitude to pupils, the personal *example* set by the head takes on a special importance. If a head wishes to emphasise to his staff the importance he places on warmth and concern for pupils, the example he sets by (for instance) making a habit of hanging around the playground and other places where pupils congregate in order to chat with them is probably more important than any amount of exhortation in staff meetings. Perhaps the next most important thing that a head can do towards promoting warmth and concern in teachers' attitudes towards pupils is to show the same attitude towards his staff.

This notion that the performance of teaching staff and hence the education of pupils is affected by the performance of the head in his role not only accords with common sense but has some support from research. In a nation-wide study of elementary school principals in the USA Gross and Herriot (1965) found a positive correlation between their measure of the principal's "executive professional leadership" and the morale of the teachers, their professional performance and the amount that pupils learned. A somewhat similar study by Revans (1965) in twenty-seven English schools measured how much pupils liked their teachers and what they thought of their effectiveness; he also looked at the attitudes of teachers in these schools towards the authority structure, focusing on how large a part teachers felt they were allowed to play in running the school. He found a significant association between teacher's perception of the school authority structure and the pupils' assessment of their teachers, both as persons and as professionals. In other words, where the teachers felt that they had a hand in the running of the school, they tend to be liked by their pupils and to be thought effective teachers. Where teachers see their superiors as remote or dictatorial, they in turn are seen by their pupils as remote and ineffective.

Like all cross-sectional correlation studies there is ambiguity as to the causal direction of these relationships. It is not certain that the direction of influence runs from the top of the authority pyramid down towards the bottom. Spurious correlations are always possible and the sceptically inclined can always pull a couple of such variables out of the hat to enliven the discussion. For example, it may be that schools in middle-class areas tend to have both pupils with favourable attitudes and better-trained teachers and administrators who have more liberal attitudes and hence that the correlation between the attitudes and behaviour of pupils, teachers and heads is a spurious product of the stratification of communities and their schools. Until there is some evidence to support these sceptical suggestions, however, the most sensible attitude would seem to be a cautious acceptance of the hypothesis put forward and the research findings cited.

Just as the behaviour of teachers towards their pupils seems to be influenced by the behaviour of the head and other senior administrators towards them so it is likely that the head's own behaviour inside his school is affected by his position *vis à vis* his superiors. They can affect the amount of time that he is able to spend inside his school by the amount of time and energy which they require him to spend on duties that take him outside the school; they can affect his internal policies if they so choose, overruling policies favoured by the head and requiring him to implement policies of their own—creating confusions as to priorities within the school; they can easily undermine his authority by entertaining appeals, protests and secret reports from staff or parents, going behind the head's back. The head's power within his school varies greatly from one educational system to another, being greater in Britain than in the USA, for example (Baron and Tropp, 1961).

Some factors affecting the head's power would seem to be: the amount of autonomy allowed to him by the controlling agency, the degree of control that he has over the hiring and firing of staff as well as the allocation of extra salary supplements and other resources and amenities in short supply which are sought by his staff, the traditional definition of his authority in the culture and how readily he can find suitable replacements for staff who leave —especially replacements who share his own outlook.

ATTAINMENTS AND OUTPUTS

As a result of the activities and interactions of staff and pupils in the framework of the official structure, various *attainments* can ensue in the form of learning increments. We have already discussed in the previous chapter various dimensions of learning attainments that may be involved. Usually, attention is focused on what is learned by pupils, presumably as a result of their participation in the school rather than on what is learned by teachers. This is in accordance with the ideology that teachers go to school to teach others, while pupils go to school to learn from teachers. On reflection, however, it will be clear that pupils learn not only from teachers but also from each other, and that teachers gain from their involvement in school, at the very least in "experience".

When we refer to outputs or attainments we are referring to something which the objective observer coming into the school from outside may (in principle) measure. Those attainments which the school is officially dedicated to cultivating (its official "goals") will be defined differently from school to school, of course. Exactly how they are defined and how they are officially assessed (if at all) will in themselves affect the strivings and attainments of pupils in the school. For maximum effectiveness the system of rewards and social control should be geared to these definitions. Both pupils and teachers will be spurred to direct their energies towards those attainments which are emphasised, praised, and concretely rewarded in their particular schools. This presupposes, however, that there is some official provision for attempting to measure these attainments (at least informally) but in many areas of attainment the only form of assessment provided is rating by teachers.

Few, if any, of the attributes which define the morally-educated person are at all easy to measure in practice. In addition though —and really more important than this—is the fact that in very few schools indeed does the official definition of goals include very many of the characteristics in our definition of the morally-educated person. This being so, there is no attempt made to measure or encourage many of these characteristics—only those which happen to coincide with the head's or teachers' personal ideas about moral education, or those characteristics which just happen to be implicated in some part of the school's structure. Thus, as an example of this, selecting pupils for positions of responsibility necessitates judgements being made about their sense of responsibility, ability to lead other pupils and so forth, even if these qualities were not regarded as among the most important goals of the school. It follows from this point that one of the first requirements that must be met before schools can be more effective at moral education, as we define it here, is that the heads at least—and as many of the teachers as possible—should come to define the goals of their school as including moral education in our sense. Only then will they have the possibility of asking themselves how they can assess and develop these specific forms of attainment by pupils more effectively.

The distinction between attainments or outputs as an objective investigator would assess them and those chosen for measurement by the school itself in its own terms is an important one. At any school those in control are likely to be unaware of many of the impacts which it has upon its pupils. Equally, they are likely to exaggerate its effect on those individual qualities which they are most anxious to influence. Moreover we must also look at the effect on pupils and teachers of the attempts by the school to measure those aspects, which it does attempt to measure, or which are measured by external assessment procedures such as university examining boards or independent testing agencies. We are calling attention here to the effects of the measurement procedures *per se*. Other things being equal, it would seem, the more attention is called to a certain area of attainment by the school's attempts to measure it and the more susceptible such an area is to precise measurements the more will the efforts of the pupils and teachers tend to be transferred to these areas from others. Exemplifying this process is the effect of impending examinations on the teaching of subjects which should ideally allow some free play of imaginative response—English literature degenerates under this pressure into the memorisation of plots and capsule characterisations.

One highly significant difference between moral education and conventional academic learning is that the latter can be measured quite easily and is, in practice, subjected to routine measurement in the school, whereas the attainments that comprise moral development generally cannot. One consequence of this is that the success of the school and of the individual pupils, as judged by people outside the school, will be based very largely on these measurements of academic learning. The absence of recognised and objective measures of moral attainment means that even the school which wishes to lay heavy emphasis on this side of the educational process will be greatly handicapped because, unlike the academically-oriented school, it cannot demonstrate indubitably to the outside world that it is attaining the results it claims. For the purposes of the internal operation of the school, the personal judgements of teachers on pupils' progress in different areas of moral development may be tolerably satisfactory, but they are not very satisfactory when schools or individual pupils must give an account of themselves to interested parties in the outside society.

Whereas the responsibilities of teachers for specific areas of academic learning can be assigned fairly precisely, it is quite different for moral education. There may be time-tabled lessons in "human relations", "thinking about moral questions" and perhaps other dimensions of learning pertinent to the morally-educated person (MEP). But the greater part of the learning in question either cannot be or generally is not effected in such an overt manner: somehow it is absorbed along with academic lessons, with organised games, with informal conversations between teachers and pupils. It is learned from participation in certain activities in a certain kind of structure or social context and in particular from relationships between pupils and teachers. The importance of the social structure of the school to a great extent lies in how it makes certain kinds of teacher-pupil contacts and relationships more or less likely to develop. Through these relationships pupils have adult models in addition to those their parents provide. The important question then becomes what qualities of personality are represented by these adult models and, in particular, how well they represent the qualities of the MEP.

This implies that *all* teachers and others who work in schools are likely to play some part in the determination of outputs on the moral education side, regardless of their intentions. Staff can opt out or be exempted from academic teaching or from administrative duties but not from moral education. All staff who come into direct contact with pupils or who influence them indirectly through their function in the school have to be taken into account, including not only teachers but also caretakers, dinner supervisors, lab. assistants, secretaries, school nurses, gardeners and so forth. Schools differ in how far they try to limit contacts between pupils and non-teaching staff. Where limitations are not severe non-teaching staff may be found to make their own contribution in addition to that of teachers in various ways.

Many facets of the school organisation have grown up for historical reasons not specifically connected with either academic or moral learning. Organised games, prefect systems, house systems, school assemblies, extra-curricular activities, school councils, are some of the notable examples. We shall look at each of these institutions and try to specify the implications that each of them has for social control, motivation and tension management, and in particular moral education.

CHAPTER 3 REFERENCES

George Baron and Asher Tropp, "Teachers in England and America", in A. H. Halsey *et al.* (eds.), *Education, Economy and Society*, Free Press, New York, 1961, pp. 545–57.

Charles E. Bidwell, "The School as a Formal Organisation", in James G. March (ed.), *Handbook of Organizations*, Rand McNally, Chicago, 1965.

Neal Gross and R. E. Herriot, *Staff Leadership in Public Schools*, John Wiley, New York, 1965.

Daniel Katz and R. L. Kahn, *The Social Psychology of Organizations*, John Wiley, New York, 1966.

Talcott Parsons, "Paradigm of a Social System", in T. Parsons, E. Shils, K. D. Naegele and J. R. Pitts (eds.), *Theories of Society*, Free Press, New York, 1965, pp. 36–41.

R. V. Revans, "Involvement in School", *New Society*, 26 August, 1965.

Willard Waller, *The Sociology of Teaching*, John Wiley, New York, 1932.

Chapter Four

THE FORMAL STRUCTURE OF THE SCHOOL

In analysing the school as an agent of moral education one may, broadly speaking, adopt one of two approaches. These are: (1) the structural or mechanistic approach and (2) the gestalt or atmospheric approach. In the structural approach, which is the one predominantly used throughout this book, one looks in turn at different facets of the school and considers how variations in the form or functioning of each one may affect the process of moral education, that is the school's impact on its pupils in the areas of moral development. This approach can produce precise and testable hypotheses.

The main disadvantage of this approach is contained essentially in the adage about the whole being more than the sum of the parts. In comparing two schools which are totally different in their ethos, one may go through a long list of specific comparisons —the number of pastoral roles, the nature of the rules and rewards, the structure of teaching groups, roles of responsibility for pupils, the nature of the school boundary, etc.—and still seem to leave important differences unstated. These are differences that can be readily (if loosely) defined in utterly non-technical terms. For example, it may be that in one school there is a warm concern with the whole pupil, while the other one is an intellectual forcing house and nothing more.

Although many of the specific structural points of comparison will reflect this monumental difference, it sometimes seems as if something important is missed if the contrast is not also summed up in this way. These two approaches differ in emphasis rather than essence, though the difference in emphasis can sometimes suggest rather different conclusions. This book mostly follows a structural approach.

In a casual look at the school, it is generally the formal structure of academic learning that strikes the observer first. Although there are differences between religious and secular schools, between schools in one-party states and those in democratic nations, still it is generally true that the formal structure connected with academic learning is more prominent than that connected with moral education in the school.

The formal structure of academic learning includes: a system for the differentiation of pupils into teaching groups; a system for differentiating teachers and allocating them to teaching groups; a scheme for dividing teaching time and specifying which teachers are responsible for which groups of pupils at specific times of the day, where they should be and what they should be doing. Theoretically there is a vast range of alternative ways of organising the academic work of a school along these dimensions. In practice there are conventions which tend to be followed by heads and school administrators, ignoring many of the theoretical possibilities. Even so, the manipulation of those alternatives which are recognised within a particular educational system for the formal organisation of academic work presents a very complex task of administration and there is an extensive literature on this subject (see Franklin, 1967). Not surprisingly, there are now experiments using the computer to try to cope with the practical problems of making a formal structure for a particular school.

The limiting case of a school with the simplest possible formal structure for academic learning is that of the one-teacher-one-room school. This is assuming that all pupils in this school are taught together as a group. But this is in practice unlikely since the school intake covers a wide range of age and ability. As soon as the one teacher begins to differentiate among these pupils, some formal organisation of the academic work has begun. When the size of the school increases to two or three teachers, the degree of formal organisation need not necessarily increase. Provided that the teachers divide the pupils among themselves in a random fashion, there would be no more formal structure than in the case of the one teacher school. So far as the formal structuring of time is concerned, the number of teachers need not affect this either. Under the arrangement whereby one teacher stays with one group of pupils for the entire day, the allocation of time to different subjects can be entirely informal. Or it can be subject to a formal plan if the governing body wishes to impose this or the teacher wishes to impose it on herself. When teachers begin to specialise, especially by subject, instead of spending the whole day with the same pupils, then some formal time-tabling is necessary in order that the movement of the teachers among groups of pupils may be coordinated. Teacher A is obliged to finish his maths lesson with class X at a certain time, because at that time teacher B is coming to teach them something else. Flexible timetabling is possible either under the one-class-one-teacher system or under the system of team teaching. However, under the system whereby teachers work *singly* and *specialise* a rather rigid and formal timetabling is necessary.

DIFFERENTIATION OF PUPILS' ROLES

Within the one-teacher school and the one-teacher classroom pupils may be differentiated by the teacher in many ways in order to structure the teaching process. Organisation on this level tends to be under the control of the individual teacher and not highly formalised. On the level of the whole school, when there is more than one teacher and they work singly, the division of pupils into teaching groups and the differentiation of teachers' roles has a formal basis.

Pupils might be grouped on the basis of their attainment, either overall or in certain subjects. In a school that was run exclusively on this basis pupils would advance from one class to the next whenever they passed the appropriate promotion test. Thus pupils of different ages could be in the same class and pupils could stay different lengths of time in any particular class. An exceptionally bright pupil would not only be working in a class with older and duller pupils but may move on to the next class before many of them. In theory it might be possible in very large schools for pupils to be grouped by both attainment and ability, so that they would tend to be promoted at the same time and to progress through the school in a group together—that is in several groups.

Instead of differentiating pupils on the basis of what they have learned, one can do this on the basis of what they have studied. On this basis all those who have worked through book one (at their varying levels of comprehesion and retention) are considered ready for book two. Similarly those who have completed the work designated for class one are ready to move on to class two. This principle is perhaps more applicable in some subjects than in others, depending mainly on how cumulative the body of knowledge in question might be. The more cumulative it is the more necessary for thorough learning of the earlier stages to be insisted upon, even if pupils have to repeat their work in certain classes. In other subjects it may be important that pupils have exhausted the interest value of a particular subject, for example a particular topic in history, and more important that they should move on to a new subject even though their grasp of the earlier one is unsatisfactory. This failure will not impede their future work so much as their failure to master an early stage of material in mathematics. This principle of curricular age may be combined with the one of attainment so that rather than making the poor achievers in class 1B repeat another year in 1B while their age mates proceed to 2B, they may be moved to 2C.

The principle of curricular age comes quite close in practice to the system of differentiating pupils by seniority in the school, that is not by their precise calendar age but rather by the number of school terms which have elapsed since their entry to the school.

Curricular specialisation gives another basis for dividing and grouping pupils in their academic learning. The curriculum branches at certain points into alternative subjects, of which a pupil can do one only, whether by choice or designation—Latin or Greek, physics or biology, etc.

The most prevalent system of formal differentiation of pupil roles in Britain is based upon a combination of attainment and curricular age or seniority. Grafted on to this basis are further principles of differentiation based on curricular specialisation, sex and other factors. Wherever attainment enters into the formal differentiation system it is necessary to take account of its diffuseness or specificity. The most diffuse system is that of streaming, which differentiates among pupils on the basis of overall attainment; the more specific forms of differentiation are those which assess attainment in individual subjects and differentiate differently for each ("setting").

The formal structure of pupil differentiation affects the interaction possibilities among pupils. Pupils are assigned to particular groups for particular lessons and those who are assigned to the same group see more of each other than those who are assigned to different groups, hence the probability of forming friendships or getting to learn about each other is remarkably different in the two cases. Where lesson groups are formed on the basis of attainment this means that pupils' interaction with other pupils who are considerably cleverer or less clever than themselves will be correspondingly curtailed. The amount of time that pupils of widely different abilities are together, in their free time and perhaps for non-academic occasions, will be less than the times when they are sorted out in this way, since the greatest part of school time is occupied by academic lessons. This will be less true for schools with a strong house system cutting across attainment division and much less true for boarding school. But on the whole the proposition that work groupings will affect the choice of pupils' friends seems a fair one.

A further dimension of this problem involves the stability or fluidity of teaching groups, that is the extent to which pupils change their companions or workmates from one lesson to another in the course of their typical day or week. At one extreme is the highly stable class in which a number of pupils spend their entire week together for all their lessons. At the other extreme there is the fluid system which reshuffles pupils many times during the day. This is most commonly in order to create more homogeneous attainment grouping by setting for individual subjects. The advantage of the stable class is alleged to be that pupils get to know one another better and feel more comfortable at school. The disadvantage would seem to be that they have insufficient opportunity for learning to get along with new pupils.

The formal organisation of academic learning is one of the focal concerns of educational theory and is closely related to other theoretical concerns. One of these is the prevailing definition of the classroom learning situation. Where this is conceived by educators mainly as a situation of passive individual learning by pupils and formal lecturing and testing by the teacher, certain approaches to formal organisation follow. The paramount concern is to achieve a homogeneous audience. However, if the teaching-learning situation is defined as one involving the active and creative participation of pupils in many forms of work, including project work, then homogeneity of attainment is no longer crucial. If, in conjunction with this approach to the nature of learning there is also a concern for the learning of social skills and attitudes of considerateness, then there is likely to be a positive preference for heterogeneous classroom groups (Taylor, 1971). If, moreover, the administrator has been impressed with the practical difficulties of attaining truly homogeneous attainment groups, and with the research strongly suggesting that a self-fulfilling prophecy operates thereby a pupil inaccurately placed in a teaching group tends to develop his abilities in accordance with that initial prognosis, there are then additional reasons for preferring a formal structure of pupil differentiation which manifestly eschews attainment as its principal basis (Rosenthal and Jacobson, 1968).

DIFFERENTIATION OF TEACHERS' ROLES

In the evolution of the school from the one-teacher-one-room school of early days to the large organisation of today the evolution of teacher role differentiation has tended to take the form of increasing specialisation on an individual basis. Instead of the teacher who is wedded to a particular group of pupils for the whole day, week and year, the teacher tends to become a movable unit who is switched from one class to another in successive teaching periods. Then from one year to the next the teacher may in theory switch to a set of entirely new classes and pupils. This poses a substantial problem if the teacher is to know anything about the pupils as individuals.

From the pupils' point of view there are problems of continuity in two directions: from lesson to lesson (subject to subject) during the same day and from year to year, even within the same subject. Under the system of departmental specialisation which has become conventional, the continuity of curriculum from year to year within a single subject is supposed to be planned by the head of the department so that continuity and progression is ensured even with the turnover of teachers. The continuity or integration from one lesson or subject to another in the course of the same day has evoked less concern. Some attempts have been made to introduce what are called "integrated studies". In its simplest version this means that what were formerly two or three subjects on the timetable with two or three different teachers become amalgamated under the control of one teacher. Thus history and geography may become "social studies" under a single teacher who has twice the time available to each of the former specialist teachers. This approach can in principle be extended to any degree up to the limiting case of the one teacher having a class for the whole day. While there are recognised to be various powerful arguments in favour of this kind of integration, a major obstacle to its implementation is the limitation on the knowledge of any one teacher. Even in the primary school this has been felt to be a serious problem and in the secondary school all the more so.

One method of organising academic work has been claimed to overcome both these problems—team-teaching (see Carlin, 1967, Polos, 1965, and Shaplin, 1967). In essence this system involves the pooling of teaching resources and the pooling of pupils likewise. In a five-form entry school, for example, instead of each of the five forms in a particular year being regarded as five separate teaching units each with their exclusive teacher for a particular subject, they would be pooled. This means that the teaching of this five-class population is (in theory) planned as a whole. It does not mean that they are taught in groups of 150, though at certain times they will indeed mass together for some joint work, perhaps to hear a lecture or view a film. At other times they will break up into much smaller groups, sometimes groups smaller than that of the original class of thirty. If they are to see a film, they can see it all together at one time instead of each of the five teachers showing it separately to each of the old-style classes. If they are to have a lecture on a particular topic they can hear it from the one teacher who can do it best.

This kind of division of labour frees the remaining teachers for that length of time during which they can be preparing their contributions to other lessons. Other lessons will find each class working under the supervision of its "own" teacher. Ideally the programme for the years' work in this subject is planned by the teachers together and executed by them as a team. The division of roles and responsibilities is more complex for team teaching than for the old class-teacher system. Instead of one teacher having complete responsibility for thirty-odd pupils for a whole year, under the general direction of his head of department, their work is both more specialised and more closely coordinated. Those who are outstanding lecturers will do more lecturing, those who are skilled in preparing visual material will concentrate on this, those whose *forte* is in organising field work will do this. In addition all will take part in the supervision of classroom work in the usual way. Each teacher can have his or her "own" class in which he or she gets to know the pupils on an individual basis, as in the older system. The pool of teaching abilities which is now available to all the pupils is a greater one and its sharing out among pupils is more equal.

From the pupil's point of view, in some ways team teaching is still further from the simple social structure of the class teacher. There is no simple routine whereby a class knows exactly what it will be doing, where and with whom on any particular time of the day. With the class teacher the pupil knows he is always with this person; under the simple departmental specialisation the pupil always knows that he will be with a particular teacher doing a particular subject at any time of the day; under team teaching, however, the pupil only knows what subject he will be taking, he may not know beforehand who will be supervising him or lecturing him, where this will take place, or with which other pupils he will be working.

From the teachers' point of view this system implies that he is no longer the exclusive king of his classroom in the old way, with the advantages and disadvantages which this implies. His autonomy is reduced, since he must fit in with the overall plans of the team, though he may have a voice in determining what these are. On the other hand, the novice's anxieties over having complete responsibility for a class without the support of colleagues may be reduced. This is especially important for the student teacher and the beginner, who can work his way from less demanding to more demanding roles within the teaching team, always with more experienced colleagues close at hand to help him out. Even for the more experienced teacher the availability of feed-back from colleagues who can observe his performance on the job can be of great value for professional growth and development. Of course there are anxieties attached to this working situation and the idea of being observed or supervised, just as there were fears attached to the isolation of the old-style teacher in his self-contained classroom. But when these can be worked through in the group context of the teaching team in private sessions, the potentialities for the development of one's individual resources as a teacher and as a person would appear to be very great.

We may note several other features of team teaching as a system of formal organisation of academic work, not specifically from the point of view of the individual pupil or teacher, but rather its characteristics as a system. Firstly, it is a more stable system in the sense of being more resistant to the effect of temporary absence or turnover of staff. The absent member of the team causes less disruption of the system than the absent class teacher. Secondly, the employment of ancillary helpers to take some of the chores out of teaching can be more effectively administered in the context of team teaching. A team can employ clerical assistance, cleaners-up and other non-professional aids more efficiently than the individual teacher normally could. Thirdly, a more finely-graded career structure for the teacher can be created, given team teaching. Instead of just one post of responsibility per subject, as head of department, there is now a ladder of responsibility through each team. There may be several teams per department, each with its leader and with as many other positions of intermediate responsibility as the head and the governors care to create.

The authority structure of the teaching team may take various forms—it may be autocratically organised by the leader of the team, who is either the department head or appointed by him or (in the case of an inter-departmental team) appointed by the head; or it may be a democratic group in which policy decisions are made by vote. The less autocratic this group is, the more feedback is likely to be utilised for the improvement of teaching practice and administrative arrangements. Either way though, team teaching tends to involve some decentralisation of decision-making away from the principal or department head into the team itself. The more democratic is the team the greater the extent of decentralisation, since this implies the sharing of the rank-and-file teachers in planning and decision-making.

There is a degree of explicitness and clarity about the relationship between the academic outputs of the school and those aspects of its formal structure which are intended to contribute to these objectives. These we have discussed in the previous section, where we also made the point that there may be *other* important consequences flowing from the formal framework of organisation within which academic work takes place. We turn now to various other aspects of the school's formal structure which are in evidence. There is not a great deal of agreement among educators as to what they hope to achieve through their house systems, prefect systems, extra-curricular activities, competitive sports, cadet corps, and so forth. Partly for this reason we shall skip the questions of what they *intend* to achieve thereby and how these structures came to be set up and shall consider only the question of how they appear to function in the school at the present time.

Some of these structures appear to have a pastoral function, meaning a general oversight of pupils' welfare in the broadest sense, including many of the aspects of moral education and more besides. Most of these parts of the formal structure also make important contributions to the administration of a complex routine and the maintenance of social control, particularly over the conduct of pupils. In the case of some of them this aspect is more apparent than the pastoral one.

MANIFESTLY PASTORAL STRUCTURES

By pastoral care we refer to the efforts of teachers to notice when some problem is bothering a pupil to the point of making him or her very unhappy or threatening to affect adversely his or her education and growth. The source of the problem may lie in the home, in relationships with friends, teachers or any others. Pastoral care involves dealing with the consequences of this problem and will often require some investigation of its origins in order to understand the pupil's state of mind and to decide wisely what can be done to help. Often, but by no means always, a personal problem of this kind will lead the pupil to behave in ways that are disruptive of the normal routine and make extra difficulties for teachers and also perhaps fellow-pupils. This will not always be so, of course, for it is well-known that many pupils who are miserable repress their feelings and outwardly conform to the social requirements—often *over*-conform. Ultimately they may get over it, or develop some quite surprising form of bizarre and deviant behaviour, which seems quite incomprehensible at first because no one was aware of the problems bothering that pupil. For this reason good pastoral work requires far more than merely looking out for behaviour problems.

Good pastoral work contributes to tension management for the school and hence to good discipline. It also contributes to the individual growth and long-term happiness of individual pupils.

This implies a contribution to good discipline as one of its consequences but it goes well beyond this.

Some schools, especially boarding schools, schools responsible for maladjusted pupils and large schools which are keen to overcome the disadvantages of their size, are found to have some arrangements which are explicitly justified in terms of providing a more personal and humane routine as well as providing pastoral care for the pupils. Such is the case with the house system in the boarding school (Wilson, 1962) the cottage system in the correctional establishment, and the provision of form teacher and homeroom in very many schools. These pastoral structures include staff roles with prescribed pastoral duties, such as the house-master, tutor, cottage parent, form teacher, and an arrangement whereby particular pupils are allocated to particular pastors. That is to say, every pupil is allocated to an official pastoral group. This kind of comprehensive pastoral system is to be distinguished from a second kind, in which certain pastoral roles may be provided, such as the chaplain or professional counsellor, but it is up to the initiative of the individual pastoralist or the pupil who has some problem to make the contact. This may be called a "consulting" system as opposed to a "comprehensive" one. It should not be thought, however, that these systems are mutually exclusive. On the contrary the most effective arrangement is likely to be where a comprehensive system is reinforced by a consulting system staffed by trained professionals. Given the tendency to professional specialisation in education, there is a natural tendency for pastoral care to be considered another specialism, just like the teaching of chemistry or physical education. This is a misconception, since pastoral care is, by definition, concerned with the whole pupil, with the pupil as an individual, who can only be known as such by someone who has had a sustained relationship with him.

If this view is accepted, it follows that the teacher with pastoral responsibilities can only be expected to be effective if he is given the opportunity for frequent contact with his charges under conditions where they have something to do together but where they are not tied down to a rigid routine of activities. Good pastoral work may be done by all teachers for all of the pupils with whom they come into contact. A teacher whose inclination is to get to know his pupils in this fashion is likely to be a good watch-dog for danger signals, regardless of whether he is *officially* defined as just their subject teacher or as their form teacher or house master. The advantage of having a formally structured, comprehensive pastoral system with definite assignment of responsibilities is that there is less danger of some pupils being left out altogether. There is the further advantage that teachers can be officially rewarded for good work in the pastoral area when this is clearly defined as their responsibility. Not to so recognise it is, in effect, to penalise the teacher who wishes to do this work.

OTHER ORGANISED ACTIVITIES

Here we are concerned with three kinds of formally organised features of school life: (1) clubs at which pupils can indulge in special interests they may have under the sponsorship of teachers, such as photography, nature study, train-spotting; (2) competitive sports, both intra-mural and inter-school; and (3) dramatic and other spectacles which are performed by pupils for the school. All three groups of activities have in common the fact that they are voluntary, they take place outside the normal school day, are not in practice open to more than a select group of participants and are supervised and controlled by teachers.

In terms of the role of the pupil, all of these activities have in common the fact that they involve an extension of this role from that of passive recipient of information and opinions emanating from the teacher in a formal classroom situation. Generally speaking, these organised activities have more relevance to moral education than to academic learning, and more relevance to social control than to either.

Having described these different groups to be found in the schools under investigation, the researcher should look at two of their features in particular. Firstly he should note the degree of pupil control over leadership and policy-making. This may vary from no control at all in the hands of pupils, as in the case of organised games for example, to some control as in the case of most extra-curricular clubs, and a high level of pupil control, as in the case of fraternities and secret societies. For the sake of perspective we may note that the informal social system of the pupils is entirely controlled by them. The second main feature to be noted in the case of all these groups is to what extent they are a direct extension of the traditional school curriculum and to what extent they represent the incorporation of some elements of youth culture into the confines of the school.

Whereas we would expect the first kind of organised group to extend the amount of time and energy invested in the school by those pupils who are already committed to their roles within the school, the second kind of group may extend the *number* of pupils who are committed to activities within the school, as well as the *amount* of commitment by those already committed.

In general, the extra-curricular groups supported by the US high school tend to be more numerous, more active and to include a greater proportion that fall towards the youth culture end of the scale than we find in the case of the average British secondary school. Hence it may be that a change of policy on the part of British schools would bring about more commitment but that this would not necessarily happen in the case of the US high school because they have already gone so far in the direction of extending the boundaries of the school and incorporating youth culture into it. In other words, the relationship postulated between these variables is not a simple linear one.

The amount of youth culture influence within these organised groups in the school, and the amount of pupil control in the same groups will, I would hypothesise, be positively correlated. Genuine pupil control will imply a policy favouring youth culture and teacher control will generally imply the reverse. A school which would tolerate a high level of pupil control is likely also to tolerate a high degree of youth culture penetration into the school and a school which will not have one is not likely to have the other, I suggest.

Voluntary extra-curricular organisations have proliferated most in the schools of the USA; they are also in evidence in British schools—even those which have a house system; they are virtually unknown in France and in Russia exist mainly in the form of school branches of the Communist Party youth movement. Sociologically these organised groups appear to perform several functions, apart from the significant fact that they occupy their members in activities which are at least harmless.

Left to themselves pupils form their own social groups, with their own leaders, their own activities and norms, their own means of sanctioning conduct that violates these norms, their own status hierarchy both within and between groups. These groups operate both in the playground and in the classroom. From the teacher's point of view the main implication of this is that, to the extent that pupils are involved in such groups they are less psychologically dependent on teacher's approval and hence they are less easy to control than they were at a younger age before these peer groups developed.

The teacher's position may be strengthened by a good understanding of the principles of group dynamics and particulars of his own pupils' group formation. It may also be helped by having in the school a range of organised groups for pupils which are attractive to them but which are controlled by teachers. The latter then have the power to exclude individual pupils from membership for bad conduct in school. (Waller, 1965, Chapters 9, 10; Bamford, 1967).

On the positive side teachers have control or substantial influence over the allocation of various privileges among the members. In selecting for sports teams and casting plays teachers commonly have absolute control. In other groups their power is less but still substantial, especially where their personal influence is needed to persuade the school to give them special dispensations to make their activities possible.

There is another side to the process. Through their participation in these activities teachers and pupils may develop a different sort of relationship from the one developed in the classroom. Ideally both are participating because they enjoy the activity itself. (In practice, of course, either or both may be doing it in order to look good in the eyes of the head). Even in the non-ideal situation, though, there are certain dynamics inherent in the situation itself. Both teachers and pupils are working together on a common goal which each has chosen; usually under much more informal conditions than in the classroom, if only because the pupil-teacher ratio is lower and the rebellious pupils have selected themselves out. Teachers and pupils begin to see each other as individuals, not just as role-players in an academic learning system.

We may suggest that the more personal relationship that tends to develop between teacher and pupils in the setting of the voluntary extra-curricular activity, which happens more often than it generally does in the classroom, is conducive to more compliant behaviour on the part of pupils. Certainly they would be less likely to act disruptively in the presence of that particular teacher in so far as they have come to like him, respect him and wish to have his approval; he may even influence their conduct in his absence. The development of such a relationship may also lead to the teacher being more sensitive and considerate towards pupils.

The school is not alone in providing recreational activities (with or without "moral uplift" as a latent purpose) for their pupils. There are commercial interests providing activities such as skating rinks, dancing, coffee bars. There are voluntary youth organisations of a non-profit and ostensibly character-building nature, which aim to attract young people into their organisation by offering attractions such as camping, musical bands or sports. The statutory youth services of the local authorities in England and Wales fall somewhere between these two approaches, being more hedonistic than the would-be "character educators" but not profit-oriented.

There has been a tendency for heads of schools in Britain (especially grammar schools) to see themselves as being in conflict with the leaders of youth organisations—let alone the commercial providers of teenage amusements. This antipathy was no doubt rooted in snobbery on the part of heads but also in a realistic feeling that homework and youth clubs are competing for the same limited evening time. Perhaps the advent of television seems to this kind of head to represent a threat of so much greater proportions that youth clubs seem benign by comparison. Be this as it may, the youth club has tended to be the haunt of the early leaver rather than the exam-taker and the recent policy of building youth centres on to school buildings and appointing wardens who are also part-time teachers has often failed to overcome the head's prejudice that the youth centre is only fit for his early leavers.

This is not always the case however. And at the other extreme there are a few schools where the head and the youth centre warden work closely together in planning the activities of the centre, which may tend to take over nearly all of the extra-curricular activities of the school. With the youth centre warden as, in effect, head of extra-curricular activities and teachers working officially for the youth service (and paid extra) for their extra-curricular activities, the division between school-oriented, exam-seeking pupils who stay after school for a few "respectable" activities such as the stamp club and the school-rejecting early leavers who attend the youth centre and shun school-based extra-curricular activities can be ended.

One of the functions of extra-curricular activities we have suggested is to give teachers an extra lever with which to extract compliance with their normative standards of conduct from pupils. Another approach to this problem on the classroom level is exemplified by the "collective" system used in some Russian schools (Bereday *et al.*, 1960). In this system the class, usually a stable, mixed-ability group of similar age, is officially given collective responsibility for the performance and conduct of all its members. Promotion comes only when *every* member has passed the required tests, so that all have an interest in helping the low achievers, unlike the system of individual competition for marks (or grades) which prevails in North America and Western Europe. In the event of bad conduct the whole class is punished collectively. So, again, the delinquent individual is pressured by his peers to conform. In various ways competition is officially arranged between collectives, which presumably tends to build up the solidarity and cohesiveness of the class as a group, makes the pupils feel that their personal interests lie in working for the group and makes them eager to pull their deviant class-mates into line.

Within a classroom in a Kiev school the following arrangements were found. Each row served as a unit with its own monitor, who supervised the row. Each week the monitors had a meeting to plan for the coming week. Each month the class had a meeting to evaluate the work of the monitors and the general state of classroom discipline. Suggestions for improvement were made. The academic progress of pupils was also considered, in particular the slow ones who were named and volunteers to help them were found (*ibid*).

The Russian collective system, operating in a society with a collectivist school and political philosophy, is based on a different form of accommodation with the natural social system among pupils from that of the prefect system. Instead of fragmenting and undermining the solidarity of the pupil group and so inhibiting its development as a distinct group set apart from the staff, which is the way the prefect system operates, the monitor system utilises and strengthens the separate identity and cohesion of each classroom group for the official social control system. This is done by structuring the promotion system and the allocation of other positive and negative sanctions on a *collective*, class-wide basis (Bronfenbrenner, 1970).

Whereas the British house system balances the individual competitiveness within the classroom against the group solidarity of the house, the Russian collective system vests all the pupil's face-to-face social relations in one group and it makes *all* rewards contingent upon the collective behaviour of members of that group. These two systems need to be compared not only for their effectiveness in terms of social control but also for their effects on the development of attitudes of caring for others, social skills in dealing with others. The danger with the collective system would appear to be twofold, from this point of view: that pupils will be inept at dealing with others outside their own class, because they are never brought into contact with these others, and that they will be extremely harsh in dealing with delinquent or under-performing members of the class who are unresponsive to their efforts because of some serious handicap.

CO-OPTING PUPILS INTO THE AUTHORITY STRUCTURE

There are various ways in which selected pupils can be officially co-opted into the authority system of the school, by being vested with the right and duty to watch over the conduct of their fellow pupils and issue sanctions (usually negative) when deemed appropriate. The best-known version of this is probably the prefect system, originally developed in the British independent boarding schools.

The prefect system works in so far as it prevents solidarity developing among pupils as a separate group and succeeds in linking them as individuals to a corporate body (the school) represented by staff and senior pupils (all prefects, past, present and prospective) and the values they stand for jointly. In the perfectly functioning prefect system the prefects are the natural leaders to whom pupils look. This depends in part on staff making sure that those senior boys who possess the individual attributes which tend to give prestige among pupils (such as sporting prowess) are made prefects, which in turn implies that they have to be motivated to accept the position and its duties. Those schools which operate the most successful prefect systems are those which have long-established traditions, that is to say that they have been doing it for a long time. Thus each new generation of pupils sees a body of prefects who possess both institutionally-given prestige and prestige based on their individual qualities and no prominent seniors who repudiate the official norms of the school or the legitimacy of the prefect system. If there are such dissident individuals at least they do not lead a dissident group. Once established in schools with highly selective recruitment a prefect system generates a tradition which makes its continuance easier than its initial establishment was. At the outset most strenuous efforts on the part of the headmasters, blessed with charismatic powers of leadership, are necessary to start an effective prefect system (Lambert, 1966, 1968, 1969; Bamford, 1967).

The breadth of the prefect's authority varies. It may be mainly concerned with maintaining order (for example: marshalling pupils to the places where they are supposed to be at particular times, preventing rowdiness and running in the corridors) and with assisting in the administration of the school (e.g. arranging duty rotas and games practices). Or it may extend far beyond this to encompass a pastoral responsibility for the pupils in his charge (e.g. censoring their reading matter, questioning the use of their leisure time and the friends they make). The sanctions at their disposal may similarly vary in range and severity, from merely being able to reprimand pupils and report them to teachers at the one extreme to being entitled to beat them at the other. So also is there great variation in the extent of their autonomy and freedom to act on their own without needing a teacher's specific approval. In general the independent boarding school prefects have the widest authority with the greatest range of sanctions and the greatest amount of autonomy. Those in state boarding schools and day schools of all kinds have less (Lambert, 1968).

Also worthy of note are those positions for pupils which control access by other pupils to certain resources (e.g. the library, sports facilities or extra-curricular activities). Although they may have very little control over policy, by virtue of their control over access to scarce and valued resources they have positions of some small power within the pupils' social system.

Another approach to the whole issue of co-opting pupils into the authority structure involves the creation of a representative school council, which discusses pupils' grievances and suggestions pertaining to changes in school rules, policies and provision of amenities; it formulates suggestions, and presents them officially to the head. The head may or may not actually sit down with the council. Representatives of the teaching staff likewise may or may not be present.

The fundamental difference between this system and the prefect system is that the school council allows pupils to participate in the *making* of policy, while the prefect system allows them to participate in administering a given policy. The two systems can readily function in the same school, though climates of educational theory seem to be such that those schools which favour prefects tend not to favour school councils and *vice-versa*. This may be considered a pity, on the ground that a full moral education could benefit from both kinds of learning experiences being available to pupils.

The prefect system grew up originally as a means to impose more effective social control on the pupils and this remains a major function which it performs when operating well. It can also be claimed to teach those pupils who occupy such positions to understand better the problems of those in authority and to teach them the responsibilities that go with the exercise of authority. The function of the school council would appear to be less one of social control than of tension management, serving as a channel for the expression of grievances and perhaps leading to remedial action. On the one hand, it enables the head and his staff to be better informed on the climate of opinion among pupils and, on the other hand, it gives pupils a means of expressing and debating their grievances. Further, it puts the pupils' representatives in a position where they are expected to formulate constructive proposals as well as just convey complaints. If the school gives them the power to influence policy, then they have the salutory experience of having to take responsibility for their ideas, and face up to the consequences when they are not successful. The earliest and strongest proponents of school councils have been the "progressive" educators going back to Homer Lane (Wills, 1964).

Whereas the role of prefect provides experience and perhaps training in the social skills of leadership or management of people, the role of school council representative is more involved with the democratic processes of discussion, persuasion and compromise. The individual prefect has the power to impose various sanctions on individual pupils, within the discretion allowed him by the rules; the council representative has no power as an individual but may participate in changing school rules—perhaps changing the role of the prefect—if a majority of the council are in agreement and if the head and staff are disposed to take heed of the council in this area.

The attitude of the head to the council is crucial. If he is kept in thrall by his governing body, their attitude is crucial too. The school council can function as a mechanism for tension management, providing feedback on grievances and leading to corrective action aimed at the causes of the discontent. Equally, it can function as a private debating society for a small number of pupils who are prepared to co-operate in play-acting a sham in which all matters of substance are either vetoed off the agenda by the head, or torpedoed in discussion when he explains that it would be "inopportune" and "irresponsible" to press them. The supposed "representatives" are given small but significant privileges; most important, they are made to feel that the head appreciates their cooperative attitude, and should any individual be "awkward" he would turn very nasty and make that pupil sorry he acted that way. Specific modes of retribution would be left to the imagination, and pupils are likely to be well aware of how important the head's personal assessment of their "character" or "promise" may be in connection with applications for jobs or scholarships.

For the council to be a truly representative body, performing an effective communication function, other preconditions must be fulfilled. Provision is necessary for preliminary discussions before each meeting between each representative and his constituents. At least two sessions are necessary; one to collect matters for the agenda and one to discuss the items raised by other groups so that the representatives know the views of constituents on those matters too. Provision is also necessary for a feedback session after the council meeting to inform constituents of the proceedings and satisfy their demands for explanations. It is probably necessary that school time be officially allotted to these purposes.

In the beginning most pupils will probably not be convinced of the value of these meetings, nor will they be socialised into the procedures of orderly discussion. The support of a teacher will often be necessary, then, if the pupil representative is to do his job of liaising with his constituents. It is therefore necessary that the teaching staff as well as the head should understand and support the objectives of the school council if it is to succeed.

A very wide range of social skills is required from the school council representative and is developed in him if the system operates well. He has not only to operate as an effective debater within the council, but also to be an effective reporter back to his constituents and an effective collector of their points of view. His most difficult task, perhaps, is to make them understand the reasons why their suggestions or demands could not be met unmodified. Learning to compromise in committee is not usually easy but even harder is to explain to one's constituents the pressures exerted in the larger system which they cannot see but which force the modification of their proposals. This is especially hard where the council is sham and the representative has sold out to the powers that be. Then the real explanation will not be given, either because of fear or because the representative has really been duped.

Despite the significant differences between the prefect system and the school council, both are means of co-opting selected pupils into the official authority structure of the school. As such, both imply drawing the selected pupils into roles which will modify the way they play their other roles *vis à vis* fellow pupils. The prefect system clearly creates a distinct social distance between prefects and other pupils, which is often reinforced by separate common rooms and other privileged arrangements. This social distance makes it easier for the prefect to give orders to and impose sanctions on the others, both hard things to do. They are hard because there was formerly some solidarity between these pupils and the exercise by one of power over the other creates the uncomfortable likelihood of the powerful one being resented and disliked for this. The pupil who is elected as council representative faces a different but analogous problem. Up to the time of election he may be an outspoken champion of his peers' demands, brooking no compromise. Upon election and induction into the realities of school politics, he may come to see that by intransigence he is likely to gain only notoriety but by compromise he may gain some small but concrete concessions. If he comes to favour compromise, whether for real gain to his constituents or as a sell-out, he has moved significantly from his initial stance and from the one his peers understand. He may find it hard to convince them of the wisdom of this change and likely to find that a gap has opened between him and them—a gap of communication and empathy which often means that he is less acclaimed by his peers as a compromiser than he was as a fire-brand. How acute this problem is depends in part on the sophistication of the constituents. Truly, though, we have here a veritable microcosm of the political process.

CHAPTER 4 REFERENCES

T. W. Bamford, *The Rise of the Public Schools*, Nelson, London, 1967.

George Z. F. Bereday, W. W. Brickman and G. H. Read (eds.), *The Changing Soviet School*, Constable, London, 1960.

Urie Bronfenbrenner, *The Two Worlds of Childhood*, Russell Sage Foundation, New York, 1970.

P. M. Carlin, "Team Teaching", in Franklin, op. cit., pp. 281–7.

Marian Pope Franklin, *School Organization: Theory and Practice*, Rand McNally, Chicago, 1967.

Royston Lambert, *The Hothouse Society*, Weidenfeld and Nicolson, London, 1968.

Royston Lambert *et al.*, *New Wine in Old Bottles*, Occasional Papers in Social Admin. no. 28, Bell, London, 1969.

Royston Lambert, "The Public Schools: A Sociological Introduction", in G. Kalton, *The Public Schools: A Factual Survey*, Longmans, London, 1966.

N. Polos, *The Dynamics of Team Teaching*, W. C. Brown, Dubuque, Iowa, 1965.

Robert Rosenthal and L. Jacobson, *Pygmalion in the Classroom*, Holt, Rinehart and Winston, New York, 1968.

J. T. Shaplin, "Co-operative Teaching", in Franklin, op. cit.

L. C. Taylor, *Resources for Learning*, Penguin, Harmondsworth, 1971.

Willard Waller, *The Sociology of Teaching*, John Wiley, New York, 1932.

W. David Wills, *Homer Lane: A Biography*, Allen and Unwin, London, 1964.

John Wilson, *Public Schools and Private Practice*, Allen and Unwin, London, 1962.

Chapter Five

INPUTS: (1) PUPILS

It is arguable that what the child learns before entering school has a greater bearing on his or her long-term development than everything learned in school (Bloom, 1964). This sort of pseudo-quantification and comparison can only be highly tendentious, however. It is more profitable to view the situation from another perspective. The effect of the school on the child is always contingent upon his (or her) earlier experiences and learning, for they have moulded his attitude towards the later experiences as well as preparing him (well or badly) to be able to cope with them more or less competently. In connection with the child's response to school experiences we must also remember the part played by genetically inherited factors which affect the range of possible development of intellectual abilities, as well as certain aspects of temperament and personality.

There is great controversy surrounding the status of genetic factors in explaining child development but some agreement of authorities may be found around the notion that in relation to intellectual development genetic factors do set limits of likely development and whether the actual development of the child approximates more to the upper or lower bounds of these limits is determined by environmental factors, primarily those of the early home environment and secondarily those of school. Thus there is a continual interaction between innate (genetic) factors, related to both intellectual ability and basic personality on the one hand, and environment on the other hand (Hunt, 1968).

It is unlikely that all pupils would perform equally well, even in the best possible school, due to these innate differences. At the same time, it is almost certain that the performance of the vast majority of pupils in school is well below their potential and that improvements in the schools themselves would lead to improved performances. Such improvement in performance by pupils may also be described as increases in the effects of school on the pupil.

Before arrival at school virtually all children, barring only the severely subnormal and physically handicapped, have completed an impressive amount of learning—mostly without formal teaching. Most impressive of all is their mastery of the basic psychomotor skills of bowel and bladder control, feeding themselves, walking and talking. Intellectual and social skills are also somewhat developed before school, though this varies greatly with the kind of adult supervision the child has had and the kind of experience in dealing with others apart from its parents or other principal guardians. Similar factors determine how much and what kind of knowledge or cognitive assumptions the child acquires before school, though for all children what they learn in the pre-school stage will be significant when they get to school. Attitudes to many different things are already starting to be learned before children come to school, though it would not make sense to talk of values being learned so early. Basic personality features are already evident before the age of starting school and so are many kind of behavioural habits. Some of these habits are a cause of great concern to the children's teachers when they violate the school's norms of conduct—for example children who are in the habit of speaking in loud voices or rushing around at high speed will come up against their teachers' strenuous efforts to change those habits.

This chapter falls into three parts. The first one contains a discussion of the major factors in home background or home environment which research has shown to affect pupils' response to school. The second section discusses the part played by children's relationships with peers on their development and their response to school. Finally, the last section of the chapter looks, not at "factors" as in the previous two sections, but at the *processes* of learning which occur as children develop. Growing up involves all of these learning processes, which are not tied specifically to home, school or other particular environments.

HOME BACKGROUND

If we take the nature of the schools we find in a particular society as "given" we may then discuss the differing degrees of readiness of pupils to fulfil the expectations which they will meet in school. If, on the other hand, we take the characteristics of pupils at the time when they enter school as "given", we may then discuss the differing degrees of effectiveness of the schools in absorbing their pupils as they find them. To make such a comparison fair, we should have to somehow equate pupils' characteristics—that is, either to look only at schools with similar intake or to statistically adjust the measurements we made.

Neither of these two opposing perspectives is intrinsically right or wrong. Which is appropriate in a particular context depends upon the purpose for which the analysis is being made. If it is being made with a view to policy implications, then it makes a great deal of difference which perspective is adopted. Taking the schools as given restricts possible policies of improvement to those which change home environment or other aspects of the pre-school situation without affecting the school. Taking the children as given, however, opens up possibilities of modifying the organisation and policies of the school to overcome these difficulties of pupils adjusting to school.

We are concerned with home background here because it is a necessary aspect to understanding the functioning of schools as we find them and fortunately it is an area which is exceptionally well researched—in fact more thoroughly than any other area in the whole sociology of education. Two distinct bodies of researchers have contributed to this accumulation of knowledge: sociologists with an interest in the manifest inequalities in educational success connected with social class differences, and social psychologists interested in differences in child-rearing practices and their consequences for child development. We shall review the main conclusions of these two bodies of scholarship in this order.

It has been shown in a considerable number of studies which all confirm one another, that the children of manual workers are on the whole less successful in school than those of non-manual (white collar) workers (Floud, 1961). This finding, however, is only the starting point of the investigation. For it remains to be shown what aspect of home background, associated with social class actually plays a causal role in affecting the child's adjustment to school. It is not the parents' social class or status *per se* but the kind of social experiences provided in the home, especially in early childhood, which tend to be correlated with social class or status.

What we are trying to find are *those differences in the home which affect differential success in school* regardless of father's occupation:

that is to say, those characteristics which successful middle-class pupils and successful working-class pupils both have but which the unsuccessful members of both classes lack. In terms of the following table we are looking for factors like X.

*Successful Middle Class**	*Unsuccessful Middle Class*	*Successful Working Class*	*Unsuccessful Working Class*
X	no-X	X	no-X

This approach can be illustrated by reference to the factor "size of family", which was found to be related to success in school. More than one study found that working-class pupils selected for grammar school tended to come from smaller families than those from the same class who were not selected. Then again the 15 *to* 18 survey found that early leavers tended to come from larger families than pupils from the same social class who stayed on longer at school (Crowther Report, 1959). Thus "size of family" is a factor that is distributed like X in the table above. However, it is not a truly *explanatory* variable such as we seek, for we cannot tell from data such as this what sort of casual process is working. Is it that children with fewer siblings have more parental attention and so develop their intellectual potential more fully? Or is it that certain kinds of parents tend *both* to plan effectively for small families *and* to have certain notions about how children should be treated? Or both? What are these "notions"? For in them might be a set of causal factors corresponding to X which would explain both the broad difference between the academic achievement of pupils from the different social classes and the exceptions or deviants from the typical behaviour for their social class.

The most promising candidate, I believe, for the role of this explanatory factor is something that we may call for short "middle-class values". By this we mean a set of orientations that equip one to cope relatively effectively with the demands of school and then later with those of work and adult life. The most important of these orientations is a *future time orientation*, as opposed to an orientation to past or present. This involves a preference for anticipating future needs and planning where possible to meet them by sacrificing (where necessary) present pleasures; a disposition to

* We shall use the term "middle class" as a short-hand term for pupils whose fathers are in non-manual (white collar) work and "working class" for those whose fathers are manual workers.

control impulses and think of the consequences before acting; and the feeling that to behave in this way is morally right. Along with future orientation we shall consider two more "middle-class values": *activism* (as opposed to passivism or fatalism) involving confidence in one's ability to control the environment to some degree and *individualism* (as opposed to collectivism or familism) involving a belief in the individual's right and duty to make his own way in the world, dependent on no one and allowing no one to impose dependence on him and tie him down.

The theorist on whose work this formulation is most directly based is Florence Kluckhohn, who devised her categories of value-orientations as a means of analysing and defining differences between cultures (Kluckhohn and Strodtbeck, 1961). The three orientations listed above comprise only part of the full scheme which comprises five value-orientation dimensions. American researchers have devised questionnaires for the purpose of comparing pupils of different home backgrounds, with different levels of success in school in terms of these orientations (Strodtbeck, 1961; Rosen, 1956) and two researchers working in England have adapted them for English pupils (Jayasuriya, 1960; Sugarman, 1966).

In a study of 540 London schoolboys of 14–15 years of age these value orientations were measured by means of a questionnaire and shown to be very useful in explaining differential adjustment to school both between and within groups from different social class backgrounds (Sugarman, 1966). Pupils responded "agree", "disagree", or "don't know" to a list of statements, some phrased so as to affirm one of the supposed middle-class values and some in the opposite direction. Thus, to score highly on *future orientation* pupils would have to disagree with statements such as "There is no sense in worrying about the future so long as you are doing all right now" and they would have to agree to statements such as "You have to give up having a good time now to do well later on" and "Most times it is better to be tactful and diplomatic instead of saying just what you think". To score highly on *activism* they would have to reject statements like "One must learn to take life as it is without always trying to improve things", and "The greatest source of happiness in life is to be satisfied with whatever you have". To get high scores for the third value, *individualism*, they would have to reject statements like "It is best to be like everyone else and not stand out from the rest" and endorse others like "Nowadays you have to look out for yourself before helping your parents".

Boys' scores on "middle-class values" measured in this way were found to be correlated with their behaviour in school in a number of ways: with their level of academic performance, both in absolute terms and also relative to others with similar IQ scores; with their conformity to the conduct norms of the school, as rated by their teachers. These value-orientations clearly are related to success in school. They help to make it happen in that boys who come to school with such values already developing adjust better to school because the expectations that teachers have for their pupils are, to a large extent, defined in terms of the three middle-class values already spelled out. They expect high levels of impulse control and deferral of gratification for future benefits after leaving school, refraining from mischief-making despite the boredom of the classroom and devoting precious evenings to homework rather than enjoyment; they expect pupils always to do their best and not to subside before the difficulties of the situation (activism); and they usually expect pupils to work on their own without seeking or giving help (individualism).

At the same time, involvement in school tends to develop these value-orientations further in pupils. Thus those who manage to become involved in school despite the lack of any initial advantages change in this way and those who started out already quite high on these values move even higher. There is evidence on this specific point from a study by James Savage and this writer in one London boys' school where we found that in the first-year boys in a high achievers' class scored higher on this measure of middle-class values than first-year boys in a low achievers' class. At this age the difference was quite small and not statistically significant but for each ascending year-group the high achievers tended to score higher while the low achievers remained much the same. Thus the gap between them increased year by year until the fourth year (the oldest group we studied).

We return now to the other side of the process, that in which value orientations function to mediate between background and differential success in school, and to the former study of 540 London schoolboys in four different schools. Can we show that these values are the outcome of certain kinds of home background or social class? We must do this to establish their status as explanatory causal variables like X in the diagram.

We measured the social class backgrounds of the boys in this study on the basis of their fathers' occupations as reported and we measured the "intellectual quality" of their homes on the basis of (1) the type of newspapers taken in the home (differentiating them not by political bias but by their "intellectual quality" or the reading age necessary to assimilate them), (2) the number of books possessed and (3) whether the parents take the children on outings to plays, museums, etc. "Social class" and "intellectual quality of the home" were correlated with each other and both correlated with the boys' achievement and conduct in school. "Quality" of home was correlated with all three of the middle-class values scales (future orientation, activism and individualism) but social class was only correlated with the future orientation scale.

For the purposes of explaining differential success in school, therefore, these three value orientations seem to represent the kind of factor we are looking for. "Intellectual quality of the home" seems to pin-point some of the features of the home which develop these values in the children better than the global measure of social class. So, if we want a factor X which is a property of the home itself, "intellectual quality of the home environment" is our nomination. If, however, we want the type of factor X which is a property of the child, derived mainly from the home and directly related to behaviour in school in a way that the former type of factor cannot be, then "middle-class values" is the nominee.

We now turn to consider the evidence of child-rearing studies by psychologists and what they suggest may be some of the more important features of parent-child relationships influencing childrens' success in adjusting to school.

An authoritative review of all the major child-bearing studies (Becker, 1964) shows that the most significant differences in child-rearing methods and their consequences can be discussed in terms of two basic factors or variables which stand out as having paramount importance. One of these variables distinguishes between parents who use "power-assertive" techniques as opposed to those who use "love-oriented" methods; the other variable distinguishes between "restrictive" and "permissive" approaches.

"Power-assertive" techniques include physical punishment,

shouting at the child and verbal threats. "Love-oriented" methods include the expression of disappointment by the parent, sending the child to his room, or other ways of showing the affectionate relationship between them is spoiled as a result of the child's bad behaviour. The love category also includes positive sanctions, such as praise and giving reasons why the parent has to ask him to do what he has asked. The general import of most studies is that love-oriented techniques are more successful than power-assertive ones in teaching children to control aggressive impulses and developing a conscience (in the sense of feelings of guilt after transgressing and willingness to confess when challenged). Although the findings on resistance to temptation are contradictory, the two features of internal control of aggression and conscience development clearly tend to make these children more susceptible to control in school and hence less prone to conflict with teachers.

The restrictiveness-permissiveness variable is based on the number and extent of parental expectations for the child across various areas of behaviour. Restrictiveness tends to lead to well-controlled, socialised behaviour—the kind that teachers on the whole favour—but also tends to lead to dependence, fearfulness and submissiveness, as well as a dulling of intellectual striving. Permissiveness on the other hand, tends to foster outgoing, sociable, assertive behaviour and intellectual striving, though it also tends to develop less persistence and more aggressiveness. Clearly, there is a conflict here between the goals of intellectual development and social development, on the one hand, and the goals of easy social control in the school and a quiet life for teachers.

Becker's analysis of this material clearly indicates that the child-rearing methods most predictive of success in school are love-oriented and restrictive. This combination tends to produce a child who is obedient, polite, neat, submissive, non-aggressive, not friendly and not creative. The next most propitious combination—or, if we are to take a less pessimistic view of the school, an alternative formula for the most successful type of background—is the combination of love-oriented and somewhat permissive methods. This kind of background tends to produce children who are active, socially outgoing, creative, aggressive in a socially skilful way, independent, friendly and ready to take adult roles. The remaining two combinations of child-rearing methods are both disastrous, though in different ways. The combination of power-assertive and permissive methods tends to produce children who are highly aggressive (but not at all skilful about it), non-compliant and frequently delinquent. The combination of power-assertive and restrictive methods tends to produce children who are neurotic, socially withdrawn, shy and quarrelsome with peers.

We have noted already the importance of impulse control, seen as an aspect of future orientation, in the child who is to be a successful pupil in school. Becker's analysis of the child-rearing studies also reveals that one of the main reasons for the greater effectiveness of love-oriented methods is that parents of this kind themselves present models of non-impulsive, controlled behaviour. Parents who treat their children impulsively tend to produce impulsive children. An important aspect of parental behaviour in this connection is the matter of administering punishment and the basis on which this is done. What distinguishes middle- and lower-class families is not the frequency with which physical punishment is used so much as the choice of situation in which to punish and the atmosphere in which it is done. The middle-class parent on the whole does not punish the child just because he or she has done something which is a nuisance, but only when the child has done something, which, if permitted to develop and become a habit would lead to a pattern of behaviour which the parents view as undesirable (Kohn, 1959). This social class difference in punishing is another facet of what we are calling the "X-type" family.

Again, this type of parent explains to the child as often as possible exactly why the punishment is being given, in terms of rules (categories of approved and disapproved behaviour) which he has broken. Of course, these rules are not only mentioned in the context of punishment. The point of mentioning them is to refer back to earlier parental statement of what kind of behaviour is being demanded. A child from the X-type family, brought up with clearly defined expectations within the family and attempts by parents to explain the norms of expected behaviour in other situations probably adjusts more readily than others to new situations outside the family—such as the very new situation of going to school. The rules themselves may be very different, but this kind of child is more highly sensitised to the existence of implicit rules in apparent chaos.

This applies not only to the official side of school life as a pupil, where the rules are many and partly formalised, but also to the informal social relationships among pupils on a peer level. In both these areas there are problems of adjustment in terms of *understanding* the expectations involved and the structure of the situation, and acquiring the skill appropriate to performing in these areas as well as the attitude and personality dispositions which makes for successful adaptation (such things as friendliness to peers, cooperativeness with adults and—yet again—impulse control).

The factor of parental consistency, though already alluded to, is worth special mention. It is essential to the X-type of parent-child relationship because we have postulated that this involves training the child to follow *rules* of conduct. Rules necessarily imply consistency. Parental (rule-governed) consistency is a necessary condition for the child to learn similar behaviour. Klein (1965; vol. 2) and Douvan and Gold (1964, pp. 490–1) have documented the importance of consistent rules, consistent enforcement and explanation of rules by parents in the development of youngsters who are responsible, controlled, non-delinquent and autonomous. Deferred gratification does not pay and will not be learned unless the future reward can be confidently expected. Parental inconsistency from one time to another, sometimes rewarding and sometimes not, prevents the development of a future orientation. This has implications for both academic learning and conformity to social norms.

One of the first features of the "X-type" family to which we pointed was the "intellectual quality of the home" assessed in terms of such indicators as the type of newspapers taken and number of books possessed. Bernstein (1965) has argued that children in this type of home acquire command of far more sophisticated forms of language and conceptual thought than do children from the typical lower working-class family. He argues further that most of what teachers say to pupils in school is said in this more sophisticated "formal language", involving an "elaborated" code. This is the form of language which uses relatively complex sentence structure with subordinate clauses to express conditional relationship, causal dependence, intentionality and so forth. It contrasts with the "restricted" code of the "private" language form which is used by people of all social classes in intimate peer groups. This kind of language consists basically of short declarative statements and many appeals for agreement such as "Didn't he?" and "Isn't that right?" These utterances which appear to be questions do not in fact call for replies. They assume agreement, just as they assume a common context of shared experience, common attitudes and values.

According to Bernstein, the middle-class child tends to be bilingual in the sense that he can use both forms of language fairly effectively, while the lower working-class child tends to be restricted to the restricted code. Coming into school, where most of the conversation between pupil and teacher takes place in the formal language (elaborated code) this constitutes a severe handicap for the child who is not fluent in the formal language. One of the main reasons why he learns less effectively in school is that he is at the same time unfamiliar with the *language forms* preferred and demanded by teachers, the language forms in which they speak to pupils, and the *modes of thought* which are made possible and tend to be associated with the use of those more elaborated linguistic forms. This handicap is a cumulative one. The more that children are tuned in to the elaborated codes, the more they improve their ability to use it and the more they learn in school as a result of using it. Pupils who are not tuned in to the use of this linguistic form learn less, develop their linguistic abilities less and therefore progressively fall behind.

This theory weaves into our argument in several interesting ways. The X-type parents' attempts to raise their child to understand certain abstract rules of good conduct both presupposes and tends to develop in the child a relatively sophisticated intellectual and language skill. It involves learning to generalise, think in abstract terms and discriminate between situations on the basis of abstract criteria. Thus the moral and intellectual aspects of child-training are closely interdependent and on both counts the X-child has an advantage in the competition of school. He has a substantial advantage in the learning situation *per se*. Over and above that he also can cope with the social conformity aspects of school more easily and hence can focus more energy and attention on the learning problem. In this sort of way the advantages of the X-home are compounded.

A more obvious but nonetheless interesting point lies in this: that for a child to have a high level of linguistic facility implies that someone—either one or both of his parents (or perhaps a parent substitute, such as a grandparent) has spent a good deal of time with him and has treated him as a "person" in the sense of someone whose questions and ideas, though naive, are to be taken seriously. Indeed this kind of child-centredness (or intellectual indulgence of the child) seems to be an important element of the X-type family in its own right (Bernstein and Henderson, 1969). Implied also and supported by independent evidence is the further point that X-type parents set higher standards for their children, or at least they expect things of them at earlier ages than other parents. Moreover they carefully grade the standards of achievement that they set their children, so that they are high enough to stretch them but not so high as to induce despair. In this way these children learn the value orientation of activism and get their motivation to try hard at a wide range of "problems", "challenges" or "tasks" (not necessarily competitive ones) such as those presented in the classroom which leave other children uninterested (Winterbottom, 1958; Klein, 1965).

To summarise, we have suggested a number of features as characterising the type of home background and the kind of parent-child relationships which tend to go with success in schools. We have also suggested a number of features of the child's developing personality which result from the foregoing home and parental conditions and which directly make possible the success to which we referred.

The parent-child relationship is affectionate, consistent in the standards of conduct which are conceptualised in terms of general rules, child-centred in the sense of spending much time on the child and "taking him seriously", manipulative in the sense that affection is withdrawn for bad behaviour by parental standards. The typical child product, resembling the typical parent has the following characteristics: adequate impulse control, future orientation, relatively sophisticated linguistic and conceptual skills, well-developed internal controls involving guilt mechanisms and ready responsiveness to opportunities to pit oneself against environmental challenges (activism).

Although our main concern here is with home background as it affects adjustment to school, we may pause to review some evidence on correlations between home background and altruism, which is of course one of the prime components of the morally-educated person. Sorokin (1954) studied the backgrounds of people nominated as "good neighbours" to a US television programme that was offering awards. These good neighbours came from large families and reported happy childhoods. Although most of them grew up in farm or working-class families, three quarters of the sample were currently middle-class and middle-income recipients. That is, they had been upwardly mobile on the whole. Their altruistic habits developed gradually and uneventfully, only for three per cent was there a sudden conversion. These "good neighbours" were no more intelligent or more highly educated than average, yet they reported very favourable attitudes to their teachers, probably indicating a close harmony in values between their homes, their teachers and themselves—one of these values apparently being altruism.

Berkowitz (1968) and Berkowitz and Friedman (1967) have shown that teenage boys from different social class backgrounds differ in their willingness to help others in a small practical way. Least willing are working-class boys; most willing are middle-class boys with fathers employed in large organisations; intermediate are middle-class boys with self-employed fathers. Sugarman (1973) showed that teenage boys' and girls' attitudes of altruism as revealed on questionnaire measures tends to correlate with the "intellectual quality" of their home background. And for an adult sample in six nations Almond and Verba (1963) have shown that social status as measured by education is correlated with placing a high value on generosity and consideration for others relative to other personal qualities. In all of these studies the aspect of home background which is emphasised is not the economic one—though the relative job *security* of the more educated and bureaucratic employees may also be important in affecting the qualities of relationships in the home—but rather the aspect of relative sophistication in family relationships as defined by many of the features we ascribed in this chapter to the kind of home that produces children who are successful in school. Although none of these studies provides direct evidence on the kinds of control methods used by parents, it is noteworthy that the study by Sugarman used exactly the same measure of home background as was used in an earlier study by the same author which showed this variable to be clearly related to academic achievement, good school conduct and endorsement of "middle-class values" such as "future orientation" or impulse control. In other words, it looks as if rather similar factors of home background are involved in producing the child who adjusts successfully to school and the child who is relatively altruistic, showing concern for others. It must be remembered, though, that our evidence on the altruism side is quite scanty, so we cannot press this parallel too far.

Our definition of the MEP (presented in Chapter Two) corresponds fairly well to some other definitions of character types which have been put forward by various psychologists. Derek Wright (1971) has brought together the more important of these definitions and offered a composite character typology, in which one type, which he labels "the altruistic autonomous character", corresponds very closely to the MEP. This type of person is altruistic not only in obvious ways, but he uses his brain to decide how to act in new situations. He has generally been brought up in a home where he had a warm and respectful relationship with his parents, who provided models of concern for the interests of others (including the child's). They did not, however, prevent him from having friendships with peers nor from having some rights of privacy in those relationships. From the juxtaposition of his parental and peer relationships with their differing normative perspectives, he is challenged to think for himself about what *he* personally believes. He may decide to adopt any of several moral positions but he remains an altruist, because his experience of personal relationships and his thinking about it lead him to the conclusion that this is a moral principle that he should abide by. His adoption of this principle and conformity to it in practice is motivated by his own need to be consistent to his own ideals. This autonomy can be seen in other areas where he may decide to follow paths not approved of by parents or friends. He has the strength that comes from a secure self-image to follow his own convictions—even when this results in disappointing those whom he would prefer to please. Wright emphasises the importance in the development of this character type of the special balance between family and peer experiences. To a discussion of peer relationships and their importance for adjustment to school, as well as for other aspects of individual development we now turn.

PATTERNS OF RELATIONSHIPS WITH PEERS

The relationship between the child and its parents does not exhaust the identifiable factors affecting development. We must also take account of the relationships between the child and other children. Going to school means learning to get on with other children mainly of a similar age, as well as all the problems of adjusting to the demands of teachers. So the child who starts school already well behind the level of social development of his peers has problems in both areas at the same time. At later ages, when the social relationships among pupils have become elaborated into a considerable social system in their own right and when the demands of the school have become in many ways more onerous, the peer group plays an important part in mitigating the strain which the official structure of the school creates for pupils. The pupil who is cut off from this source of tension management —of relief and relaxation with his peers—is at a disadvantage.

Yet the importance of development in terms of peer relationships is not only that these relationships are useful to the child but that certain important things can be learned perhaps more effectively through peer contact than in other ways. Thus from their data on four-year-olds, the Newsoms (1968) conclude:

> ". . . it is largely through interaction with his siblings or with other children of the neighbourhood that he first learns about personal possessions, lending and sharing, asking permission, waiting for another child to finish and taking turns. Through social play with his peers, he begins to realise that it will sometimes be necessary for him to give in to another child. . . . Such experiences often provide the child's first introduction to the concepts of fair play and social justice. . . ." (p. 104)

It would be a mistake to think of the role of parents and peers as being quite separate and distinct. For one thing, the child-rearing methods used by parents in the first few years will affect the amount of difficulty the child has in getting along with others because of the behavioural tendencies and personality features which the child has acquired as a result. Thus, for example, the excessively shy child and the excessively aggressive child will each find their own difficulties in getting along with peers and making friends. So too will the child who is "spoiled" by parents and is not taught to accept the kind of restraints which others in the society will expect.

For the young child, parents also play another kind of role affecting their child's interaction with his peers. They may intervene directly to affect both the frequency of contact and the kind of companions their child has, for example by taking him to play with other children, putting the child into an organised playgroup or nursery school, or—at the other extreme—by keeping him away from other children. The parents who turn their child out of the house with orders to keep out of their way and not to get into trouble (either on his own or in the custody of an older brother or sister) are equally creating the conditions for certain kinds of relationships with peers to develop rather than others.

As well as affecting the child's life with his peers in this sort of way, parents may intervene to supervise and stage-manage the actual early encounters, coach the child beforehand as to what to expect and what to do, console him after things have not gone well and try to explain how he might have handled the situation better. The exercise of these kinds of parental functions may be welcomed by the child in the first few anxious years, tolerated later and highly resented after that. To some extent, of course, this depends on the kind of relationship the child and parents have.

Coaching is appropriate where the child is new to a certain kind of experience with peers and does not know what to expect or what will be expected of him, or where he has already made some mistakes and does not know what he has done wrong. If there were no parents to tell him, for example, "You were too rough" or "You kept taking the other boy's toys and would not give them back", he might have to suffer repeated and painful rebuffs before learning his mistake. Too many such experiences may easily lead a sensitive child to withdraw from further attempts to play with other children.

For example, when the child has acted selfishly and inconsiderately towards a playmate, being rejected as a result, the coach's explanation may help the child to see this. In so far as the child makes a habit of talking about his social experiences with such a person who really does understand them better, he will learn to understand the nature of social relationships, their obligations, rewards and the interdependencies among people in society.

Although this in itself may not necessarily have a practical pay-off immediately, it does mean that the child's understanding of social affairs is developing more rapidly and in later years, when he will find himself in more complex social situations, he will then be better able to understand and handle them.

Through continued and developing relationships with peers children tend to acquire social skills and insights which can stand them in good stead in relationships with other children too. Unless their relationships are very rigidly restricted to a small group of other peers which does not change over many years, they are not just investing in relationships with particular individuals but in skills and capabilities which are transferable. Just as important as these skills and capabilities is a developing understanding of how the realisation of their own goals depends on gaining the co-operation of others and how, simultaneously, the others need them (see Bossard and Boll, 1960, Chapters 26 and 27). The peer relationships discussed here may take place in school, outside, or before the child starts school.

The highly restricted peer group is well-known in lower-class urban areas of stable populations. There, parents commonly exercise no control on the child's behaviour outside the home, unless to tell an older sibling to look after him or her. Thus children of similar age who live within a few houses or flats of each other form a closed group or gang. Conflict between these groups, which is quite common in the absence of parental intervention, hardens the boundary around them and discourages changes of membership from one group to another. Members of this kind of group are commonly from families of the power-assertive type and are themselves aggressive in disposition. Most of this aggressiveness is turned on those outside the group. They also tend to be emotionally very insecure and to therefore cling to their fellow members all the more desperately. They highly resent being separated from one another in school and when they are together are extremely difficult to control because, not only are they as individuals non-responsive to rebukes from teachers, but in the presence of other members of the group they are so much more concerned with the responses of their mates and responding to *them* that the expectations, rebukes, or praise of others is barely heard (Short and Strodtbeck, 1965).

Another kind of difficulty in adjusting to school is that found by children who have had insufficient experience in learning what is needed to get along with peers. Because their attempts to join in playing with others are clumsy or because, once invited, they cannot follow the unwritten rules of games and just hanging around together, they are social isolates. To the extent that the school attempts to organise pupils to work in groups, some of the difficulty of the social isolate may be alleviated. This will depend, though, on careful coaching by teachers—both of the isolates and the more sociable pupils who must be induced to accept them. It remains true, of course, that pupils who are more able at managing relations with peers will perform better in group work situations than other pupils. The hope, however, is that the difference between them will diminish over the long term as the isolates gain more experience under favourable conditions.

Our discussion so far has focused mainly on the early years of childhood, mainly pre-school years, and on considerations of peer relationships which apply almost regardless of age up to the time of leaving school. We turn now to consider some of the particular features of peer relationships in the adolescent period and how they affect the individual's response to school. From roughly the age of thirteen years, certain features of teenagers and their relationships with each other become apparent. A need to assert some independence from adults becomes apparent and tends to express itself by counter-alliances with peers rather than immediate individual autonomy. Around this age teenagers, especially boys, are encouraged to think about future careers and pressures for achievement and extended future orientation, sometimes in a competitive context, begin to build up. Around this time also boys and girls become interested in each other and the desire for popularity, which is not restricted to any age group, at this time takes on a more determined character as boys vie with each other for the attentions of particular girls and girls likewise strain to make themselves attractive to boys (Parsons, 1954; Erikson, 1963; Mays, 1965).

All these factors combine to make the teenage peer group loom large in the lives of the teenagers and, by the same token, in the lives of their parents and teachers. In these groups they find support for their assertion of independence from parents, enjoyment and relaxation from the stresses of the official side of school life and worrying about the future, as well as some structuring of the boyfriend and girlfriend rat-race. Boys and girls in their respective groups set agreed norms of conduct for their own social life—partly by passing on the norms accepted among teenagers of a year or two older than themselves and partly by their own tacit modifications. They also exchange a certain amount of information about technical matters such as make-up, dating, birth control and so forth, and about the reputations of members of the other sex. Obviously there is a delicate balance between the needs and desires of group members for social support in these matters and the reality of competition against each other for the attention of the opposite sex.

Poignant as some of these problems are, our prime concern in this chapter is with the implications of peer relationships for adjustment to school. The dominant thesis in relation to this question, due to the work of Coleman (1961), is that the effect of the peer group system in secondary schools is to temper very considerably the effectiveness of the official pressure for academic attainment. In a survey of eight high schools in the Midwest of the USA, Coleman asked pupils between the ages of thirteen and seventeen years a variety of questions, concerning their own values and attitudes, concerning membership in the "leading crowd" of pupils in the school and concerning the attributes which they perceived to be important in gaining membership of that "leading crowd". Membership of these "leading crowds" is a prerogative of boys who are personable and distinguished at sports, and girls who are popular with these boys. Exceptional academic achievement is in no way a qualification for this elite status. This interpretation is supported both by the perception of pupils in general and by a comparison of the values expressed by leading crowd members and non-members.

It is true, though Coleman skates lightly around the point, that leading crowd members do tend to have higher academic grades than non-members. But this could be explained by the fact that they tend to come from homes of higher social status in general. Coleman's claim is that their academic performance would be greater than it is but for the value system among the peer groups in school which emphasises athleticism, personality and sociability rather than intellectual or academic excellence.

Strong confirmation for this thesis that academic performance tends to be depressed by involvement in high school peer group life comes from a later study by McDill and Coleman (1963) in which they followed a panel of pupils over four years. They found that pupils belonging to the leading crowd were more likely than non-members to develop less favourable attitudes toward academic achievement over this period of time. At the same time they tended to become more positive in their intentions of going to college. Both of these attitude changes may be attributed to the effects of membership in peer groups with a common value system. Alternative intepretations are conceivable but on the whole seem less likely than this one.

Coleman is concerned exclusively with the implication of peer groupings for *academic* performance in school and ignores other implications which are less discouraging from the teachers' point of view. As we have discussed in Chapter Four, the involvement of pupils in sporting and extra-curricular activities in school makes them more susceptible to social control within the official structure. It would appear that the "leading crowd" discussed by Coleman base their elite status in the school to a very large extent on their position in the school sports teams and as leaders in other activities officially sponsored by the school and hence under official control. So, although teachers may not be able to affect the value system of the leading peer group in the school or their influence on other pupils without radical changes in the structure of the school, they can operate within the existing system to make sure that pupils who enjoy this elite status are models of conformity to the rules and expectations of the school. Pupils who do not meet this requirement to a sufficient degree can be removed or suspended from their positions on the school team or other activity which is the basis to a large extent of their status among the other pupils. Thus the peer group structure among pupils can play an important part in maintaining social control.

It also fulfils a number of important functions for the pupils themselves, which we mentioned earlier—breaking free from parental apron strings, cushioning the strains of achievement and planning for the future, and facilitating the dating and mate-selection process. Further, it may be suggested, that the existence of this kind of peer group life at school makes pupils more content with their lot and more ready to comply with the official demands of the school.

The term "youth culture" or "teenage culture" is sometimes

applied to describe the activities and implicit values found among teenage peer groups. The concept is a somewhat contentious one because it is difficult to draw a boundary around this culture and also it is doubtful whether we should think of a single youth culture or several distinct sub-cultures. An earlier study by Hollingshead (1949) of just one high school in the same area as the Coleman study, shows clearly the existence of two distinct peer group systems each with its own sub-culture: one for the mainly middle-class, college-bound teenagers, centred around the social activities and sports of the high school and one for the lower-class early leavers with their activities centred around street corner, candy store and skating rink. The middle-class youth culture clearly corresponds to the one studied by Coleman. Let us give a little attention to the other youth culture, that of the early leavers—those whom the school have failed or those who have failed in school, according to which way one prefers to look at it.

Hollingshead's research was done over twenty years ago but, though fashions in clothes and music have changed and perhaps the bowling alley has replaced the skating rink, I see no reason to suppose that the basic character of the youth culture of the "non-strivers" has changed. Then as now, in many different societies, this sub-culture is visibly identifiable by its distinctive styles of dress and adornment, music and dancing, slang and other mannerisms, which invariably contrast quite clearly with the styles accepted by most adults in the same society. Alongside this aesthetic rebellion there is a rejection of certain values quite fundamental to the school and middle-class, adult society. One of these values which is rejected is that of deferred gratification or future orientation—replaced by spontaneous enjoyment, hedonism or present orientation. The other value rejected is that of the young being subordinate to all adults—the assertion being that teenagers are "grown up" in the sense of being equal in status to adults though (they would be quick to insist) different in kind.

The hypothesis that teenagers who identify themselves with the life-style of this sub-culture would also endorse the values hypothesised and that these teenagers would be manifestly less well-adjusted to school was tested in the London survey of 540 fourth-year boys cited earlier in our discussion of middle class values (Sugarman, 1967). Involvement in the life style of "teenage pop culture" as found in London in 1964 was measured by several indicators, all contained in the same questionnaire. The first presented a list of activities that seemed to be part of "making the teen-scene". Respondents taking part (boys only) were asked to mark the ones that applied to them. The list included: regular listening to pop music radio stations, wearing teenage fashions, being keen on dancing and hanging around coffee bars. These items corresponded very well to the hedonistic aspect of the sub-culture. Other questions were asked about smoking and going out with girls. These two areas seemed to be important for their symbolic connotations of being "grown-up". Since the three indicators (making the teen scene, dating and smoking) were quite well intercorrelated, they were used together in a combined measure.

A high level of involvement in this sub-culture was found to be associated with a tendency to reject deferred gratification or future orientation values, as measured by the questionnaire which we discussed in the previous section on middle-class values. On the whole then, this style of life does tend to be associated with a certain set of values, in conflict with those preferred by the school.

As for adjustment to school, we find that high levels of involvement in the teenage non-strivers' sub-culture tends to go along with unfavourable attitudes to school; it tends to go along with being an under-achiever, that is, having a record of academic performance which is low in relation to that of other pupils who have a similar IQ as measured three years earlier; it also tends quite strongly to go with having a poor conduct record, as reported by the form-teacher or house-master (Sugarman, 1967).

High levels of involvement in this sub-culture were found mainly among boys from homes of lower social class and poorer intellectual quality. Although home background is a fairly good predictor of adjustment to school in this study, involvement in this sub-culture is a considerably better one. In other words, where pupils' adjustment to school is not what would be expected on the basis of their home background, this is likely to be revealed in the pupils' level of involvement in the teenagers' non-striving sub-culture.

There seems to be a process whereby the styles in this sub-culture become progressively more extreme as those of yesterday are borrowed by teenagers and young adults who wish to enjoy the aesthetic styles without any commitment to the values which accompany them for those who are most highly committed. This means, of course, that one's measures of involvement rapidly become out of date. This does not affect the general proposition, though, that there is this sub-culture among many pupils in school and their slightly older peers who have dropped out of school, with its own symbols and life-style, supporting a rejection by pupils of two of the most fundamental expectations attached to the role of pupil in the school.

Of course there have always been pupils who broke school rules, were mischievous and hated school. What has happened more recently, so it seems, is that this new sub-culture has crystalised the deviant tendencies of a number of pupils into a contra-culture, presenting the new contra-role of "teenager" in rivalry with the official, school defined role of "pupil". This cultural efflorescence no doubt softens the pains of failure (in terms of the school's criteria) for those who would have failed anyway and may add to the number of determined rebels some who would have been too faint-hearted to have rebelled very strongly against the demands of the school in the absence of the moral support conveyed by this contra-culture.

In reconciling these results with those of Coleman, a number of points must be kept in mind. Firstly, he talked of membership in a leading crowd versus non-membership, whereas we in the London study spoke of involvement or interest in a number of activities and self-reported behaviour. In other words, Coleman is talking primarily about elite group membership and secondarily about the group's activities and style of life; we have been talking primarily about a style of life or, more strictly, about identification with a style of life, which may in some cases be only an attitude measure. In the second place, Coleman is talking about an elite status group among pupils which probably does not exist in British schools with their much less developed social and sporting activities compared to the American high schools. Their teams perform in front of large paying crowds from the local community, accompanied by brass bands and cheer leaders.

The sub-culture studied among the London boys surely exists also in the American high school, as Hollingshead's work suggests. Finally, as I suggested in the discussion of Coleman's findings, I do not believe that the implications of teenage culture for the schools are entirely pessimistic. Just as the emergence of this culture has made the pupil's alternative to the school clearer for him, so at the same time it has made the nature of the teacher's adversary clearer to him too. Teachers who wish to try to reach across the cultural divide to make contact with their pupils—even the alienated ones—can now easily find out quite a lot about the things that interest these pupils and can find some way of approaching these difficult pupils through their own contra-culture. This does not mean that teachers should dress up in teenage style clothes, adopt their slang and all conflict will be ended. However, the exploitation of this culture by mass media and other commercial interests have brought it into the public domain as never before. It is therefore more accessible to teachers than ever before and it is up to them to find the appropriate way of using this knowledge in an educationally constructive way (Lippitt, 1965).

PROCESSES OF LEARNING

In the previous two sections we have discussed some of the major factors associated with home and peer relationships which affect the child's response to school, meaning his capacity and motivation to comply with its expectations and to learn from his experiences in school. We are, therefore, discussing how the child learns from earlier experiences with parents and peers various things which affect the way he learns later from school. Our analysis so far is, however, seriously incomplete—for we have discussed only factors affecting learning but we have said nothing about how they affect it or *what* is being affected. In other words, we have so far ignored the processes of learning. It is important to our analysis that we should at least outline the major processes of learning which take place in the home, peer group, school and other situations. We have said a good deal about situational factors and will say more. But before we can proceed to the last stage of our analysis, suggesting how situational variables affect aspects of learning crucial to moral development, we must indicate what these processes are and, so far as possible, which ones appear to be most important in different situations and for different dimensions of learning.

1 *Imitation/Modelling.* From its earliest years the child imitates the behaviour of its parents and later on other "significant others".

It imitates a wide range of behaviours, from the smallest mannerisms to basic attitudes and beliefs. Children not only imitate parents but also peers—especially those slightly older—and where they look up to a particular teacher they may take him or her as a model too (Bandura and Walters, 1964).

Early learning of this kind has consequences for later learning in school and adjustment to school. Whether the balance of consequences is to facilitate or impede adjustment and the kinds of learning officially expected depends on what kinds of habits, behavioural and mental, are learned from early models. If we regard teachers as models who should be imitated in some respects for successful adaptation to school, a second crucial fact is how far the child's earlier and concurrent models resemble teachers or otherwise affect his readiness to take the teachers as models for imitation.

2 *Drill*. We shall see later how important a place routinisation has in the classroom as a means of maintaining social order under difficult conditions. Drill or routinisation teaches habits to the child and induces a form of conformity. It would seem however that these habits and this conformity are to a high degree situationally specific and that (for example) learning to walk on the left-hand side of the corridor and not to run in school may be effectively taught without any carry-over to other situations at all. This is not to deny its value within the school though.

3 *Formal Teaching*. Learning can take place in the context of a formal teaching situation in which the teacher addresses a class of pupils whose scope of responses is restricted. On a somewhat less formal level, parents and peers may also function as teachers for short periods on an *ad hoc* basis. In or out of school teaching is most effective when it follows up the child's spontaneous interests aroused by his own exploration and discovery.

In the long term, heavy exposure to both drill and formal teaching by lecture may affect attitudes, values and possibly personality attributes—not so much as a result of the *content* of this teaching but more as a result of the *passive role* in which the child is cast by these methods. A great dependence on these methods would seem likely to induce passivity, dependence and a tendency to unthinking obedience on the part of the children—hardly conducive to becoming a morally educated person who can think for himself.

Formal teaching also includes learning situations less rigid than the formal lecture. As we shall see in our analysis of the classroom, teaching can incorporate ideas that come spontaneously from pupils so that there is more of a dialogue between teacher and pupils, though always with the former in control. This version of formal teaching is more successful than the more rigid kind (see Flanders, reviewed in our next chapter).

Explicit teaching, which may be in a formal context of lecturing, preaching or in a less formal discussion framework, plays an important part in the learning of universalistic moral principles, in so far as these are found in the culture in question. It seems that in the cultures of economically-advanced societies there is more effort expended in stating and preaching moral principles as such—as opposed to a body of traditional norms ("the ways of our fathers", etc.) stated in terms of many *specific* injunctions of a low order of generality and abstraction.

Exposure to this kind of formal teaching probably is most important late in the child's development, for the kind of moral education which we are concerned with here. That is to say, that in the absence of successful experiences with the other forms of learning discussed here, this kind of formal teaching—whether by preaching alone or with discussion—will not produce morally educated people. On top of successful learning of these other kinds, though, this formal presentation may play a useful part in integrating the various internalised normative standards of the individual into a whole that is more meaningful to him and so helping him to think in terms of more general principles in terms of which to decide choice situations.

4 *Operant conditioning*. The teaching machine best exemplifies the principles of this learning process which has been best demonstrated in the work of B. F. Skinner (1953). This learning process involves two concepts: an action or judgement ("operant") which is followed immediately by either a reward or no reward. Operants which are rewarded tend to be repeated (or learned); those which are not rewarded are not.

Routine intellectual operations, informational data and a wide variety of psycho-motor skills have been successfully taught and learned by teaching machines and programmed learning texts, which operate on the same principle. It is possible in theory for a human teacher to operate in the way described. When, however, a machine or other device can be programmed to present a series of carefully graded steps in a lesson, each followed by a test item with a built-in reward for the right answer, there are certain advantages. Each learner can proceed at his *own* pace, unlike the situation of formal lecture or class teaching. The teaching machine, unlike the human teacher has infinite patience, never tires, treats all learners alike without favouritism and without any memory of past mistakes or past delinquencies.

Operant conditioning functions all the time, though in a less rigorous and planned form than the teaching machine. It is another way of defining the familiar process of social interaction in which people act more favourably to those who do things they like than those who do things they do not like and so tend to encourage behaviour which they (and others) like over behaviour they dislike. This rewarding or reinforcing plays a part in the child's imitation of parents, friends and other models. In so far as they approve of imitation they spontaneously reward him for it.

5 *Avoidance conditioning*. Basic to this learning process is the extreme dependence of the small child on his adult socialising agent for all resources—but especially for love and approval. The more love and approval the child is accustomed to get, the greater is the anxiety aroused by the fear of losing it. Avoidance conditioning uses this sanction to teach impulse control and internalised conformity to social norms, even when the subject believes there is no danger that others will know about his delinquency.

The kind of learning involved here has been explained by Aronfreed (1968) and by Trasler (1962) in terms of a model of "passive avoidance conditioning". It can be demonstrated in the laboratory by first teaching an animal that food can be obtained by pressing a lever and then introducing an electric shock mechanism which delivers a shock when he presses this lever. Even when hungry, the animal soon learns not to press the lever. In the same way, the child learns that certain goals and certain avenues to goals are forbidden and will be punished. Stealing would be such an example and the extreme disapproval of his parents (loss of love) corresponds to the electric shock. Having once committed the forbidden act or come close to it and having been punished, *any stimulus* which is associated in the child's mind with the forbidden act serves to arouse all the anxiety associated with his fears of losing parents' love. In this way the impulse to forbidden conduct is inhibited.

We do not even need to postulate the exercise of foresight in this case. The mere thought of the forbidden act triggers off the associated anxiety and, since temptation is recurrent, the conditioned state renews itself and does not decay with time, unlike learning based on operant conditioning. Whereas operant learning depends on continued reinforcement for retention, avoidance conditioning does not decline and indeed requires very substantial efforts to change a pattern once it has been laid down. As any psychiatrist knows, this is a serious problem for people who grew up in families where avoidance conditioning was used too effectively to implant guilt feelings which are highly crippling to the adult.

Avoidance conditioning in the human is necessarily a more complex process than in the case of the rat. This is basically because the social world in which the child will live involves very many norms and expectations, specifying the behaviour expected in different situations, and the correct classification of the situations in order to determine which norms apply is a complicated business. The rat had to learn one simple and specific taboo—not to press a certain lever in a small cage—ever. Certainly parents do try to teach their children prohibitions which are as specific, for example never to go near the open fire in the living-room when it is alight, or never to touch father's razor.

Often however, parents try to combine teaching the child a specific prohibition like this with teaching him to avoid a more general class of acts of which this is only one example. Thus a child who has been punished for taking biscuits from the kitchen without permission may be told not only not to take biscuits again but that he must learn not to take any things that don't belong to him without permission. Stated in this way, the rule or prohibition requires a very considerable degree of conceptual ability on the part of the child. He may be able to grasp the idea that he must not take things that belong to his parents but not be able to generalise this to things that belong to a brother or sister.

9

Or having mastered that stage of abstraction, the child may fail to realise that this applies not only to things that belong to individuals but also to public property or amenities, for example flowers in a communal garden.

It is possible, though very much less efficient, to train the child by means of avoidance conditioning attached to specific acts without this attempt to generalise the lesson. In fact parents who are themselves unable to think abstractly and generalise can only operate in this way. The very young child and the child of low intellectual ability can only be taught in this more specific way—though in the former case, the degree of generalisation can be increased as the child's intellectual powers develop. And one of the factors which will contribute to developing these powers of generalisation and abstraction is having his behaviour criticised in terms of these general rules and requirements rather than in terms of specific unexplained prohibitions.

The effectiveness of avoidance conditioning is determined by a number of factors. Minimally it is determined by the strength of the emotional bond between child and the socialising agent, by the agent's consistency and willingness to withdraw affection as a sanction and by the agent's and the child's abilities to abstract and generalise.

Normally parents and guardians are the only ones who have a strong enough emotional bond with the child for it to be used as the basic sanction for avoidance conditioning. It is not, however, a bond that can be assumed to exist always—and often it is missing—because it needs to be carefully cultivated. The child has first to be induced to look at the early socialising agent as a source of love, then to be made aware that this love may be withheld or tempered in some way when he does something which is strongly disapproved of. He will then be highly sensitised to cues indicating disapproval on the part of the parents. The pain associated with *actual* loss of love gives rise to anxiety over the *possibility* of this and constant alertness for cues indicating parental disapproval.

In so far as children with this kind of pre-school conditioning associate their teachers with their original socialiser on the basis of similar expectations, methods of control and other surface attributes, their teachers are able to trigger off the same fund of anxiety—albeit less effectively than parents. This is the major reason for the greater susceptibility to discipline in school and home of children reared by love-oriented methods, which we noted in the first section of this chapter.

6 *Discovery*. The child's natural curiosity leads him to explore the environment around him, both by experimenting on it and by just observing. Thus he learns many things about the world and society in which he is living even without any effort on anyone's part to teach him. In fact his curiosity may lead him to discover things which the adults controlling his life do not want him to know about. Restrictions may then be placed on his freedom to explore and discover, not only for this reason but also for his physical safety. The extent to which children are allowed to explore and discover for themselves and the extent to which their curiosity is encouraged by conscientious attempts to answer their questions, seems likely to affect not only how much they learn about the world around them but also to affect the development of their intellectual powers, which they are developing in solving problems that they themselves want to solve (MacDonnell, 1972).

As educators have come to be convinced of this, much greater efforts have been made, especially in primary schools, to set children to work discovering and exploring for themselves certain areas of knowledge, with the teacher fulfilling the role of advisor, custodian of various tools and resources and evaluator and not just the traditional role of lecturer. At the same time some parents have become aware of the importance of discovery learning and a whole new sector of the toy industry has developed producing "creative toys" for pre-school children.

Discovery learning is probably the most important way in which all of us form impressions about the attitude of other people towards us. We receive a variety of signals, of which the most important are generally not overt verbal messages but are either non-verbal or cues which are implicit in verbal messages whose overt content refers to something else. We learn about their attitudes towards us from their tone of voice, facial expressions, physical proximity and contact, the amount of time they find to spend with us bearing in mind their circumstances and so forth. Equally the child may be affected more by the way he feels he is treated by others, than by what they say to him. From the way he is treated he will infer the attitude of his parents, teachers and his peers—sometimes he will infer them incorrectly, but he will be affected by what he *thinks* their attitude is, even if he is mistaken. His teachers may tell him, for example, that they will always be willing to talk about things that are bothering him, but if when he tries to do so he always finds they are "busy" then he will conclude that they do not in fact care about him. If the headmaster appears to take an interest only in the star sportsman and to ignore all other pupils, they will infer that the only form of accomplishment which he values is in sports.

This is not to say that pupils are alert to every single gesture and act of their teachers. Indeed many must go unnoticed. But what is being argued is that the predominant overall pattern of behaviour by teachers and head towards pupils tends in the long run to have its effect on them. If this pattern runs in the same direction as the behaviour of parents, the effect will be all the greater.

This process works both ways, though it is more glaring and easily seen in this direction, where it works contrary to the declared policies of the school. However, it works equally in the benign direction. The pupil who is talking to his housemaster about something that troubles him and sees that he sends other callers away (including adults) will be inclined to believe that the housemaster really is concerned with his pupil's problems; when pupils see that their art work is displayed prominently in the school they will feel that this work is valued; when they notice that the headmaster spends as much time in praising this work as he does in praising the winners of scholarships and the scorers of goals they may then (and only then) conclude that he truly values efforts of this kind.

In similar ways we learn about the attitudes of our parents, friends, teachers and others towards many other subjects—even when they do not state them explicitly (and even when they would wish to conceal them from us). As Jules Henry (1965) has expressed it, human beings do not perceptually filter out the "noise" that accompanies the messages which others intend us to receive. We can and do receive signals on several channels simultaneously. In this sort of way, for example, children may learn that their parents think that certain kinds of newspapers, music, hobbies and jobs are preferable to others. And in so far as there is some consistency running through these attitudes and values, the child is likely to react to them, either coming to accept them himself or reject them depending on the nature of his relationship.

(Note that this interpretation of the attitudes of a model is different from the imitation of specific, overt features of the model which we described earlier.)

Because of this process whereby people read implicit messages which may not have been intended by the sender, the range of influence which socialising agents may have over their subjects can be very much more extensive than they either intend or realise. For instance, the fact that certain topics are consistently avoided—that they are never spoken of and that conversations which are heading in their direction are redirected—tells a great deal about the attitudes held towards those topics. In the formal setting of the school there may be rituals which carry *heavily* emphasised messages—often about status inequalities which are emphasised by differences in uniform, rigid orders of precedence in entering or leaving rooms, obligatory forms of address between members and so forth. Other clear messages can be carried by other aspects of the school organisation of a non-ritual kind. For example the existence of a streaming policy and along with it a policy of allocating the poorest facilities and the least qualified teachers to one of these streams consistently indicates to all (especially to the pupils in that stream) something about the attitude of the staff towards them.

It may be objected that this policy exists out of dire necessity or is the legacy of a previous regime and should not rightly be used to infer the attitudes of the present staff. However, if most of the staff involved in implementing such a policy strongly believed in the equal status and value of the pupils in the different streams it would surely strike them repeatedly that this was inconsistent with their beliefs and they would do something about trying to change it. Only when the values built into a particular organisational arrangement are broadly in keeping with the values of those who administer it (or when they have no values about such matters) does it seem to them that there is anything "neutral" about the arrangement. To the pupils on the receiving end, although they may not be capable of articulating their perceptions, such arrangements are likely to convey a feeling that they are felt to be worth less than those who receive more favourable treatment.

It is not being argued here that pupils and children have such sensitive perception that they read meanings into every single nuance of unspoken communication. Rather it is being argued that when a variety of implicit signals are in agreement in conveying the same message, that message is likely to be understood by those whom it concerns—even if others (including those who send the message) remain unaware of them.

This learning process of independent exploration leads the child to form ideas about the normative expectations that operate in his society and other aspects of the way relationships among people seem to be patterned. This discovery learning proceeds alongside the deliberate efforts of socialisation agents and in some areas overtakes them. In other words, we must not overlook the *active* part the child plays in his own socialisation. He does a lot of observing and working things out for himself. Roger Brown (1967) suggests that this aspect of learning the social conventions and rules may be compared by analogy to the way in which children learn language. Although the young child may be given some formal instructions in grammar, long before this he has worked out for himself some interpretation of the basic rules of language use in his society, without very much formal guidance from others, except in so far as they correct his utterances when they go against convention. Thus by observation, imitation, correction, inference and much imaginative ingenuity the child learns to use the language of his social group more or less as do the older members of the group. What he learns is not merely to reproduce specific sounds, words and sentences which he has heard from others, but the ability to make sentences of his own which he may never have heard from others. By analogy this may be a model that can be applied to the process through which the child learns how to get by in his social group. Conceived in this way the socialisation process involves a considerable initiative and intellectual effort on the part of the child rather than just a passive soaking up of teaching.

CHAPTER 5 REFERENCES

G. A. Almond, and S. Verba, *The Civic Culture*, Princeton University Press, Princeton, NJ, 1963.

Justin Aronfreed, *Conduct and Conscience*, Academic Press, New York, 1968.

A. Bandura and R. H. Walters, *Social Learning and Personality Development*, Holt, Rinehart and Winston, New York, 1964.

Wesley C. Becker, "Consequences of Different Kinds of Parental Discipline", in H. L. Hoffman (ed.), *Review of Child Development Research*, Vol. 1, Russell Sage Foundation, New York, 1964.

Leonard Berkowitz, "Responsibility, Reciprocity and Social Distance in Help-giving", *J. Experimental Soc. Psych.*, IV, 1968, pp. 46–63.

Leonard Berkowitz and F. Friedman, "Some Social Class Differences in Helping Behaviour", *J. Personality and Soc. Psych.*, V, 1967, pp. 217–25.

Basil Bernstein, "A Socio-linguistic Approach to Social Learning", in J. Gould (ed.), *Penguin Survey of the Social Sciences*, Penguin, Harmondsworth, 1965.

Basil Bernstein and D. Henderson, "Social Class Differences in the Relevance of Language of Socialization", *Sociology*, III, Jan., 1969, pp. 1–20.

Benjamin Bloom, *Stability and Change in Human Characteristics*, John Wiley, New York, 1964.

James H. S. Bossard and E. S. Boll, *The Sociology of Child Development*, Harper, New York, 1960.

Roger Brown, *Social Psychology*, Free Press, New York, 1967.

Central Advisory Council for Education, England, 15 *to* 18, H.M.S.O. London, 1959. (The Crowther Report.)

James S. Coleman, *Adolescent Society*, Free Press, New York, 1961.

Elizabeth Douvan and M. Gold, "Model Patterns in American Adolescence", in H. L. Hoffman (ed.), *Review of Child Development Research*, Vol. 1, Russell Sage Foundation, New York, 1964, pp. 469–528.

Erik H. Erikson (ed.), *Youth: Change and Challenge*, Basic Books, New York, 1963.

Jean Floud, "Social Class Factors in Educational Achievement", A. H. Halsey (ed.), *Ability and Educational Opportunity*, O.E.C.D., Kungalv, 1961.

Jules Henry, *Culture Against Man*, Random House, New York, 1965.

August B. Hollingshead, *Elmtown's Youth*, John Wiley, New York, 1949.

J. McVicar Hunt, "Environment, Development, and Scholastic Achievement", in M. Deutsch *et al.* (eds.), *Social Class, Race, and Psychological Development*, Holt, Rinehart and Winston, New York, 1968, pp. 293–336.

J. L. Jayasuriya, "A Study of Adolescent Ambition, Level of Aspiration and Achievement Motivation", unpub. Ph.D. thesis, University of London, 1960.

Josephine Klein, *Samples from English Cultures*, 2 vols., Routledge and Kegan Paul, London, 1965.

Florence R. Kluckhohn and F. L. Strodtbeck, *Variations in Value Orientations*, Row, Peterson, Chicago, 1961.

M. L. Kohn, "Social Class and the Exercise of Parental Authority", *American Sociol. Review*, XXIV, 1959, pp. 352–66.

Ronald Lippitt, "The Youth Culture, the School System, and the Socialization Community", in A. J. Reiss (ed.), *Schools in a Changing Society*, Free Press, New York, 1965.

Edward L. McDill, and J. S. Coleman, "High School Social Status, College Plans and Interest in Academic Achievement: A Panel Analysis", *American Sociological Review*, XXVII, Dec., 1963, pp. 905–18.

Arthur MacDonnell, "The Competent Child", *Harvard Graduate School of Education Assoc. Bulletin*, XVI, Spring, 1972. (Report on "Pre-school Project" of Burton L. White and Jean Carew Watts.)

J. B. Mays, *The Young Pretenders*, Michael Joseph, London, 1965.

J. and E. Newson, *Four Year Olds in an Urban Community*, Allen and Unwin, London, 1968.

Talcott Parsons, "Age and Sex in the Social Structure of the United States", in *Essays in Sociological Theory*, Free Press, New York, 1954, pp. 89–103.

B. Rosen, "The Achievement Syndrome", *American Sociol. Review*, XXIV, April, 1956, pp. 352–6.

James F. Short Jr., and F. L. Strodtbeck, *Group Process and Gang Delinquency*, University of Chicago Press, Chicago, 1965.

B. F. Skinner, *Science and Human Behavior*, Free Press, New York, 1953.

Pitirim Sorokin, *The Ways and Power of Love*, Beacon Press, Boston, 1954.

Fred L. Strodtbeck, "Family Integration, Values, and Achievement", in A. H. Halsey *et al.* (eds.), *Education, Economy and Society*, Free Press, New York, 1961, pp. 315–47.

B. N. Sugarman, "Social Class and Values as Related to Achievement and Conduct in School", *Sociological Review*, XIV, Nov., 1966, pp. 287–301.

B. N. Sugarman, "Involvement in Youth Culture, Academic Achievement and Conformity in School", *British Journal of Sociology*, XVIII, June, 1967, pp. 151–64.

B. N. Sugarman, "Altruistic Attitudes in School", *Journal of Moral Education*, II, Feb., 1973, pp. 145–56.

G. Trasler, *The Explanation of Criminality*, Routledge and Kegan Paul, London, 1962.

Marian Winterbottom, "The Relationship of Need Achievement to Learning Experiences in Independence and Mastery", in J. W. Atkinson (ed.), *Motives in Fantasy, Action and Society*, Van Nostrand, Princeton, NJ, 1958.

Derek Wright, *The Psychology of Moral Behaviour*, Penguin Books, Harmondsworth, 1971.

Chapter Six

INPUTS: (2) TEACHERS

BACKGROUND, TRAINING AND APPROACH TO TEACHING

Having discussed some aspects of the early social experiences of pupils which affect the way they respond to situations in the school ("pupil inputs"), we now turn in a similar vein to look at teacher inputs. Unfortunately we know a good deal less about the effect of differences in background, personality and training on the behaviour of teachers in school.

We know from the work of Floud and Scott (1961) that the social origins of teachers in England and Wales are overwhelmingly from the middle range of the class structure, modest non-manual and superior manual occupations. Out of all those who entered teaching since the Second World War only ten per cent come from families in the professional and administrative categories. This implies that the great majority of teachers have experienced a significant but moderate degree of upward status mobility relative to the social status of their parents and this mobility goes back at least two generations in the families of most teachers. This success, certainly in the last generation of the teachers, has been achieved through the medium of the educational system. Thus they are likely to be convinced of the efficacy of formal education for success in life—perhaps over-convinced of it, bearing in mind that its connection with success in other fields of work is by no means so direct.

One specific connection between mobility experience and attitudes of teachers has been documented in a study by Himmelweit (1955), who found that teachers who had experienced the most upward mobility tended to have the most authoritarian attitudes and to be most likely to agree that "the wrong kind of child" was getting into the grammar (selective secondary) schools. They perceive a problem of (what they feel to be) inappropriate attitudes and behaviour on the part of certain pupils. It is interesting that it should be *these* teachers who feel this most strongly. It is unlikely that very many of these teachers themselves once displayed such non-conforming behaviour. More likely, when they were the age of these pupils, they were much more conforming to the expectations of their teachers, perhaps while being rather painfully aware at that time that they were differentiating themselves from the majority of their peers of similar socio-economic circumstances. It is, I suggest, because the struggle to succeed in school was much harder for these teachers from humbler social origins—not only economically harder but also emotionally—that they became rather harsher and less tolerant in outlook than many of their colleagues. They have invested too much in this struggle for them not to take the rules of the competition very seriously.

At least as important as the attitude differences between different types of teachers is the overwhelming basic similarity in the attitudes and expectations which teachers bring to school with them. They are all representatives of "middle class culture" and they come face to face in school with a population which is, at best, only partly socialised into this culture by virtue of age and of which a great proportion is hardly at all socialised into it because their homes have not exerted any significant influence in that direction, and their prior schooling has been able to achieve precious little. The overwhelming majority of teachers believe in the importance of neatness, thrift, planning for the long-range future, individual striving—especially in schoolwork, politeness, ambition and success in terms of the socially-agreed hierarchy of occupations, care of property, punctuality, verbal articulateness, sexual modesty, and sportsmanlike conduct; they abhor physical violence and cheating. More than a few researchers have documented the wide cultural differences existing in both Britain and the USA between the middle class culture, as represented by teachers and school and the lower working class culture of the poor urban areas. (For Britain, see Klein, 1965, vol. 1; Jackson and Marsden, 1962; and Mays, 1962; for the USA see Becker, 1952; Hollingshead, 1969; Havighurst and Neugarten, 1957; and Whyte, 1943).

Thus, even apart from the conflict inherent in the teacher-pupil situation as a result of the fact that teachers attempt to control and restrict the behaviour of the pupils very considerably, there is a further tension in this relationship due to the cultural gulf that looms between most teachers and most of their pupils. As we have indicated, this cultural gulf has an age dimension and a social class or status dimension. Even where pupils come from homes very similar to those of their teachers, there still exist differences in norms and interests due to the age differences between them. The most serious gulf, however, exists when both factors are involved—with the social class or status one at its widest. This is the situation of the teacher in a lower class neighbourhood school or in a streamed school where the pupils who are culturally most alien to the school are congregated together in certain classes. The teacher who faces a class of children whose families are recent immigrants from Asian or African countries, or the white Anglo teacher on an American Indian reservation faces these problems of a non-shared cultural background only to a slightly greater degree (if indeed it is greater) than the teacher in a slum area.

Having established some of the background to the teacher's working situation *vis à vis* the pupils in terms of the twin problems of control and cultural differences, we may proceed to consider some factors that differentiate among teachers in their approach to the job. Some correlations between teacher's behaviour and pupils' development were reviewed in Chapter One. It is not to be assumed without any further thought that the direction of causality is always *from* teacher's behaviour *to* pupils' behaviour and attitudes and never in the other direction. Teachers do vary their approach according to which group of pupils they are teaching—especially their techniques of discipline and control. And it is likely that teachers' general style of teaching is affected by the kind of pupils with which they mostly find themselves faced—that is, they would have developed other styles if they had found themselves working in different kinds of areas with different kinds of pupils. On the whole, though, it seems appropriate to think in general of "teachers" as a set of independent variables and "pupils' development" as a set of dependent ones. Pupils are at a more malleable stage of their growth than are teachers; pupils are less able to move from a situation which they find intolerable and teachers have more scope to co-ordinate and plan their mode of dealing with pupils than the latter have of doing this—though ineptitude on the part of staff and lack of leadership may sometimes reverse the position. Where pupils do have a relatively influential causal role that is more often one of setting severe limits to what teachers can accomplish rather than influencing them in an enduring way—though this may sometimes happen too.

Data on teachers' attitudes are important because we know that, in certain areas at least, teachers' attitudes are correlated with their classroom behaviour and both are related in some ways to pupils' development. Authoritarian attitudes among teachers have been shown to correlate with teachers' classroom behaviour; teachers' attitudes to pupils have been shown to correlate with teachers' performance as assessed by observers and by their pupils (Getzels and Jackson, in Gage [ed.], [1963] p. 523, p. 509), and teachers' attitudes to a variety of teaching issues (physical punishment, noise, eleven plus selection, etc.) have been shown in the NFER survey of streaming to be related to a number of aspects of pupils' attitudes to school and self (Barker Lunn, 1970).

These three types of variables are brought together in a single research by Harvey and his associates (1968). They assessed differences among teachers of infants in their modes of cognitive organisation or thought styles, observed their behaviour in the classroom and also assessed the behaviour of their pupils. Ninety teachers and 118 classes were studied. Cognitive styles are analysed in terms of a distinction between "concrete" and "abstract" styles. Concrete style is defined in terms of three factors: (1) the need for a high degree of structure and order, (2) the need for a high degree of simplicity and certainty and (3) a belief in "divine fate control". (The two questionnaires used to assess the conceptual styles of the teachers in the study did not involve specific reference to issues of school or education.) In their observed classroom behaviour the more "concrete" teachers were found to be less resourceful, more dictatorial and more punitive than their more "abstract" colleagues. Pupils taught by the more abstract teachers, compared to those taught by the more concrete ones, were significantly more involved in classroom activities, more active, higher in achievement and less concrete in their own responses; they were also less nurturance seeking, more cooperative and more helpful—but not significantly so than pupils of the more concrete teachers.

There is thus ample support in empirical research for the common-sense assumption that the nature of teacher input into the school plays a highly important part in determining the effectiveness of the learning process and hence the nature of the school's output. Unfortunately we know little about the determinants of teachers' differing dispositions. The Himmelweit finding about highly mobile teachers clearly links up with the finding of Harvey and associates and also those reported by Getzels and Jackson in that authoritarianism in the sense used by Himmelweit is very similar to Harvey's notion of extreme "concreteness", high scores on authoritarianism and low scores on the MTAI scale of attitudes to pupils.

The effects of teacher training can be shown in relation to scores on the MTAI (Minnesota Teacher Attitude Inventory) which measures attitudes to pupils from the standpoint of a tender-minded, human relations approach to teaching: thus elementary teachers have higher scores than secondary teachers; female teachers score higher than male teachers; counsellors score higher than school administrators. Teachers in training show an increase of MTAI scores over time, suggesting that the emphasis in training institutions is in the direction of tender-minded, "progressive", human relations approaches. On moving to work in the school, an interesting thing happens. After the first year in secondary school, the scores of teachers drop—at least from the second to the fifth year of their teaching careers. Those who are working in primary schools, however, show the opposite trend—their scores increase. The continuity we see at the primary level of education training and work situation does not obtain at the secondary level, where the effect of exposure to the work situation (including the attitudes of older and more experienced colleagues) tends to erase the attitudes to teaching learned in training. These findings, reported in Getzels and Jackson have been supported by a parallel but smaller investigation by Findlayson and Cohen (1967).

THE AUTHORITY OF THE TEACHER

The question of authority is a central one in any analysis of social systems, not least in the analysis of the school. Given the general finding of some degree of order and predictability in the way people behave and some regularity with which some people give instructions and others follow them (albeit less completely than the former would often wish) how can we explain this? In the case of the school how do heads come to have authority over their staff? how do the controlling agencies have authority over the heads? and in particular how do teachers achieve and maintain authority over pupils? By "authority" we mean two things: both the actual control over the behaviour of others and the recognised right to do so both in the eyes of those who are controlled and those who look on.

Education committees of LEA's in Britain (school boards in the USA) control their schools both by virtue of laws which legitimate their control but also because they control the finance and can enforce their decisions through the law courts if necessary. Similarly the head's authority over his staff derives from legally constituted contracts of employment which the staff enter into when taking up the job. The teacher's authority over pupils is a more subtle and complex matter. Legal factors are present, in the sense that parliament has caused schools to be created and compelled parents to send their children there up to a certain age. However, this authority merely suffices to get the children through the doors and into the school, it does not suffice to control their behaviour once they are there. How then does the teacher establish and maintain authority over his pupils in the school?

Three bases of authority or modes of compliance are distinguished by Etzioni (1964): "Coercive" compliance based on the fear of physical violence or death for disobedience; "remunerative" compliance based on the hope of material or economic rewards for compliance and "normative" compliance based on the feeling that one "ought" to obey the person who has given the orders because of the character of one's relationship with him. Some organisations are clearly based on a predominant reliance on one of these approaches. Thus the prison is mainly based on coercive compliance, the factory on remunerative compliance and the Church on normative compliance. In all organisations, however, there is overlap between the categories—not least in the school. Not only do we find that different types of schools lean to one way rather than the other, but within a type of school we find that pupils of different kinds respond to orders on the basis of different modes of compliance. In public boarding schools and religious schools normative compliance is the rule. In grammar schools remunerative and normative compliance are both involved. In the top stream of the secondary modern school the same modes of compliance are found and in lower streams there is an element of coercive compliance.

While this set of distinctions enables us to make some interesting comparisons, two criticisms may be levelled against it. Firstly, the category of normative compliance covers a very wide range of diverse situations. It includes under the same heading both situations where pupils conform to a teacher's orders because he occupies the position of teacher and situations where they comply because they respect him as an individual and wish to earn his approval, although they would not do this for other teachers. That is, personal and positional authority are used together here, while in terms of the carry-over from one teacher to another their implications are very different. The second criticism is that the scheme omits an extremely important mode of compliance, namely the habitual conformity to a set of expectations which are highly routinised and have become traditional. If asked why they comply to such expectations, the people in question would say "that's just the way we do things here" or "that's how it's done". Arguably, this is part of the normative compliance category, in which case we come back to the criticism that this category is all too wide and heterogeneous, including all acts of compliance based on the desire to earn "prestige, esteem, love, acceptance" from the person who has given the orders.

In the school classroom it is particularly clear how the effective teacher creates a social order by deliberately routinising the activities of the class. (Waller, 1965, chapters 14, 18; Shipman, 1968, chapters 6, 7; Smith and Geoffrey, 1968, chapter 3; Jackson, 1968, chapter 1).

Given the basic facts of the teaching situation—the crowding of pupils into the classroom where they grossly outnumber their teachers—only on the basis of some form of routinisation can order be maintained by the teacher. There is a "calling the class to order" routine. This may be the rule that when the teacher enters the room all stand silently in their places, or just that silence falls when teacher calls for quiet. There are routines for getting ready for written work; routines for distributing material, and so forth. If these routines are made very clear and the children are drilled in them at the very beginning and if class activities are restricted at the outset to only those which are highly routinised, the teacher's mastery of his class is made easier. An unspoken assumption sinks into pupils' minds that would read (if verbalised) "teacher say, pupil do". Smith and Geoffrey suggest that the teacher may make a point of giving many simple and readily complied-with directions early in his encounter with a new class. This has the effect of helping to establish the "teacher say, pupil follow" frame of mind. When this has been established, the teacher who wishes to engage the class in less authoritarian activities, such as discussion, project work and so forth, may proceed with this on the sound basis of the respect of his pupils for his determination to maintain order and his ability to do it.

Where there is an extreme dependence on routinisation as the basic pattern of classroom interaction, it seems clear that this is likely to produce an attitude of unthinking passivity on the part of pupils, and to inhibit completely any development of creative or original thought—in fact any tendency to "think for oneself" is likely to be squashed. The conclusion to be drawn from this is not that routinisation is something to be banned from the classroom, for this would make any kind of social order well-nigh impossible. Rather the conclusion is that the teacher should not rely too much on routinised forms of classroom activity, but should mix in with them other kinds of activity that give more scope for the pupils to think for themselves and to use some imagination—for example discussion and project work.

Some careful research on teaching styles and their consequences by Flanders (1964) has shown that different teachers teaching the same subjects to similar children vary considerably in the extent to which their teaching styles encourage or inhibit pupils' participation and that the extent to which they do this has a marked effect on both the amount of learning that takes place and in the pupils' attitudes. Observers sitting in the classrooms and watching the teachers, classified their interaction with their pupils into a set of precisely defined categories:

(1) Teacher lectures or expresses own opinions.
(2) Teacher gives direction.
(3) Teacher gives criticism or justifies use of own authority.
(4) Teacher asks questions.
(5) Teacher clarifies pupils' ideas and uses them in problem solving.
(6) Teacher praises and encourages pupils' action.
(7) Teacher makes constructive interpretation of pupils' feelings or attitudes.

Categories 1 to 3 represent teacher's statements which tend to inhibit pupil participation. These he calls "direct" methods. Categories 4 to 7 tend to expand pupil participation and these are called "indirect" methods.

A total of thirty-one teachers were studied, half of them teaching maths and half of them teaching English or social studies. The pupils being taught were thirteen to fourteen year olds. The observers were specially trained to use the classification scheme with a high degree of accuracy and reliability. They all underwent between twelve and eighteen hours of intensive training.

The maths teachers were observed during six one-hour periods and the English and social studies teachers were observed during six two-hour periods. Firstly, an overall classification was made of all the teachers on the basis of an indirect/direct ratio, that is the proportion of their statements which fell in the indirect compared to the direct. These observations were made in the beginning, the middle, and at the end of a two-week period.

Although some teachers clearly made far more use of the indirect statements than other teachers, there was no teacher who made exclusive use of one or the other.

Teachers who made more use of the indirect methods had superior academic achievement in their classes compared to the more direct method teachers, teaching the same subject with the same curriculum material to pupils of the same age. This was true for both maths and English and social studies. Teachers who made relatively more use of indirect methods had pupils with more favourable attitudes to the teacher, the class, and learning activities in general. These attitudes were not only more favourable but also more constructive and non-dependent. These differences were especially marked in the English and social studies classes. The indirect teachers also had fewer discipline problems.

Although Flanders stresses the fact that all teachers use both kinds of methods, he also points out that the indirect teachers are better at playing the direct teacher role than the direct teachers are at playing the indirect role. In other words, teachers who on the whole make more use of indirect methods, are also more flexible in their teaching methods. They switch roles more easily and presumably can therefore make more fruitful use of the changing flow of happenings in the course of their lessons. They "ask longer, more extended questions" and far more often; they were "more alert to, concerned with, and made greater use of statements made by students . . . they skilfully integrated student ideas into the content discourse of classroom communication" (Flanders, pp. 209–10). None of this is incompatible with the limited use of routinisation at certain phases of the lesson to establish and re-establish the teachers' authority.

Teaching techniques in the classroom cannot provide a complete answer to the problem of the teacher's authority, though they may account for some of the difference between teachers in their effectiveness in establishing this authority. We must also take account of other important factors that are not bounded by the classroom wall. As pupils grow towards adolescence they tend to question many of the features of their lives which they were prepared to take for granted earlier. One of these questions they are liable to raise (even if not in an explicit form) concerns the purpose of their going to school and complying with all the expectations that are laid upon them there. Those pupils who are aspiring to careers which they know require them to pass certain examinations for which the school is preparing them can give a fairly satisfactory answer to this question but for those pupils with different sorts of aspirations there is no satisfactory answer. For them school work does not lead towards a meaningful goal. Only in so far as they can find an intrinsic interest in the work, gratification from the working context (from peers or teacher or both) or in so far as their membership in the school gives access to other gratifications (not directly linked with school work) such as positions of influence in the school, membership of enjoyable extra-curricular activities and so forth, can they quell their dissatisfaction with the requirements of school.

In other words, along with the variability due to teaching methods there will be further variability in pupils' acceptance of teachers' authority due to differences in their aspirations or career goals. There will also be differences between schools with similar kinds of pupils based on the availability within the school of other forms of gratification for pupils. Thus the more that classroom working practices make possible satisfying kinds of peer group collaboration, the more positions of influence there are available for pupils, the more appealing kinds of extra-curricular activities and social events there are at the school and the more scope is provided for pupils to choose to study subjects that interest them in ways that foster and do not kill that initial interest, the more will teachers' authority be buttressed in the sense that pupils will be less motivated to rebel against the school and against the teacher's authority.

Another reason pupils might (but do not often) have for respecting the authority of teachers would be to the extent that they see them as providing a valued form of help in coping with the problems of growing up. This may take the form of informal conversations between teachers and pupils outside of lessons or in the lessons when pupils are working on their own, or it may take place within the context of the lesson in a formally planned way. In the latter case discussions may arise in the context of English, social studies, religious education or "general studies". The discussion may begin on a quite general topic (such as capital punishment or poverty, for example) or on a specific but impersonal topic (such as Henry VIII's divorces). This discussion may then turn into one that has much more bearing on the lives and concerns of pupils if the teacher encourages this. Pupils might bring up for discussion problems that have bothered them, either in general terms or in some detail.

This kind of discussion can be very valuable for pupils because it enables them to share experiences and develop their ideas about problems which concern them but which, it seems, they rarely discuss among themselves outside of school. Such a discussion, if sensitively guided can help them to clarify their ideas in ways which they might not have seen, left to themselves. If discussions of this kind go hand-in-hand with a developing informal relationship with the teacher in the way suggested before, they are likely to be more effective. Not only will the teacher's knowledge of the pupils as individuals enable him to guide the discussion more sensitively, it will also enable them to trust him more and they will also be able to follow up the discussions in more private conversations afterwards if they so desire. The point is that such discussions are not only of intrinsic value to the pupils in their growing up but they also put the teacher-pupil relationship on a different basis. This basis is one in which the strivings or gropings of the pupils towards adulthood are recognised and aided, rather than being repressed by demands that the pupils conform to a passive and meekly obedient role as is so often the case in the secondary school.

In so far as pupils develop such a relationship with a teacher (this does not mean *all* of their teachers) they are less likely to rebel against his authority or, perhaps, that of his colleagues.

So far we have discussed the question of the teacher's authority within the frame of reference of the individual teacher in his or her classroom, without taking much account of the context in which the teacher functions. Some of the most important elements in this context are the teacher's colleagues, his head or principal, the parents of pupils, and the local community.

The teacher's colleagues are important for his authority on several levels. Firstly, some degree of consensus between teachers as to what rules they will insist upon and enforce most energetically is very helpful to each of them, particularly one who is new to the school. A teacher's reputation among his colleagues, if extreme, can be communicated indirectly to pupils if his colleagues are indiscreet or vindictive.

The head or principal plays a most important role in relation to this problem of the teacher's authority. Teachers feel very strongly that the head should support them with any problem they have in establishing their authority over pupils, including situations where the parents intervene to take their child's part (Becker, 1954). The head serves as the ultimate punitive agent in the school and the manner in which he performs this role can make a big difference to the problems the classroom teacher has with his most disruptive pupils. He can also (rarely) be a court of appeal from the teacher's ruling.

The role of parents in supporting or challenging the teacher's authority is significant but not nearly as pervasive as that of colleagues, head or, of course, pupils. The attitude of parents towards authority is, in part, reflected by the way they exercise authority in the family and hence prepare their child to have certain broad predispositions to respond in certain ways to their teachers in school. Another part of the parents' influence may be exerted through the explicit explanations and instructions they give their children prior to starting school and concurrently with their schooling. Explicit instructions to the child to behave well in school are worth far less than are a few years of appropriate socialisation prior to school. Musgrove and Taylor (1969) studied parents in two areas of a city, one area heavily middle class and the other one working class, and found that in the latter area, more parents claim that they tell their children to cooperate with the teacher than in the middle class area, as these parents consider it unnecessary, in view of the way they have raised their children.

Especially pertinent is the way parents respond to the information that child and teacher have clashed. Do they tend to take the side of the child or the teacher? Or do they try to look fairly at the evidence?

Though it is somewhat dangerous to generalise, it appears that teachers get the most ready support from parents from the lower middle class and "respectable" working class. Lower class parents more often take the child's part, assuming the school to be hostile to people like them. Occasionally they overreact in support of the school, threatening or delivering harsh punishment to the child for acting disrespectfully towards teachers. In general, though, families in this social stratum do not give much support to their children's teachers, at least partly because they feel uncomfortable in dealing with them, see them less than do other parents and hence understand the teachers' perspective less well.

At the same time, teachers generally feel more uncomfortable in dealing with lower-class parents, when they do see them, than they do with other parents. And, it must be admitted, some teachers and heads are prejudiced against these children and do treat them unfairly. Parents of the upper middle class may be extremely supportive of teachers. Compared to lower middle-class parents, though, they are less inclined to accept without question whatever the teacher or head may say. They tend to be more self-assured, partly because of their higher standing in the community and they tend to be more knowledgeable about educational methods and philosophies than the lower middle-class parents on account of their own superior education. Some teachers are not as comfortable in dealing with upper middle-class parents as they are with lower middle-class ones, while others value the greater understanding of their aims which they tend to find from upper middle-class parents in general (Becker, 1952a).

Upper-class parents are generally hard for the average teacher to deal with, on account of their condescension and assumption that they will get their own way (Hollingshead, 1949). In Britain, though not in the USA, it is rare for the *average* teacher to deal with such people, for they patronise the private sector of education fairly exclusively, where they encounter teachers who come (relatively) closer to their own social status and (more important) who remind them of the teachers who stood over them in their own school days. One factor which tends to make the middle-class parent relatively supportive of the teacher's authority is that there tends to be a greater degree of concordance between their views on the aims and objectives of education, than there is in the case of teachers and lower status parents (Sieber and Wilder, 1967).

PERSONAL AND POSITIONAL AUTHORITY

The distinction between "positional" and "personal" authority which we outlined in Chapter Three has some important implications for these problems of the teacher's role. The teacher who bases his authority in the classroom on successful use of routinisation—and we have suggested that all teachers do to some extent—is to this extent exercising positional authority. He is claiming respect on the basis of his position and role within the school. In dealing with a new class, we believe, most teachers rely heavily on routinised procedures to lay the foundation for their authority and hence start out their relationship with each new class on a basis of positional authority. After the initial phase, however, teachers may go on to establish a more personal relationship with their pupils. They may go about this in one of two ways: by presenting themselves to the class in general as an individual whom they can like and/or respect—as distinct from an anonymous entity playing the role of teacher; or by entering into a set of one-to-one relationships with individual pupils in the context of the classroom and extra-curricular activities and making informal contact in various situations, mainly in school but possibly outside too.

On the teacher's role are two sets of pressures, pulling in opposite directions, one towards a preference for a personal relationship with pupils and the other towards an impersonal, positional one. The latter implies a relationship between teacher and pupil, governed by universalistic standards, impartially applied. Such standards define not only right and wrong answers, good and bad work in the area of academic learning, but also they define good and bad conduct in terms of the procedural rules laid down by the teacher for his classroom, laid down by the head for the school in general and in terms of the less specific standards of approved conduct on an "ethical" level. That these standards are universalistic and apply equally to all is fundamental to the officially proclaimed value system of the school. Terms of disapproval and condemnation (such as "favouritism") exist to describe behaviour which involves illegitimately importing personal considerations into areas where universalistic judgements are required. This is most dramatically seen in the case of formal examinations in the school, but in less formal ways such judgements are made many times in every lesson by all teachers.

Pressures in the direction of developing more personal relationships between teacher and pupil derive from the desire of pupils themselves to be treated as individuals and to have some allowance made for their individual characteristics, special interests and handicaps. They also derive from the awareness of teachers that pupils can be more readily motivated by teachers with whom they have a more personal relationship—provided that it is on balance a favourable one. With this kind of relationship, a teacher is likely to have a better knowledge of the abilities and deficiencies of each pupil and hence the most effective way of helping him to use the former and to overcome the latter. In areas of development besides academic learning the personal relationship is even more important. Only from such a basis and the interpersonal trust that depends on it can pastoral work of any value be done in schools.

Many other roles beside that of teacher are bedevilled by similar conflicting pressures between the pattern of impersonal, universalistic standards and that of personal, particularistic ones. In the teacher's case the problem may be seen as one of developing enough personal and particularistic affectivity in the relationship to motivate both parties to maximum effort, while not going so far as to make it too painful and difficult for the teacher to make unfavourable objective, universalistic judgements of his pupils' work and conduct when necessary. The difficulty is two-fold; maintaining objective perception and having the emotional toughness to convey unfavourable judgements to those whom one cares about and does not wish to disappoint. The judge, magistrate or external examiner can afford to play a role of total impersonality and total commitment to the universalistic standard. The fan cheering his hero and the supportive friend, can totally embrace the particularistic and affective pattern, abandoning all universalistic pretences. The teacher, because of his professional responsibility to educate his pupils to universalistic standards and to prepare them as well as possible for life in a society where they will be judged by universalistic standards, has no such easy way out.

Some analyses of American high schools have led to the conclusion that pupils exert considerable pressure on teachers to enter into personal relationships and to base their authority more on this nexus than on the impersonal and universalistic authority of the position itself. In line with this they tend to withhold compliance from teachers who lay claim to a purely positional authority (Bidwell, 1965). It should be noted that the main study in which this pressure was reported (Gordon, 1957) was conducted in only one school in a prosperous suburban area in the USA. The pupils in question were therefore of high school age (thirteen–seventeen years) and possibly more sophisticated in social skills than the average secondary school pupil.

These pressures may draw the teacher into a position fraught with difficulties. Soon he could find himself responding to pupils less in terms of their academic performance and conformity to conduct norms and more in terms of their personal attractiveness and social power. In the situation that could arise here, the traditional role of the "teacher's pet" is radically redefined. Traditionally the teacher's pet has often been a pupil who makes unusually great attempts to win the teacher's favour in order to compensate to himself for low popularity among the peer group. Or, if the one is not a cause of the other, at least the two have tended to go together. The new version of the teacher's pet is a pupil who is very popular among his peers and active in many of their common activities, frequently as a leader. Indeed one of his motives for seeking the friendship of the teacher may be the need to gain special indulgence when academic work is graded because his active extra-curricular life has accompanied a neglect of academic work. At the same time, the active part this kind of pupil plays in extra-curricular activities at school brings him into contact in informal settings with the teachers who sponsor those activities, and hence provided additional opportunities to develop friendly relationships. It is suggested by Gordon that techniques of manipulating teachers become part of the pupil sub-culture in some high schools, being informally communicated from one generation of pupils to their successors in the next year, without each group having to discover for themselves either the general principles of "how to succeed in school without really trying" or the specific weaknesses of each particular teacher and how to take advantage of them.

Gordon also found that teachers could employ either of two strategies to get themselves out of this difficult situation. They could revert to the positional (universalistic) authority traditionally expected of the teacher and ignore the wishes of the pupils in this respect. He suggests that only those teachers who had strong backing from their principals could in fact succeed in this strategy. On the other hand they could play along with the personal (particularistic) role and use their control of academic grades (marks) to keep the upper hand to some extent. They might then "allocate grades so as to disrupt the student social structure, thus arousing students' anxiety, and subsequently to reduce this anxiety by affective reinforcement of desired behaviours" (Bidwell, pp. 980–3). We need not enter into a discussion as to how typical a situation this may be. Suffice it to note that it can exist—to whatever extent—and even if not typical, it reflects certain pressures and tendencies which are widely present in the teaching situation.

Several features of the teacher's working situation make it especially difficult for him to handle problems such as the one we have just discussed. Generally the teacher works in isolation from his professional colleagues—even from other adults (Sexton, 1966). In a sense his working situation is one of cultural deprivation. Generally there is not a high level of appreciation of his efforts on the part of his clients (pupils) and this makes him somewhat vulnerable to manipulation by individual pupils who do show some appreciation. Both of these conditions are rare among professional workers and the combination certainly makes for a uniquely difficult working situation.

One change in the organisation of schools which would alleviate this situation to some extent would be a change in the widely-held convention that no teacher should "intrude" in another one's classroom and that no class should have more than one assigned teacher. Team teaching represents one breach in this tradition; another approach, more direct and requiring much less disruption of the existing school structure would be an arrangement whereby each teacher spent even one of his free periods each week visiting one of the classes that he teaches while they are being taught by another teacher. This would achieve two results, both potentially valuable to the teacher's working efficiency. One result would be to make available to the teacher being observed the informed comments, criticisms and observations of a professional colleague. This kind of feedback on one's role performance on the job is notoriously lacking in the usual teaching situation. Secondly, the teacher-observer can see what different approaches his colleagues use and extend his own repertoire. Thirdly, he can see pupils whom he teaches reacting to other teachers, learn more about them and more about the effectiveness of his own methods. If the allocation of pupils to classes is fluid (i.e. shifting from lesson to lesson) then teacher-observers can see pupils whom they teach not only reacting to different teachers but also in different peer settings and possibly playing different roles in the informal social system of the classroom.

This relatively small investment of time will thus contribute on two levels to increasing the efficiency of teachers who take part: by getting to know more about their pupils and acquiring that knowledge sooner; also by improving their teaching skills in general. Regular staff meetings for the exchange of the knowledge gained on both of these levels, rather than leaving it to be exchanged on an individual, one-to-one basis between teachers, might increase the pay-off still further. The staff meeting could function not only as an information pool and exchange, but also as a supportive group to which a teacher who was having difficulties on the job (including difficulty in handling the role strain concerning authority discussed above) could turn for sympathy, advice and moral support. It may be alleged that staff meetings and informal staffroom cliques serve this function to a small extent already, but not, I believe, nearly to the degree to which they usefully could.

SELF-FULFILLING PROPHECIES

Education is a highly evaluative process. That is to say that teachers or other socialising agents are constantly engaged in evaluating the behaviour of those in their charge and responding to this behaviour in ways which communicate their evaluation, either explicitly or implicitly. Teachers are evaluating behaviour both in terms of their norms of conduct and in terms of performance standards for work. These evaluations are generally communicated by explicit verbal statements (such as) "that's a nice drawing", "hold your pencil nearer to the end", "don't talk to your neighbour so much" or "is that the way to behave in this classroom?"

There is also another kind of evaluation made by the teacher in relation to what he or she believes each pupil is capable of. On the basis of various immediate cues such as the appearance, manners and other superficial behaviour of pupils, as well as knowledge of their "record" in school, teachers rapidly form some initial impressions of their pupils and working hypotheses about what they can expect from each. With a completely new class and with very little information to go by, it makes sense for teachers to be alert for signs which seem to indicate that certain pupils are testing the limits to which they can go in this teacher's class. Since no teacher can possibly keep in check all the non-conforming acts of thirty or more children, they will usually concentrate on those few who are thought to be potentially the most disruptive. "Concentrating" the teacher's attention may take various forms, from a show of sympathetic interest to "making an example" of an individual pupil. In terms of the expediency of social control, it may be effective to employ "overkill" tactics on one or two selected pupils. However, such methods can be extremely hurtful to the victim especially when the teacher was mistaken about the pupil's intentions and he was not in fact "trying something on". The result of such a mistake may have important consequences for the way that the relationships between this teacher and this class develop—quite apart from the scar it leaves on the individual unjustly treated. A pupil martyr may be created. Or the teacher may find that he has fallen victim to a "put-up job".

In the classical form of this situation several pupils who are members of a closely-knit peer group select another pupil (usually an isolate) as a stooge and lay a trap for him very stealthily, such as the traditional drawing pin on the chair. When events go according to plan, the stooge falls into the trap and creates a disturbance in the classroom (for example, by crying out in alarm or falling noisily to the floor). The conspirators have concealed any clues as to their guilt and when the class bursts into uproar all the teacher sees is the unfortunate stooge writhing in discomfort. If he decides to make an example of him, he will be reinforcing the pupil social system in which the stooge is an outcast, reinforce the prestige of the conspirators and create in the minds of the pupils who realise what happened the impression that he can be easily fooled. This is not perhaps, a trap into which most teachers would fall but it is certainly one that has ensnared many inexperienced and unperceptive teachers.

With respect to academic learning, teachers also tend to form initial impressions about what different pupils are capable of. It is perhaps not so urgent for them to form their working hypotheses regarding academic learning as it is to form their hypotheses as to which pupils represent the greatest potential threat to law and order in the classroom. Nevertheless it is a pervasive feature of classroom culture that teachers offer some evaluation—however cursory—of every piece of academic work done by every pupil and almost every statement made by them in the class.

The teacher's prediction of each pupil's likely future learning curve enters into his evaluation of the pupil's work only because of the ideology that what is to be evaluated is not absolute performance but effort or performance relative to ability. We do not expect a "dull" pupil to learn as much as an "intelligent" or "able" one. And hence we do not blame them for not doing so. We blame them only for falling short of what we think is a "reasonable" level of performance for their individual capabilities. Ironically, this well-meaning, liberal attitude has lead to illiberal consequences as the abilities of pupils who have not hitherto done well or for some reason are not thought to be capable of doing well, are under-estimated; their teachers expect little of them; they perceive and accept this definition of themselves and conform to it, hence achieving less than they would have done had their teachers expected more from them.

Rosenthal and Jacobson (1968) have summarised a wide variety of studies conducted in various situations to test this hypothesis, including studies of experiments that were supposedly being conducted with rigorous controls to ensure objectivity, that is to ensure the elimination of the expectancy effect. In many instances it can be shown that the expectation of the observer, experimenter, therapist or teacher tends to affect the results they report. In some cases this is shown to be a result of unconsciously biased observation and in other cases there is impartial observation and assessment but there is an interpersonal process whereby the subject's actual behaviour is modified in response to the expectations of some person or persons.

Rosenthal and Jacobson then describe an experiment which they conducted in a California infant school by manipulating the expectations of the teachers and watching for the effects of their pupils. The teachers were told that the research was intended to develop a test for "late developers". They thought that the test being given to their children was such a test but in fact it was a standard but not well-known IQ test. The researchers were attached to eminent institutions and the teachers had every reason to believe what they were told. After the tests had been administered for the first time, each class teacher was given a list on which appeared the names of some of their children who were alleged by the researchers to be "late bloomers" on the basis of the tests and therefore should be expected to show unusually high intelligence gains in the near future. In fact the names of these children had been selected by random numbers. They were no different from their peers in the control group—except in one thing, namely that their class teachers had been led to expect that they would register greater gain in learning than their peers.

At the end of a year or rather less, the children were retested and their scores compared with the earlier testing. Had the pupils designated arbitrarily as "late bloomers" gained more in IQ than their peers in the control group? Yes, apparently they had and the gains were clearest among the youngest two age groups. Taken singly the difference between experimental and control groups was not significant in years three to six. However, combining all years together gave a statistically significant difference. Hence the authors claim that their study confirms the hypothesis that teachers' expectations regarding pupils' level of achievement makes a difference to the actual achievement of those pupils.

Unfortunately, a close examination of the methods of this study shows it to have flaws so serious that the whole study must be set aside as invalid. This does not mean that the hypothesis is untrue but merely that this study cannot be used to sustain it. The reason that we summarise it here, only to reject it, is that it has become well known and widely cited, as if it provided conclusive support for the hypothesis. It is important to make it clear that this is not so and merely to ignore its existence would not serve this purpose.

The faults in the study are pointed out by Thorndike (1968) in a short but trenchant book review. Firstly, he points out, the entire experimental effect appears in only nineteen subjects (the "spurters" or experimental pupils in grades one and two). Secondly, and far more seriously, when the mean IQ scores quoted in the report are examined, some very bizarre things emerge—one class with an incredibly low mean score and remarkably low means for the whole first year. This leads Thorndike to conclude that the testing, on which the whole experiment rests, was wrongly performed in some way which cannot be determined. Furthermore, when he extrapolates from some of the IQ means reported to raw test scores this gives grotesque results—one control group with impossibly low test scores and one experimental group with impossibly high scores, that is scores that would appear to be technically impossible on the test that was used. On these grounds, Thorndike concludes, we cannot use this study to support any hypothesis. Is it too ironical to suggest that Rosenthal, Jacobson and their associates were too eager to produce supporting data for the hypothesis they *expected* to be supported?

Rosenthal and Jacobson summarise the results of another research by Beez, not previously published. His subjects were sixty children in a pre-school education programme ("Head Start"). Each child had only one teacher who taught him or her the meanings of certain symbols. Half of the teachers, randomly chosen, were led to expect good symbol learning. The difference in actual attainments of these children in symbol learning as tested by an independent researcher who did not know which child had been designated into which category, showed highly significant differences in the expected direction. Pupils whose teachers expected more from them in fact learned more—although they were no different from their peers. This study introduced a more powerful manipulation by designating some children as good learners and some as poor learners, whereas the Rosenthal experiment merely differentiated between "late bloomers" and the rest, avoiding the ethical problems of actually depressing the success level achieved by certain pupils.

The story by Beez is valuable for another reason, in that he demonstrates one of the mechanisms through which teacher's expectations operate to affect the amount that pupils learn. He measured how many symbols each teacher tried to teach each pupil and found that teachers who were told to expect good symbol learning tried to teach their pupils considerably more symbols. Yet this was not the only factor operating, for even when he controlled the number of symbols that teachers tried to teach, there still remained differences in learning between pupils in experimental and control groups.

As yet we have little idea as to the mechanisms through which teachers' expectations affect pupil learning. Various suggestions can be made though. Teachers' expectations can influence pupils' own expectations as to what they are capable of. They can also influence pupils' expectations as to what will be considered satisfactory by their teacher: those whose teachers will be satisfied with little will probably give little, those whose teachers require more will probably give it. Teachers may allocate their time differentially among pupils according to their expectations from them. How this works will depend on the teacher's value system: some will feel that the disadvantaged should have more of their time and others that the gifted should have more of their time. But either way the point is that for each teacher his assessment of pupil's capabilities influences his behaviour towards them.

In the course of this chapter we have shifted the nature of our analysis. Having begun with an interpretation of the background of teachers and some of the factors in the school which influence their conceptions of their role, tied in with some published empirical studies, we shifted to a more speculative kind of analysis. This is one of the hazards of pioneering work such as this, that there are vast areas where the work of preceding researchers is no help. Having made the maximum use of their work, one is then on one's own and in trying to open up a huge new territory (such as the role of the school in moral development) one can only rigorously research the problems one at a time. Meanwhile, however, I believe that it is important to try to map out this new territory by indicating what seem to be the major questions and, where an informal investigation suggests certain answers or hypotheses, to offer these for consideration, too. Even if they are wrong, as some are bound to be, they should stimulate discussion and new research by other workers. The following chapters become even more speculative, as we enter the realms of the unknown even more deeply.

CHAPTER 6 REFERENCES

J. Barker-Lunn, *Streaming in the Primary School*, National Foundation for Educational Research, Slough, 1970.

Howard S. Becker, "Social Class Variations in the Teacher-Pupil Relationship", *J. Educ. Sociol.*, 1952, pp. 451–65.

——, "The Career of the Chicago Public School Teacher", *American J. Sociol.*, LVII, 1952, pp. 470–7.

——, "The Teacher in the Authority System of the Public School", *J. Educ. Sociol.*, XXVII, 1954, pp. 128–41.

Charles E. Bidwell, "The School as a Formal Organization", in James G. March (ed.), *Handbook of Organizations*, Rand McNally, Chicago, 1965.

William Boyd and Wyatt Rawson, *The Story of the New Education*, Heinemann, London, 1965.

Amitai Etzioni, *Modern Organizations*, Prentice Hall, Englewood Cliffs, NJ, 1964.

D. S. Findlayson and L. Cohen, "The Teacher's Role: A Comparative Study of the Concepts of College of Education Students and Head Teachers", *British Journal of Educational Psychology*, XXXVII, Feb., 1967, pp. 22–31.

Ned A. Flanders, "Some Relationships among Teacher Influence, Political Attitudes, and Achievement", in Bruce J. Biddle and W. J. Ellena (eds.), *Contemporary Research on Teacher Effectiveness*, Holt, Rinehart and Winston, New York, 1964.

J. Floud and W. Scott, "Recruitment and Teaching in England and Wales", in Halsey, Floud and Anderson (eds.), *Education, Economy and Society*, Free Press, Glencoe, Illinois, 1961.

Blanche Geer, "Teaching", in D. L. Sills (ed.), *Internat. Encycl. of the Soc. Scs.*, Free Press, New York, 1968, Vol. 15, pp. 560–5.

J. Getzels and P. W. Jackson, "The Teacher's Personality and Characteristics", in N. L. Gage (ed.), *Research in Teaching*, Rand McNally, Chicago, 1963.

C. Wayne Gordon, *The Social System of the High School*, Free Press, Glencoe, Illinois, 1957.

O. J. Harvey *et al.*, "Teacher's Beliefs, Classroom Atmosphere and Student Behavior", *American Journal of Educational Research*, V, 1968, pp. 151–66.

Robert J. Havighurst and B. L. Neugarten, *Society and Education*, Allyn and Bacon, Boston, 1957.

H. T. Himmelweit, "Socio-Economic Background and Personality", *International Social Science Journal*, VII, 1955, pp. 29–35.

A. B. Hollingshead, *Elmtown's Youth*, John Wiley, New York, 1949.

Brian Jackson and Dennis Marsden, *Education and the Working Class*, Routledge and Kegan Paul, London, 1962.

Philip W. Jackson, *Life in Classrooms*, Holt, Rinehart and Winston, New York, 1968.

Josephine Klein, *Samples from English Cultures*, 2 vols., Routledge and Kegan Paul, London, 1965.

D. McIntyre and A. Morrison, *Teachers and Teaching*, Penguin, Harmondsworth, 1969.

Frank Musgrove, *Patterns of Power and Authority in English Education*, Methuen, London, 1971.

Frank Musgrove and P. H. Taylor, *Society and the Teacher's Role*, Routledge and Kegan Paul, London, 1969.

Robert Rosenthal and Lenore Jacobson, *Pygmalion in the Classroom*, Holt, Rinehart and Winston, New York, 1968.

Patricia C. Sexton, *The American School*, Prentice Hall, Englewood Cliffs, NJ, 1966.

M. D. Shipman, *Sociology of the School*, Longmans, London, 1968.

S. D. Sieber and D. E. Wilder, "Teaching Styles: Parental Preferences and Professional Role Definition", *Sociology of Ed.*, XL, Fall, 1967, pp. 302–15.

Louis Smith and W. Geoffrey, *Complexities of an Urban Classroom*, Holt, Rinehart and Winston, New York, 1968.

Robert L. Thorndike, Book Review of "Pygmalion in the Classroom", *American Educ. Research Assoc. Journal*, Nov., 1968.

Willard Waller, *The Sociology of Teaching*, John Wiley, New York, 1932.

William F. Whyte, *Street Corner Society*, Univ. of Chicago Press, Chicago, 1943.

Chapter Seven

HUMAN RELATIONS IN THE SCHOOL

Pupils come to school with attitudes shaped by earlier social experiences; teachers come into the school with their attitudes and dispositions shaped not only by the normal social experiences, but also by a planned training for the job. In addition they have been through a process of selection for their present positions. The school is an organised framework within which these people will play certain roles and engage in various activities *vis à vis* one another. Pupils will be grouped according to a pre-determined plan and teachers will be allocated responsibility over these groups for definite amounts of time and given certain tasks to accomplish with them.

Thus for much of the time during the school day, the activities of pupils and teachers mostly take place within the confines of a number of separate and non-intercommunicating classrooms. In between lessons, when pupils and teachers are moving from one part of the building to another, it becomes more apparent that these individuals are operating within a system larger than the classroom and as big as the whole school. The rules which are supposed to govern behaviour at these times are different from those which suffice for the self-contained classroom. They must cover such matters as not running in the corridors, walking down only one side of the stairs and other matters of basic "traffic control". Methods of enforcement may also need to be different too.

THE CLASSROOM: TEACHING STRATEGIES AND APPROACHES

The classroom may be viewed as a social system within the larger system of the school, with the same features which we noted in the case of the school. Let us consider a single lesson. The teacher corresponds to the head as chief executive. He has to establish and maintain the boundaries of his system (the lesson), to keep his pupils within the official normative limits and keep intruders out.

Inputs are provided from the larger system (the school): pupils, books and other supplies, time and a programme of work. The teacher has a certain amount of autonomy as to what rules and procedures shall be set up within each class but certain limits are set by the official structures of the school, the policies of the head, and by the school's traditions. The attainments of pupils are assessed periodically, certainly at the end of the year when the output from a year's work in a certain subject may be regarded as the input into the next year's work, or when the pupil leaves the school for the world of employment.

As a result of their training and the more or less clear expectations of the head, most teachers define their task as increasing the pupil's learning attainments in two areas: academic learning and moral education. Though very few teachers would repudiate either academic learning or moral education as basic goals, there are great differences in the relative weights they would assign to each.

An observer sitting in the classroom sees the teacher do many things: distribute supplies, lecture, joke, ask questions, give orders and so forth. Some of these actions are directly related to the two goals just discussed. When the teacher is explaining how to do long division or talking about the Norman Conquest, the goal is academic learning; when the teacher is rebuking one boy for punching another or discussing the culpability of Macbeth, it is moral education. It is possible that neither teacher nor pupils recognise this connection between their classroom work and the goals they claim to hold, but it exists from an objective point of view nonetheless.

Working towards either of these goals presupposes the existence of order and discipline in the class (social control) and many of the teacher's actions are directed towards securing this state of order, for example giving warnings and inflicting punishments on individuals who misbehave. Because the teacher's ability to keep his classes in order is the most readily visible performance aspect of his role, both the teacher and his superiors tend to be highly concerned about it. This is reasonable except in so far as it ignores the possibility that the teacher's *means* of keeping order may be such as to interfere seriously with either academic learning or (more likely) moral education, or both.

From the point of view of the naive observer it is difficult to see what the effective teacher actually does to maintain social control in his classroom. Good order is constantly maintained by creating an understanding with his pupils that certain things are not done and will not be tolerated in this class. In part it is a technique of bluff. A class that was determined to defy its teacher could always do so and if they used a modicum of intelligence could do so without much cost to themselves. A class where every pupil is banging his desk lid or scraping his chair leg, or humming cannot be stopped by his teacher. Most punishments available to the teacher involve singling out one or two pupils and "making an example of them". Those punishments that include the whole form tend to involve punishing the teacher as well, for instance keeping them late after school.

The teacher maintains his control of the situation by, firstly, not antagonising the class as a whole, and secondly by creating the impression of forcefulness and "no nonsense". The teacher who fails on both of these points is hopelessly lost. If he fails on decisiveness he may be lost too, doomed by mischievousness rather than malice. Decisiveness means keeping the upper hand or retaining the effective right to define a situation in the classroom. There is a body of teachers' folklore and precept, propagated by old hands in the profession, which aim to establish precisely this result. They warn the newcomer, for example, to stride majestically into the classroom, flinging open the door; to begin a lesson with a new class by setting them some work which only requires the barest minimum of equipment, so that there is no confusion of pupils running to search for items that they do not have, which can provide cover for much mischief-making.

A second prerequisite for the attainment of the teacher's goals (cognitive learning and moral education) is the need to build up the motivation of pupils for the work required and to remove emotional and interpersonal factors that might be impeding work (tension management). This is the function of the "expressive" group leader by contrast with the "instrumental" leader who organises people for the actual work itself (Brim, 1958).

Normally the teacher will be the instrumental leader of his class. But who will be the expressive leader? The different strategies of teachers with respect to this problem reflect, I believe, fundamentally different orientations to the teaching role and lead to significantly different outcomes for the classroom life of the present, for the amount and quality of cognitive learning and for the nature and effectiveness of moral education.

We can make a distinction between those who present themselves mainly as teachers of *subjects* in the old-fashioned academic style on the one hand and on the other those who present themselves mainly as teachers of *children* in the new-fangled, so-called progressive fashion. Let us call them *traditional* and *progressive* for short (see Waller, 1932, Ch. 18).

The traditional teacher's approach to the problem of expressive leadership or coping with the problem of tension-management in the classroom tends to be either to ignore it or to attempt to deal with it by means of activities closely controlled by himself. This is in line with this kind of teacher's general approach to his role in the classroom, which is characterised not just by a fondness for straight backs, folded arms, silence during private work but also for the lecture, question and answer sessions and pupil's comments being restricted to responses to teacher's demands. The skilful and sensitive traditional teacher provides opportunities for tension management by means of the occasional joke (by teacher), by programming an activity that the pupils enjoy towards the end of the lesson, by conducting the class in a collective recitation or question and answer session (which can build up to a very powerful rhythm—almost a chant) or through some other activity which is under the teacher's complete control.

With the teacher who ignores the tension management problem or fails to cope with it satisfactorily, I hypothesise, expressive leadership falls into the hands of certain pupils. If this teacher is fierce and effective in keeping discipline, jokes and foolery will be restricted to times when the teacher is absent but then they will tend to be really riotous. If these pupils have other teachers whose ability to control a class is not so good, they will give these teachers a miserable time since they will come from their lessons with the repressive teacher with a heavy backlog of unrelieved tensions.

The progressive teacher tries to cater for the class's need for expressive leadership in a different way—again characteristic of his general approach. He or she compromises with the pupils to a greater extent than the traditional teacher; allows some talking while they are working privately; encourages pupils to contribute their points of view to a discussion and contrives to work them into the topic if they are not altogether relevant; asks more open-ended questions than the traditional teacher; lectures less and states his own opinions less. He or she senses which pupils have problems of various kinds and varies accordingly the way they are handled. This includes varying the roles that different pupils are encouraged to play in school, both in the classroom and outside. The skilful progressive teacher may virtually conduct the class like an orchestra. Knowing who are the aspiring comedians in the class and what kinds of jokes each one specialises in, openings can be made for those pupil comedians who can be trusted not to be disruptive. When humour appears in the progressive classroom it is more likely to be from pupils and less likely to be disruptive than in the traditional classroom. With progressive methods the teacher-pupil relationship is more cordial, more personal or diffuse and the whole classroom as a group is more cohesive with higher levels of conformity to official norms when teacher is not present (Flanders, 1964).

We cannot consider each classroom in isolation, however. What each teacher does and which of these two approaches he adopts is a personal choice. But the likely results of either approach, which we have tried to suggest above, presupposes a uniformity of teaching style throughout the school. That is to say, that either approach can only be expected to produce the results suggested if it is being adopted in a school where most other teachers follow the same approach. This is because pupils form their own notions of what is to be expected from teachers and what constitutes "proper" teaching. The odd progressive teacher in a mainly traditional school, even though he plays his role in a way which would be considered highly competent in a progressive school, is likely to be defined as incompetent by his pupils in a school where traditional approaches predominate. Thus, instead of establishing a more harmonious relationship with his pupils than the traditional teachers, the reverse is quite possible. The pupils define him as "soft" and incompetent. Accordingly they play him up as if he were a traditional teacher failing to be strict enough.

How the teacher reacts to this clash of expectations will depend upon several factors: the amount of self-confidence, determination and skill he possesses as well as the amount of intelligence, sensitivity and tolerance the pupils have. He may persist in his progressive approach or take the line of less resistance and become a traditional teacher. Another important factor determining the outcome of the clash will be the attitude of his teaching colleagues, who can hardly avoid disapproving of his approach and at least implying "I told you so". There is, however, a considerable range of tolerance which they may show, from sympathetic but disapproving interest to outright ridicule or even harassment.

The situation of the odd traditional teacher in the mainly progressive school is basically similar, though inverted. He too will appear odd to his pupils who are used to a different kind of teaching. They will resent his attempts to clamp down on the relatively informal interchange with the teacher to which they are accustomed. This traditional teacher, who finds his pupils responding in an unexpected way, may react in different ways. He may panic and redouble his efforts at repression or he may sense that these pupils have established customary limits to their questions, jokes and discussion and conclude that he can modify his usual discipline. Thus he becomes a progressive teacher—at least for the duration of his stay in this school. In both cases of the "odd man out" the adjustment is bound to be hard for the teacher—and also for his pupils. The probability of the teacher in this situation resigning at the earliest possible moment are likely to be well above the norm and even for those who are fortunate enough to have supportive colleagues and relatively tolerant pupils are likely to show anxiety and strain symptoms well above the norm. It must be emphasised that these are only hypotheses.

Tentatively, I would suggest that pupils used to a progressive approach will react to the unexpected traditional teacher with less hostility than one will find in the case of pupils who are used to a traditional approach and find themselves confronted with a progressive teacher. This is an extrapolation from the finding that children reared by repressive or punitive methods behave more aggressively when they are not supervised than do those who are reared more leniently (Becker, 1964).

We should not think of the distinction between these two approaches to teaching as just or mainly a personality distinction. While it may be true that one can characterise individual teachers in terms of these variables, it must also be remembered that a teacher may teach quite differently after moving to a different school and even within the same school the same teacher might vary his or her approach with different classes.

NORMS FOR TEACHER-PUPIL RELATIONS

It goes without saying that pupil-teacher relations are highly variable, complex and very hard to define. This would be true even in the school system which attempted to define and regulate this relationship very precisely. In fact, in many societies the teacher is permitted a good deal of latitude in the way he plays his classroom role. Certainly this is true in Britain and the USA. The endless combination of different personalities that meet in the classroom will produce endlessly different situations and relationships. In spite of this, it is possible, at a very broad level of generalisation, to say something about the general social norms which define the relationship of pupil and teacher in many systems of formal education, including that of Britain.

Regarding the behaviour of teacher towards pupil, three main prescriptions seem to be fundamental. The first is that of impartiality between pupils; the second is concern for the welfare and well-being of one's pupils; and the third is that the teacher should act in accordance with his professional understanding of what the well-being of the child requires rather than giving in to the actual wishes and desires which the child may express. Between the first and second of these prescriptions there is a tendency for conflict. Whereas impartiality implies that the teacher maintain a marked social distance from his pupils, the requirement of concern for pupils implies that he should not remain too distant and aloof from them. Clearly to reconcile these two requirements is a most difficult problem and one which lends itself to many different solutions, none of them free from difficulty. On the pupil's side, the main general requirement is one of respect for a teacher and deferential behaviour, implying a social distance. This expectation is not enforced to its full extent until the pupil has had several years at school to become adjusted to the requirements of a formal school setting.

Within the broad limits of these general expectations, we can plot differences in teacher-pupil relationships along several dimensions. One such dimension we have already discussed, namely the difference between traditional and progressive teachers. We can also differentiate among teachers on several other variables.

In particular there is the distinction between *wide* and *narrow* teacher-pupil relationships. A wide relationship exists where the teacher tries to get to know his or her pupils as individuals, finding out their interests, home background, ambitions, relationships to peers and other teachers, as well as their academic performance and conduct in school. At the same time they present themselves to their pupils as individual people (adults) who are also subject teachers and are not afraid to let their pupils know something about their background, previous experiences, interests and personality, in so far as they are interested. The narrow teacher-pupil relationship is one where their interaction is exclusively in terms of the work being undertaken, whether it is a learning task or an administrative one, with the personalities of teacher and pupils being kept out of the picture as far as possible.

This factor of the breadth of the teacher-pupil relationship is not the exact same as the one we discussed earlier under the heading of progressive versus traditional classroom strategies. Each refers to a different aspect of the relationship. It may be hypothesised however, that the kind of teacher who favours a wide relationship will also tend to favour a progressive strategy and the one who favours a narrow relationship will also tend to favour a traditional strategy. Exceptions will take the form of traditionals who play a wide role outside the lesson and progressives who vanish at the end of lessons.

We should not think of these distinctions as being based exclusively on differences in teachers' personalities. While it may be true that one can characterise individual teachers in terms of their general disposition to adopt one or another approach in their teaching, it may also happen that a teacher changes his or her methods of teaching quite significantly after moving from one school to another where the kind of pupil which predominates and/or the expectations of the head were quite different. Even within the same school, the same teacher might vary his or her approach according to the average age, ability and/or general attitude of the class.

Nor should it be assumed that the decision as to which kind of relationship will develop lies entirely with the teacher rather than the pupils. The wide relationship requires two willing parties to make it successful but only one unwilling party to veto it and make it impossible. However the more common situation, I suspect, is probably the one where pupils would like to have a more wide relationship with their teachers but many of the teachers are unwilling.

INFLUENCE OF THE SCHOOL'S FORMAL STRUCTURE

In two earlier chapters we have outlined some of the variations possible in the formal structure of the school. We must now consider how such variations may affect the probability of teacher-pupil relationships taking different forms.

One aspect of the formal structure of academic work is highly relevant here. That is the degree of departmental and subject specialisation among teachers. This will affect the amount of teacher turnover in the course of a day which pupils experience. The less turnover there is, the more likely is a wide relationship. Even at the extreme of specialisation, however, a wide relationship is still possible. It is less probable, though, and the chances are that it will be less wide. Other features of the school's formal structure must be taken into account as well.

The existence of an official pastoral structure, with adequate facilities made available to those who occupy pastoral roles, will increase the probability of wide teacher-pupil relationships occurring with these particular members of staff. If those who occupy pastoral positions are also subject-teachers, then they may succeed in establishing wide relationships with their pupils in spite of the highest degree of subject specialisation.

The degree to which extra-curricular activities proliferate at the school and the proportion of teachers and pupils who are involved in them will again affect the probability of wide teacher-pupil relations existing in the school. As in the case of the official pastoral structure, the same teachers can be both subject-teachers and supervisors of extra-curricular groups. Thus wide teacher-pupil relationships are still possible despite a high order of specialisation.

It must be remembered, however, that it is unlikely that all the members of a particular class will also happen to be members of the extra-curricular group which is run by this teacher. (The same applies to the teacher who also fills a pastoral position, assuming that the composition of pastoral groups cross-cuts that of teaching groups, which is generally true except sometimes in the case of form-teachers and their form). This means that in several of his classes a particular subject-teacher may find some pupils who are members of his out-of-school group or his pastoral group. With them it is relatively easy for him to establish a wide relationship in the class and the question is whether the remaining pupils in the class will follow suit. This depends rather on the prevailing climate of the school and whether the broad or the narrow teacher-pupil relationship is the prevailing one. If it is the narrow one, then it is possible that a split will exist among the pupils in each class, some responding to the teacher in a broad fashion and others in a narrow one. This clearly breaches the expectation of impartiality on the part of the teacher. Seeing this, the teacher may revert to a narrow relationship for the duration of his lesson.

The degree to which pupils are co-opted into the authority structure of the school will affect the relationship between those pupils who are co-opted and certain of their teachers. The positions occupied by these pupils, whether as prefects or as school council representatives or some other kind of position, will bring them into closer and more frequent contact with certain teachers, for example the house masters, staff representatives on the school council, the head and any deputy who oversees the discipline of the school.

Even more than the frequency of interaction between these pupils and teachers, and the reduction of social distance between them, there is the fact that these pupils are committed by virtue of their social positions to the same values as the teachers, and have set themselves apart, to some extent, from the general body of pupils. This fact makes it possible, though not at all inevitable, for wider relationships to develop between these pupils and teachers, since the similarity of their values means that social distance is not necessary in order to preserve the required professional integrity of the teachers and the pupils, on their side, are likely to be more forthcoming.

School rules may affect the teacher-pupil relationship in various ways in so far as they preclude or permit certain activities. For example, the rule that classrooms must be vacated and locked during lunchtime would prevent the form-teachers from hanging around in their classroom and chatting with members of their form. Similarly the practice of teachers eating lunch separately from pupils rather than sitting down at the same tables with them will affect the frequency of teacher-pupil interaction and the probability of wider relationships developing.

We have discussed various factors pertaining to the social organisation of the school on the assumption that they operate uniformly throughout the school. In practice, however, each of these factors may apply differentially through the structure of the school. In particular, each year group in the school may be organised along different lines; the degree of departmental and subject-specialisation commonly varies with seniority in the school; the nature of the pastoral structure may differ for seniors and juniors; the range and nature of extra-curricular activities frequently varies with age; the availability of authority positions for pupils is likewise generally related to their age; school rules commonly differentiate among pupils on the basis of age, permitting to seniors various activities which are prohibited to their juniors. All of the points which we made about the possible effects of these factors of social organisation on the teacher-pupil relationship will apply here also. For example a lower degree of subject specialisation in the teaching of juniors will favour the development of wider teacher-pupil relations between junior pupils and their teachers than between seniors and their teachers. On the other hand, the greater availability of authority positions to senior pupils will tend to widen their relationships with teachers compared to juniors. These factors must all be balanced out against each other.

Between houses in the same school there may also be differences in social organisation in so far as the teachers in charge of different houses are permitted some autonomy in the way they may organise their houses, or in so far as their social organisation has been determined by previous traditions.

A third basis on which the social organisation of schools may vary internally on a systematic basis, that is independently of the personal inclinations of individual teachers, is based upon the different work situations inherent in different subjects on the curriculum. Differences in the organisation of classes in PE, practical handicrafts, experimental science, field work subjects and book-work subjects will be quite apparent. The whole rhythm and pattern of teacher-pupil interaction is quite different in these different work situations. In the PE class all may be doing the same activity in unison under the orders of the teacher, or they may be divided into several groups each performing the same activity. In the handicraft class all may be using the same tools and materials but working at their own pace, and there is some scope for the teacher to wander around the class chatting to different pupils. In the practical science class, in common with the handicraft class, there is a large safety problem, because of the tools and materials being used, which must preoccupy a significant part of the teacher's attention. The science teacher must also ensure that each pupil or group of pupils is performing their experiment correctly, doing the right things in the right sequence. The need for pupils to concentrate intently on what they are doing is probably greater in this class than in the handicraft class, so that the opportunities for chatting are less. Of course all science work is not practical experiments. Perhaps half of the science class' time is spent in "read and talk" learning situations, which may be the exclusive method used in teaching other subjects such as English, history, geography.

When class teaching methods are used, that is when the teacher is addressing the whole class as a unit, there is little scope for wide relationships. This possibility arises only when pupils are set to private work and the teacher may then talk to individuals. When project work methods are used the amount of time spent in class-teaching is much reduced and the amount of time available for the teacher to talk to pupils as individuals or in small groups is very much greater. In referring to the difference between class teaching and project work we are talking more of a difference in teaching methods than a difference dictated by the nature of the subject.

NORMS FOR PUPIL-PUPIL RELATIONS

The *official* norms of the school governing pupil-pupil relationships are generally very thin. Not only are they few in number but usually they are entirely implicit, so that one only knows what they are by waiting for someone to breach these tacit expectations. Then we find that there are a few expectations which are widely found. Thou shalt not bully other pupils (either for fun or profit), steal from them, engage in sex play with them, or encourage them to do anything which is in itself forbidden by school rules. In many situations pupils are not expected to help each other with their school work. Not only are examinations defined as assessments of individual capability, but homework is usually defined as an individual responsibility and so often is class work. Where group work methods are employed this will not of course be true. Nor will it apply in schools which run on the Russian collective system. But strictly individual work is the rule throughout the great majority of schools and situations.

Other expectations govern the *informal* relationships of pupils with their peers, for this is when *their* expectations of each other count. The paramount and most universal of these expectations is that pupils should not sneak or inform on other pupils. There are other values too which operate among pupils and pattern the way in which they classify and evaluate each other. These values vary, not so much between schools, as between groups of pupils within the same schools.

The operation of peer groups in more easily seen in the secondary school than in the primary school, for friendships and affiliations among pupils become more stable in adolescence. Before that they tend to shift rather often. A study by Hallworth (1953) in one grammar school, covering 150 pupils in eleven different classes, examined the "natural history" of peer grouping. Over time, he found, they became larger and better integrated, and patterned essentially in similar ways on three socio-metric criteria.

> "There was a growth from mutual choices, through small or loosely knit structures, to a large group centred around a nucleus of some four or five individuals, one of whom was particularly overchosen."

Each group had some common values and norms which were recognised by the members and which were reflected in differences between the groups in their rates of absenteeism from school, early leaving and academic marks. In a detailed study of just one of these forms, Hallworth found that IQ did not correlate significantly with marks, but the status of the pupil in his peer group did.

The peer groups which form among pupils, including about sixty per cent or slightly more of all pupils, may be classified (from the outsider's point of view) in various ways, or along various dimensions.

One dimension of differentiation would be based on behaviour relative to the official performance norms of the school. An earlier generation of British schoolboys talked of "swots" and "slackers".

Today these terms are not used and no replacements have established themselves to the same extent.

A second dimension concerns behaviour relative to the official conduct norms of the school. Pupils of all types often refer to certain of their peers as "crawlers", meaning that they were too cooperative or ingratiating with teachers by *their* standards. Pupils with good conduct records are also not slow to point out which others were known for "mucking about" in class.

Several more dimensions are defined in terms of values deriving from pupil sub-cultures. One concerns pupils' solidarity *vis-à-vis* teachers. This norm, which is probably more universal in its acceptance than any other, severely condemns the pupil who "splits", "sneaks", or "squeals". A second aspect of pupil solidarity *vis-à-vis* the teachers concerns how far one differentiates oneself from the mass of pupils, presumably seeking special rewards, by being helpful to the teachers. This is the action of the "crawler" and is highly disapproved.

Another fairly universal value among pupils, in terms of which they judge each other, seems to be amusement. The pupil who can bring fun and laughter to his peers is highly esteemed, especially if he can do this in the tedium of the classroom. Tastes in humour differ, however, and the boy who is esteemed as a wit in one group may be stigmatised as a gross buffoon by members of another group. There are even groups of pupils who are sufficiently committed to the official pupil role that they withhold approval from classroom comedians, if not to actually disapprove of them, where their humour is not integrated with the teacher's attempts to direct the lesson.

A basis of distinguishing among one's fellows, quite commonly used, relates to style of dress and leisure. A few years ago one could refer to the fairly sharply defined sub-cultures of the "mod", the "rocker" and the "square". New fashions arise every few years.

The last dimension to be mentioned concerns how "hard" or tough the boy in question is thought to be. Being hard involves pushing other people around as well as getting into fights. Hard boys are aggressive and truculent. That may get them into fights they were not looking for, but they also go out of their way to pick fights with other hard boys. Among them the term "hard" carries favourable connotations and proving one's hardness by fighting successfully with other boys wins esteem in such a group.

At the other end of the "hardness" dimension are the "sissies". Somewhere in between these extremes is the majority of schoolboys for whom fighting *per se* carries no special glory but who do feel that sometimes a boy has to stand up and fight another who is pushing him around. One who consistently refuses to do this is defined as a sissy—and not just by the hard lads (Sexton, 1969, Ch. 9 and Waller, 1942, Ch. 13).

A study which I carried out in 1965 (Sugarman, 1968) involved interviewing eighty boys in three London schools concerning their own peer groups and the others of which they were aware in their school. In a separate part of the same study questionnaires were completed by over 500 boys in the fourth year of four schools, from whom the eighty were a systematic sample. From the questionnaires it was clear that pupils tended to form peer groups with other pupils who resembled them in terms of IQ, home background, academic performance in school, conduct, level of involvement in youth culture and other variables. The aphorism "birds of a feather flock together" is true for teenage boys at any rate.

As for the activities of these groups or their peer group culture, the interviews suggested that, although pupils might be aware of differences in the attainment and conduct of their peers, these differences did not give rise to differential evaluations or status rankings *within* peer groups. This was what the boys themselves maintained in response to direct and indirect questions.

So far as the data from interviews went, the content of pupils' peer group cultures appeared to be focused around activities which were basically recreational or distractions from the official demands of the classroom, both in terms of work and conduct. Each group has its own customary activities: playing soccer in the playground with an old tennis ball, telling jokes and discussing the weekend's sports and TV highlights, smoking behind the lavatories, harassing smaller boys, or whatever it may be. And the norms which did come to light in this part of the enquiry were mostly focused on these activities.

In several of the peer groups which occupy themselves with games, especially soccer but also cricket, fives, "he" and "feet-off-the-ground", several interviewees reported a group norm that all should respect the rules of the game and not cheat. Everyone should be a "good sport". Anyone who was not, would be thought of badly and might have sanctions imposed on him. According to one account critical remarks would be made; he would find that when teams were being picked, he was one of the last to be chosen (even if he was a skilful player); when they were playing his own team-mates would refrain from passing the ball to him; and members of the opposing team would be rougher than usual in tackling him. Cases were reported from this and another sports-centred group in another school of members being barred from playing because of unacceptable ("unsportsmanlike") conduct.

Another type of peer group consists of those who walk around and/or hang about at some appointed place and talk. Sports and television were the topics most often discussed and another recurrent topic concerned happenings in school, the moods and eccentricities of teachers and the behaviour of other pupils in class. Occasionally but not often mentioned were careers and future plans. Aside from these fairly general topics, members of some groups had special interests that they discussed, such as the youth club, new clothes and pop music. The values and norms of groups like this cannot have the same functional connection with their collective activities as in the case of the sporty groups just mentioned. However, we have reports of norms such as the following: one should not boast (except in joke); one should not insist on things being done the way *he* wants if others are unwilling; one should not sulk, quarrel, or fight with other group members; one should not criticise one member to another; one should share things with his mates in the group (as one pupil expressed it, "If one of them has a cigarette and the others haven't, he should share it").

The third and last type of group (actually a sub-set of the previous one) that can be identified on the basis of this data is the "hard group". It was possible to classify five groups as hard in the sense that members reported that the achievement which would be most admired is that of a good fighter, in preference to either an outstanding sportsman or a good scholar.

To rely entirely on the respondent's own insight is always a dangerous business for the researcher, apart from being an abdication of his professional role. In this study a second method was used to explore the workings of the schoolboy's peer group.

All the fourth-formers in the four schools had answered questionnaires designed to reveal indirectly a number of facets of peer group dynamics. They were asked "at school which other pupils do you usually go around with?" from which the patterns of association amongst them could be reconstructed. They were asked which other pupils they would choose to sit next to in class, from which the popularity of each boy among his peers could be estimated. Also they were asked which pupils they would choose to have as "a leader for some group activity at school". The school records provided information on pupil's IQs, as tested at the age of eleven and their performances in recent school exams. Lastly, teachers gave ratings on pupils for conduct in class. From all of these data we were able to sort out these boys into sixty-two groups who apparently went around together in school and to classify the groups in terms of the average academic performance and conduct ratings of their members.

Because it was difficult to equate the standards of exams from one school to another, we did not look at academic achievement levels in absolute terms but relative to the boys' measured IQ. Within each school they were divided into relative IQ levels and into relative achievement levels. We then determined who was in a higher achievement level than his IQ would have predicted, who was in a lower one and who was in the same one. These we called "over-achievers", "under-achievers" and "middle-achievers".

Four types of group were differentiated on the basis of whether most members were high or low on achievement and good or poor on conduct.* We then proceeded to examine how these boys expressed their preferences for "someone to sit next to" and someone to be a leader. Our purpose was to test the hypothesis that between the four types of group there would be differences in the kind of boys emerging as most popular or chosen as leaders. These differences would reflect different norms and values in the different groups, which would also be reflected in differential pressures on members to behave in different ways—whichever way was favoured in their group and rewarded by popularity or respect. To put it simply: do some peer groups reward high achievement more than others? do some reward good conduct, while others reward poor conduct in the teacher's book? In

* High achievers, good conduct; high achievers, poor conduct; low achievers, good conduct; low achievers, poor conduct.

groups of mainly high achievers the high achievers received more choices as leader than did high or middle achievers in groups of mainly low and middle achievers. This supports the hypothesis of differential peer group norms relating to achievement. The data on popularity gives partial support to the hypothesis. The corresponding hypothesis of peer group norms in respect of conduct is *not* supported though.

Here we can only speculate, but since in the poor conduct groups all conduct ratings are low, it is possible that the boys with the lowest ratings of all in these groups are socially maladjusted and not only unable to conform to the standards of their teachers but even to those of their peers. So they are not popular.

What we find when we examine leadership votes is equally surprising. Over all the groups there is a very slight association between *poor* conduct ratings and receiving higher numbers of leadership votes. Although this relationship is very weak, it is interesting that it is in the *opposite direction* to the one between popularity and conduct. Poor conduct is actually more strongly related to high leadership votes in the two relatively good conduct groups than it is in the other two.

Taking these two sets of findings that relate to conduct together, we see a clear difference between the principles on which these boys choose their friends and their leaders. It seems from this data that boys who get into trouble with teachers are apt to be chosen as leaders (in all groups—especially those characterised by good conduct ratings) but they are not desired as seat-mates or class companions. This may imply a restriction as to the esteem accorded them or it may just represent prudence on the part of fellow-pupils who enjoy having them in the class to liven things up and respect them for their nerve, but prefer not to have them as seat-mates to get them personally into trouble.

In any event, it is clear that on both leadership and popularity criteria we must reject any hypothesis that conduct-related values or norms (as defined) operate in these groups.

Pupils get into trouble for doing things that most of them enjoy doing: reading comics under the desk or talking to their pals during lesson, flicking paper pellets, answering the teacher back and so forth. Let us speculate a little about the effects of peer group membership on pupil behaviour in the classroom and how this relates to the efforts of the teacher to maintain order.

Peer group membership is likely to contribute, I should guess, to an increase in most of these forbidden activities but especially, perhaps, to the more active ones that involve communicating with other pupils. Whereas the delinquency of non-members more often takes passive forms of inattentiveness. Faced with the immediate problems of social control in the classroom, the effective teacher penalises active forms of deviance before passive ones. Hence peer group members stand in greater jeopardy of poor conduct ratings on these grounds alone, not to mention the following further reason.

Many adolescents seem to enjoy or even crave the chance to assert themselves as individuals, to do or say something that indicates that they are not just to be treated as one of a stereotyped category, such as "teenager" or "members of fourth-year English class". Hence we find them talking back to the teacher, whether humorously or aggressively. If the teacher is competent, however, he should be able to control the average fourteen-year-old pupil with the sanctions he has at his disposal. One commonly-used sanction involves shaming or embarrassing the offender in front of the class. Now this technique is only really effective if most pupils in the class cooperate with the teacher.

A pupil who belongs to a solidary peer group can feel that his friends stand behind him while the teacher holds him up to ridicule, hence its effect on him as punishment or deterrent is very much reduced. While the importance of these processes varies between peer groups of the different types, I suggest that it operates to some extent in all of them.

The search for "pro-school" peer groups which reward good conduct at the same time as they support academic effort is, I believe, doomed to disappointment. But it may be some consolation to know that the average anti-school peer group is often less virulent in its effect than is commonly supposed and the way its members act in class is strongly influenced by the approach of the teacher, especially by the fact of whether his classroom strategy is what we earlier called "progressive" or "traditional".

We have now discussed the variations in norms and values in pupils' peer groups, that is the *direction* of their influence upon those who are their members. We must not forget that in addition to differences in direction there are differences among peer groups in the strength of their effect. The peer group at school which is also the out-of-school peer group is likely to be more influential than the one which operates only at school. The peer group which shares a member with another group is likely to have less influence over him than one which has his exclusive loyalty. Then again, the length of time over which a group of pupils have stayed together is likely to affect the strength of their mutual influence over each other.

INFLUENCE OF THE FORMAL STRUCTURE

In trying to account for these kinds of variations in the patterning of pupil-pupil relations in the school, we have to allow for two sets of causal variables and for their interaction. Firstly, there are the variables of home background and pre-school peer group experience, which we discussed in another chapter. Secondly, there are factors to do with the social organisation of the school, which will be our concern now.

The formal structure of academic learning will determine whether class composition is stable or fluid. That is, to what extent pupils change their work-mates from lesson to lesson in the course of a day. This is likely to affect the patterning of pupil-pupil relationships in several ways. The more stable is the classroom group, the more cohesiveness it is likely to develop and the greater sense of its boundary *vis-à-vis* other class groups in the school, though this depends to some extent on the role of the teacher in fostering this in-group feeling and on the overall reward system of the school. The teacher, by frequently comparing the class to other classes and encouraging them to think of themselves as a group distinct from others, may heighten this tendency. Similarly where the school is organised so as to allocate many rewards and punishments on a collective basis to whole classes rather than individual pupils, as in the Russian collective system, this again heightens the tendency to cohesiveness and a strong in-group feeling.

The result of such a highly developed in-group sentiment and class cohesiveness is likely to be twofold. On the one hand there will be strong peer group pressure within the classroom for conformity to peer group norms. These may or may not be in line with the expectations of the teacher. The other likely result, I suggest, is that pupils in such a class will develop relatively little considerateness and tolerance for others outside of their group, compared to other pupils in a more fluid classroom situation.

Another aspect of the formal structure of academic learning which has some bearing on our question is that of the basis for pupil differentiation into teaching groups. This is commonly discussed as the question of streaming or non-streaming. It has been shown in several studies of streamed secondary schools that within each different stream there develops a normative climate dominated by a certain group within the stream. This has the effect of polarising the attitudes, conduct, and performance of the pupils, over time exaggerating their initial differences from one another (Hargreaves, 1967; Hollingshead, 1949; Lacey, 1966).

The formal academic structure of the school is able to influence peer group patterns because it determines to such a large extent which pupils will spend their time together for the greater part of the school day. Groupings among pupils that form in their break and lunch-times, when they are absolutely free to choose their companions, tend to remain within the work groups as determined by the formal academic structure. Only in neighbourhood schools where pupils may bring into school previously developed friendships from the neighbourhood or their previous primary school are there exceptions to this general rule.

The effectiveness of the pastoral structure in affecting peer group patterns, I would think, is proportional to the amount of time that pupils are required to spend in pastoral groups. Therefore, the residential school is at a great advantage in this respect because most of the pupil's out of classroom time is generally organised on a house basis. However, the day school whose pastoral structure is inevitably weaker may still make a significant impact on peer group patterns. Even if it is not able to modify the principal friendship choices of pupils, they may still influence their social and moral development by influencing their range of interaction and scope of interaction on a secondary level. That is, pupils may be brought together with other pupils differing from themselves in age, ability or in other ways, who may not be their principal associates but with whom they may have regular patterns of interchange and from which both may learn an increased tolerance and understanding of each other.

The provision of extra-curricular activities may affect pupil-pupil relationships in several ways. In the first place, these groups may be the means for isolated and friendless pupils to find a social life for themselves. Secondly, they may be the means whereby pupils get to know other pupils outside of their normal friendship group in the school. Thirdly, they may bring it about that a group of pupils who normally associate together with a certain pattern of role relationships may considerably modify these relationships when they join a certain club or activity and some of them reveal talents and skills which were previously unrecognised and which lead to a shift in leadership, status and other features of their role relationship.

The existence in the school of a system for co-opting selected pupils into authority positions can have the most far-reaching effects on pupil-pupil relationships. As they are intended by the teachers to operate, these systems (exemplified by the prefect system), transfer the loyalty of those pupils selected from the pupil group to that of the staff. When it is not operating in this way, it may deprive those pupils who would have been leaders among their peers of this status, because they are perceived as having "sold out", without giving them any new status of authority in the eyes of fellow pupils. It may also happen that those pupils selected for authority positions use their authority not in terms of the official expectations of staff but more in terms of the expectations of their peers. This entails a complete breakdown of the system as planned by the official powers in the school.

In the school where a representative school council operates, this may support and be supported by the structure of pupil peer groups in the following way. The representatives elected will tend to be pupils who have high status among their peers at large. If the council is perceived by pupils as being effective and able to win worthwhile benefits for them, this will tend to further increase the status of council representatives among their peers. At the same time, one of the assets of the effective representative is the fact that he has ready communication with his peers who are also his constituents.

The extent to which the school fosters competition and cooperation among pupils may also affect pupil-pupil relationships in the school. Generally speaking, cooperative work improves the level of mutual liking, sympathy and tolerance among pupils compared to competitive working situations (Deutsch, 1949). This is assuming that the competition is on an individual basis. An alternative arrangement is to have competitions between groups of pupils. In this case, the element of competition may serve to increase the motivation of pupils for the task, provided that they are reasonably equally matched in their ability to perform. Given the increased motivation, all the social mechanisms of control among the pupil group (depending on the level of social cohesion already developed among them) come into play to reward those who further the group's progress towards winning and to suppress, often harshly, all behaviour which detracts from this.

CHAPTER 7 REFERENCES

Wesley C. Becker, "Consequences of Different Kinds of Parental Discipline", in H. L. Hoffman (ed.) *Review of Child Development Research*, Vol. 1, Russell Sage Foundation, New York, 1964.

Orville G. Brim, Jr., *Sociology and the Field of Education*, Russell Sage Foundation, New York, 1958.

Morton Deutsch, "An Experimental Study of the Effects of Cooperation and Competition upon Group Process", *Human Relations*, II, 1949, pp. 199–231.

Ned A. Flanders, "Some Relationships among Teacher Influence, Pupil Attitudes, and Achievement", in Bruce J. Biddle and W. J. Ellena (eds.), *Contemporary Research on Teacher Effectiveness*, Holt, Rinehart and Winston, New York, 1964.

H. J. Hallworth, "Sociometric Relationships among Grammar School Boys and Girls between the Ages of Eleven and Sixteen Years", *Sociometry*, XVI, February, 1953, pp. 39–70.

David H. Hargreaves, *Social Relations in a Secondary School*, Routledge and Kegan Paul, London, 1967.

August B. Hollingshead, *Elmtown's Youth*, John Wiley, New York, 1949.

Colin Lacey, "Some Sociological Concomitants of Academic Streaming in a Grammar School", *B.J.S.*, XVII, September, 1966.

Clark Moustakas, *The Authentic Teacher*, Howard A. Doyle, Cambridge, Mass., 1966.

A. S. Neill, *Summerhill: A Radical Approach to Education*, Gollancz, London, 1961.

Patricia Cayo Sexton, *The Feminized Male: Classrooms, White Collars and the Decline of Manliness*, Vintage Books, New York, 1969.

Barry Sugarman, "Social Norms in Teenage Boys' Peer Groups", *Human Relations*, XXI, February, 1968, pp. 41–58.

Barry Sugarman, "Teenage Boys at School", unpublished Ph.D. thesis, Princeton University, 1965.

Willard Waller, *The Sociology of Teaching*, John Wiley, New York, 1932.

Chapter Eight

THE SCHOOL AND MORAL EDUCATION

In this chapter we shall link the definition of the morally-educated person with our discussion of human relations in the school, suggesting how specific aspects of human relationships between teachers and pupils, pupils and pupils within the school contribute to the development of the specific qualities which we have taken to define the MEP.

In Figure 1 we depict in simplified form the kind of variables under discussion and the kind of relationship we are trying to trace amongst them. An arrow pointing from one box to another indicates that we are interested in the causal influences of the one set of variables (from which the arrow originates) on the other set of variables (to which the arrow points). Thus, for example, the arrows leading from the box "*Formal structure of the school*" represent the causal influence of these variables upon others to which the arrows point ("*Pupil-Pupil relations*", etc.). We are interested in the way that *variations* in the former set of variables tend to produce *variations* in the latter.

The boxes labelled "*Teachers*" and "*Pupils*" represent these two categories of input into the school and the arrows leading from them represent the effects produced by differences in the nature of the inputs on teacher-pupil relations and pupil-pupil relations. On the far left side of the diagram is a box labelled "*Head*" from which a number of arrows emanate, indicating the fact that—to a greater or lesser extent—the head has some personal control over the formal structure of the school, the recruitment of teachers as well as pupils, and over teacher-pupil relations. The head in turn is influenced and pressured by sources lying outside the school which are not shown. To this extent the diagram appears to exaggerate the power and freedom of action enjoyed by the head. This diagram does not attempt to show *all* these dependencies and interdependencies among these categories of variables. The purpose of our analysis here is to emphasise those aspects of the schooling process which contribute most directly to moral education.

Fig. 1. THE SCHOOL AND MORAL EDUCATION

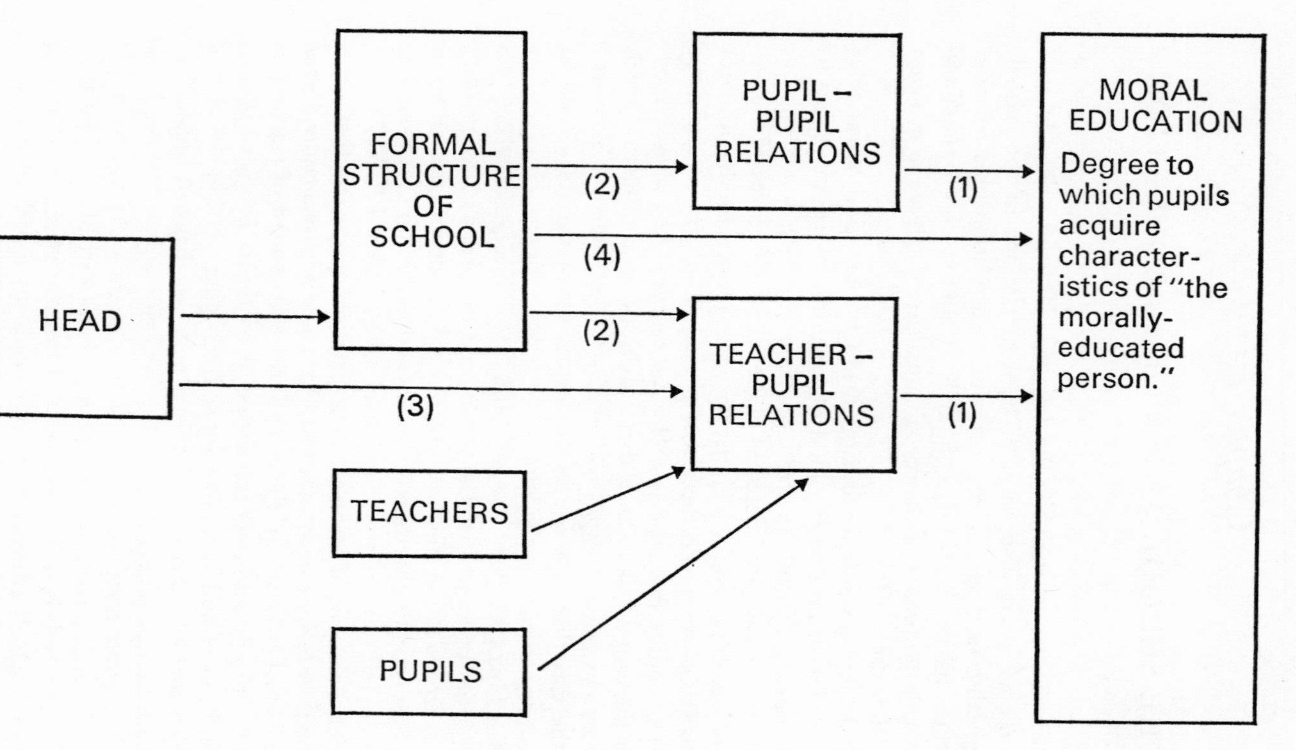

The bulk of this chapter is divided into three parts, dealing with the contributions to moral education of: (1) teacher-pupil relationships; (2) pupil-pupil relationships; and (3) certain aspects of the school's formal structure acting directly rather than acting through (1) or (2). Before entering upon this threefold break-down, though, we must note a major point that bestrides all three subsections. Kohlberg (1966) suggests that one of the most important environmental factors which may contribute to facilitating the development of moral judgement is the range of opportunities the individual has for social interaction and role-taking. He also puts forward two other factors which belong in section (3), extending the pupil's understanding of how the social system works (mainly important for pupils from deprived backgrounds) and deliberately exposing pupils to moral concepts one stage ahead of their current status in order to speed their development. These last two factors will be discussed in the proper place, but the first one (role-taking opportunities) calls for some comment here.

Citing the earlier work of Mead (1934) and Piaget (1948), Kohlberg presents role-taking as the fundamental process in human social interaction. Role-taking involves "the tendency to react to the other [person] as someone like the self and . . . the tendency to react to the self's behavior in the role of the other" (p. 398). The interaction between the self and the other (who is seen to be like the self but who is not the self) sometimes produces conflicting claims between individuals. People respond differently to these moral conflict situations, taking the role of the other (mentally) and responding to it in different ways according to the stage of moral judgement they have reached.

Since moral development, for Kohlberg, is fundamentally a process of changing one's mode of role-taking, the most important stimulant to moral development, he concludes, must be the extent of "role-taking opportunities". These he defines in terms of the amount of social interaction and communication the person experiences, plus his degree of centrality in the group's communication and decision-making structure. The more democratic the group, the more role-taking both members and leaders do in accommodating to each other's varied points of view. Also, the more responsibility the individual has through occupying leadership positions (especially in democratic groups) the more role-taking he has to do, since the leader has to take the roles of all other members.

This hypothesis leaves many questions unanswered—such as, do certain kinds of role-taking opportunities have specific value for stimulating advancement, or are all "opportunities" of equal value, their effect being simply cumulative? Nevertheless the hypothesis is based upon a theoretical assumption of respectable lineage and has a ready plausibility. More than this, Kohlberg cites several findings which are consistent with it: the fact that orphanage children are retarded in moral judgement relative to both children in families and kibbutz children; that punitive and rejecting families tend to produce delinquents, who tend to be backward in moral judgement; that families using "inductive discipline" (explaining to the child the consequences of his behaviour) more often have children who internalise their moral judgements; that peer-group isolates are retarded in moral development relative to matched peer-group leaders. (In the last two examples there may be some question as to the direction of causation.) In each example it seems that the subjects who had the greater opportunities for role-taking were more advanced in moral development.

The implications of this hypothesis for the school are to make us look at every structural variable from a new point of view—how it affects the scope of role-taking available to pupils. The more varied roles that pupils can play, the more they can participate in decision-making; the more they can share in leadership; the more they can be helped to be very open-minded about the role-taking they actually do, the more their development of moral judgement may be expected to be advanced.

TEACHER-PUPIL RELATIONS AND MORAL EDUCATION

The teacher-pupil relationship represents perhaps the most crucial area of the "school influence" on pupils. It is also probably the most complex part, since variations in the nature and quality of this relationship are determined to some extent by the formal structure of the school directly, a certain amount by indirect implications of the formal structure and a great deal by "definitions of the situation" which are established informally and tacitly between each teacher and his or her pupils.

In an earlier chapter discussing teaching in the classroom we made two distinctions among the various different approaches that teachers take. In one we distinguished between *wide* and *narrow* teacher-pupil relationships and in the other we distinguished between *traditional* and *progressive* classroom strategies. We shall argue that both wide and narrow teacher-pupil relationships have important contributions to make to moral education, though of a distinctly different kind; the wide approach is most necessary in the early years of the child's career in school and the narrow approach becomes important only later on; at any time, though, it can only make its contribution to moral education provided that the pupil still has some kind of wide relationship with some teacher as well. At the final stage, however, the wide relationship may engage only a very small proportion of his time, unlike the early years, when one wide teacher-pupil relationship occupies most of their school hours. Where classroom strategies are concerned, we continue to maintain that the balance of advantages lies with the progressive one and we will confine our discussion in this section mainly to issues related to the wide versus narrow aspect of the teacher-pupil relationship.

It is worth repeating a caution made in our earlier discussion of approaches to teaching. When we refer to "wide" and "narrow" teacher-pupil relationships we are not suggesting that teachers could or should be classified as one or the other; nor even that they could (even in principle) be placed along a dimension from "wide" to "narrow" which would represent a uniform style of teaching. We do not assume such a high degree of consistency in teachers' approaches, though *some* teachers may be like that. What we believe to be true for more teachers or many teachers—and a situation which we will argue to be favourable to moral education—is that a single teacher can vary his approach, not only with different classes but also with the same class at different times.

When we speak of the alleged contributions of "wide" and "narrow" teacher-pupil relationships to different aspects of moral education, we are not talking about two sets of alternative benefits. Nor are we *necessarily* talking about two sets of benefits that pupils may receive from two different sets of teachers—though often it will work like this. We are talking about the benefits that *may* be available to pupils from *each* of their teachers as their relationship shifts its character from wide to narrow and back again.

Just as friends and spouses can relate to each other differently at different times, according to the requirements of the situation—sometimes being mainly oriented to the accomplishment of a task and other times more to the enjoyment of each other's company—so can pupils and teachers vary the nature of their relationship from time to time. The pupil who enjoys a narrow relationship with a teacher with whom he has earlier enjoyed a wide relationship will trust him more, be more receptive to him and so learn more from him at least in some areas.

Concern for Others

In learning to care about other people (one of the key attributes of the MEP) the most important factor is the experience of being demonstratively cared for oneself, especially in the early years of infancy by one's parents or other full-time caretakers (Bowlby, 1953). A wide and personal relationship with the first teacher is necessary if a child is to expand the range of people for whom he has this concern and affection. His infant school teachers can be added to the short list of individuals for whom the small child has such feelings and so can some of his classmates. Since the social structure of the infants' classroom is basically the summation of each pupil's relationship with the teacher, peer groupings being highly ephemeral, the attitude of the teacher overwhelmingly determines the atmosphere of the classroom and the response of pupils to it (Anderson, 1945). To make the point negatively first, the narrow form of teaching style does not exude obvious concern for the pupil and leaves frustrated many of their basic needs. This frustration generates hostility and perhaps aggression against other members of the group, against the teacher (probably in indirect ways), in either case expressed either against the person or the property of these others. By contrast, the wide-style teacher, who conveys to her pupils the impression that she cares about them, creates a relationship in which these pupils want to please her and do as she wishes. The model she provides is one of kindness and consideration for others, and she rewards them for acts of kindness to each other by smiling more warmly upon them. Thus is the attitude and practice of concern for others developed in the wide teacher-pupil relationship (Aronfreed, 1970; Krebs, 1970).

The same point applies in a modified form with older pupils. Given the specialised division of labour among secondary teachers, which is so common, the issue is more complex. How much of their relationship with each of their teachers is wide in nature, within the limits of the short amount of time they spend together? Do they have a truly wide and personal relationship with at least one teacher (who may be a form teacher or tutor group teacher as well as a subject teacher)? Can one wide relationship alone produce the same effects as a number of fairly wide but limited relationships with several specialist teachers? For pupils in the latter years of schooling we are assuming that specialist and somewhat narrow teacher relations are necessary, not only for reasons of academic learning but also for reasons of moral education which we shall come to shortly. We still assume, though, that some wide relationship is still necessary—even though limited in terms of the time it occupies.

Concern for other people is closely related to other aspects of the morally-educated person as well. It would seem to be interconnected with the development of sensitivity to the feelings of others and the ability to "read" them accurately, the social skill involved in responding to them effectively and the kind of alertness to people which makes one quick to notice distress signals. We are distinguishing here between alertness to distress signals or how much attention people pay to other people, on the one hand, and how accurately they can interpret these signals when their attention is called to them, on the other hand.

The concept of concern for other people and their rights is not restricted to other people in one's immediate social environment. Indeed an individual who had very high regard for other people's interests in this narrow context but had little regard for those outside it would have to be classified as someone with low to moderate concern overall. The high-concern person, who has concern for other people and their interests both in immediate situations and remote ones, may fall into one of two main categories, developmentally speaking. He may have developed from a childhood enjoying wide and emotionally satisfying relationships with parents and others, later learning to extend his concern to gradually widening circles of others, radiating out from the core contexts of social experience.

Another kind of person has high concern for categories of people remote from immediate experience but not very much (compared to the former kind of person) for those in immediate situations, not much more than he has for unknown, anonymous persons. In the case of this second kind of person, it seems as if his rather academic concern for remote groups—which may be perfectly genuine and confirmed by his efforts on their behalf—is for him a substitute for more emotionally involving personal relationships. This contrasts sharply with the previously mentioned type, whose concern for strangers grows out of and is based upon his relationships with people in his immediate experience and his attitude towards them. The second kind of person does not believe that "charity begins at home". What experiences and preconditions tend to produce such a personality type is much less clear than in the case of the former type and we shall here confine our attention exclusively to that type.

Universalism

We now turn to consider the factor of universalism and a number of related qualities of the MEP which are not likely to develop very far within the context of the purely wide teacher-pupil relationship and which seem to require the social context of a more narrow and highly task-oriented relationship to bring them out.

One of the qualities which probably can only be developed by pupils in the context of a narrow, task-oriented teacher-pupil relationship is the ability or social skill to play such impersonal and highly specific roles—to enter into relationships in which two people interact for the sole purpose of getting a specific task accomplished. In terms of child development the narrow, task-oriented relationship only comes after the child has learned to engage in wider and more personal kinds of relationships. One of the most difficult things a child has to learn is to apply universalistic standards to judge the performances or qualities of individuals who are known intimately and either strongly liked or disliked (Dreeben, 1967; Parsons, 1961).

This brings us to the area of moral thinking or judgement which is also involved here. Thinking about moral choices in terms of universalistic categories and standards is an important attribute of the MEP and one which can probably only be learned through experience of a narrow task-oriented relationship. What is involved here is learning to hold in abeyance the overall personal impressions that one has of an individual—whether favourable or unfavourable—while one evaluates his performance or attributes. Being able to make such objective, universalistic judgements is a necessary but not sufficient condition to answering the question "how should I act towards that person?" This kind of judgement has to be made as part of the role-taking process to which we referred earlier. Mentally taking the role of the other enables the individual to become aware of the demands the other person wishes to place upon him. He must then make a judgement as to what he should do so far as fulfilling those demands or expectations.

Dreeben (1967) has argued that the school tends to foster universalism (along with certain other values) by virtue of the "tasks, constraints, and opportunities" presented to the pupil. He does not differentiate among schools but, by examining the factors in the school which he treats as constants and reconceptualising them as variables, we may perhaps advance our own analysis. Following Parsons (1961), Dreeben sees the school essentially as a bridging institution between family and the adult world of work and citizenship. As a result of going to school, they suggest, children tend to learn universalism, individualism, the achievement or "mastery" orientation and functional specificity or narrow relationships. At any rate, they learn these normative orientations more from school than they would by remaining within the family. (Whether they would learn them better from work, the army or some organisation other than school, is a question they do not consider.)

What, then, are the features of school which, Dreeben claims, tend to develop universalism? The main factor is the grouping or differentiation of pupils by age and other criteria and treating them as if they are essentially similar, subordinating their evident individual differences to their organisationally defined identity. (In the family, by contrast, the child is treated as a unique individual.) In the classroom much of pupils' behaviour is publicly visible to their class-mates. It is, therefore, easy for them to evaluate each other (by various more or less universalistic criteria), especially as they are witnesses to the public evaluations made routinely by teachers. In several other ways the school makes it easier for pupils to learn to use universalistic categories: by providing for the formation of more diverse relationships, more transient and time-bounded ones (with teachers and other pupils), and for learning the difference between social positions and the persons who occupy them.

Translating these factors into variables, we may suggest that universalism tends to be learned effectively to the degree that schools group and classify pupils and treat them in undifferentiated categories. (Pupils generally resent such treatments when taken to an extreme, though, which can cause serious problems of social control.)

The learning of universalism also appears to be facilitated by witnessing, participating in and being subjected to public evaluations based on universalistic criteria. It should be noted that the criteria used in the teachers' formal evaluations and those used in pupils' informal evaluations are generally completely different, though both may be universalistic. The purer these criteria are in universalistic terms and the more frequent the evaluations (up to a point), the more effectively is universalistic thinking learned. These, at any rate, are some hypotheses about how pupils come to accept the right of others to treat them as members of a category and their own right and obligation to treat others in this way—at least for certain purposes.

Not specifically mentioned by Dreeben but obviously important in this context is the functionally specific relationship the pupil has with those of his teachers who practise a narrow approach to teaching. This is, on the whole, a new experience for the child and it is one which is closely related to the learning of universalism because the more impersonal, business-like or task-oriented atmosphere of the narrow teacher-pupil relationship makes it easier for all to formulate objective universalistic judgements.

One important aspect of universalism in moral thinking and role-playing is that of positional authority by contrast with personal forms of authority. The most significant examples of personal authority are, of course, the child's parents and his early, wide-style teachers. It is important for pupils to have some experience of working under narrow-style teachers because their authority is clearly based on the position they occupy within the social structure of the school and not basically upon the qualities of their personality or personal relationship with the pupils.

The narrow teacher-pupil relationship introduces the pupil to an authority system that is fundamentally different from the one they have been familiar with in the family. With this kind of teacher the expected behaviour is defined in terms of impersonal general rules which specify the required conduct in terms of general categories of persons and situations. This is fundamentally different from the primordial duties to particular persons which children learn in the family. Some families, especially those of the middle class, do indeed have clear rules for the children. (This is one factor accounting for the different degree of difficulty which children from different home backgrounds experience in adjusting to school.) But even children from middle-class homes find in school an authority system, with a set of rules more extensive and more impersonal than anything they have been used to.

They also find that positions of authority in the school are occupied by a large number of interchangeable adults, instead of the two familiar parents who represent authority in the family. There the rules, even if they are formally stated, are backed by the *personal* authority of the parents. In the school, by contrast, the rules are presented as having an authority in themselves. This again is something which is graduated throughout the school from early to later years. In his first years in the school, the child associates the rules of the classroom with the *person* of this teacher, much as he associates the rules of the home with the persons of mother and father. In later years and increasingly through the school, though, as the child is exposed to a larger number of teachers for a briefer and briefer span of time, his relationship with them tends to become narrower and less personal and the common school rules which all these different teachers enforce become less and less dependent on the personal authority of the individual teacher. In other words, they become seen more and more in terms of universalistic principles.

This brings us to the matter of the nature of the rules themselves, which we consider in a later section. For now suffice it to say that if the rules in a particular school are in fact arbitrary and not rationally based, two possible consequences are likely to follow. Either the pupils' learning of universalism will be retarded or, if they can see the arbitrariness of the rules (having managed to acquire a sense of universalism despite this handicap), a problem of alienation from school will develop.

In the development of moral thinking, direct teaching with guided discussions of moral issues can play an important part too. The teacher who has a wide relationship with his pupils has a better knowledge of their backgrounds and private interests as well as the level of sophistication appropriate for the discussion. Other things being equal, therefore, the wide teacher should be able to run a better discussion. Kohlberg and his associates have argued and produced some evidence to support the point that pupils will fail to understand attempts at moral instruction which are phrased in concepts too far beyond their present level of development; and that they will not learn to develop their moral reasoning if approached at a level of sophistication below the one they have reached; that the most appropriate level at which to aim, in order to advance development, is one that is one stage only ahead of the pupil's present development (Turiel, 1966). In the absence of formal testing procedures for this (they do exist but are not generally used as of yet) the teacher is forced to depend on his informal and intuitive assessments of pupils.

Apart from the value of the narrow teacher-pupil relationship for helping the pupil to play this kind of role, which is widely found in adult life, it contributes in another way to moral education. Before people can learn to analyse moral problems and weigh up the implications of different decisions, certain kinds of intellectual perspective are required. They must be able to distinguish between act, intention and consequences (Piaget, 1932); they must be able to see consequences that are not very concrete or immediate as well as those that are. They must be able to grasp the idea that the same individual can fall into different categories at different times and in different situations: at one time a listener, at another time a speaker; at one time a winner, at another time a loser. They must be able to envision themselves in the position now occupied by another (Mead, 1934). They must be able to see how rules and moral principles exist in the abstract tied to situations and roles rather than to individual persons; how rules are social arrangements for which reasons can be given in terms of their utility and against which reasons can similarly be brought, rather than outcroppings of some moral absolute or higher power and that there are often institutionalised procedures through which these rules can be modified by those who go about it in the right way (Piaget, 1932). What we are talking about here (in part) is developing a *rational* or *functional* way of looking at social arrangements.

People who look at social institutions in this "rational" or "functional" way may be persuaded to comply with new and distasteful restrictions and to cooperate with individuals whom they dislike. They may also come to decide that restrictions they once accepted on the strength of their traditional authority or as a favour to individuals can no longer command their compliance. This approach to moral thinking is conducive to flexibility and cuts two ways: it conduces to readier adaptation to changed conditions and also to readier abandonment of existing allegiances when they seem not to be rationally justified.

This way of moral thinking and view of social reality tends to develop in the context of overlapping and narrow rather than wide and exclusive relationships. The fact of concentration on task achievement puts a premium on rational or functional means-ends thinking which expands from the area of technical or engineering matters to the area of social relationships among those who are supposed to be working together to accomplish the task, then to many other of their relationships.

"Character"

A further set of qualities required by the MEP and developed more in the context of the narrow teacher-pupil relationship may be called "moral toughness", "KRAT", in John Wilson's terminology (Wilson *et. al.* 1967) or "character" in the jargon of traditionalist moral education. Some rather extreme situations which exemplify these qualities at a high level would include: risking physical danger for a highly valued goal, the inflicting of necessary pain on oneself or others when necessary in order to administer treatment for injury or illness; telling a friend a painful truth that he should know for his own good; or standing out from a group of friends who are demanding a show of loyalty when one's conscience indicates the need to act differently from what they propose. This same quality of "moral toughness" is required in more modest quantities in a multitude of more mundane situations—in fact every time that a person resolves on a course of action which he defines as "right" but which he is not entirely enthusiastic about following, either because it requires him to do something that is hard or unpleasant or just because it distracts him from more pleasurable pursuits. What we are calling "moral toughness" could equally well be called "living up to one's good intentions".

Where there is a strong emphasis on the performance of specific tasks in a relationship between two people, there are implied definite standards of task performance and these are relatively objective and verifiable. This is more true with respect to some kinds of tasks than others: for example where the task is to solve a mathematical problem, perform a scientific experiment, translate a text, or build something to a specified plan. In the cases of such tasks it is relatively easy for the teacher to pass judgement and the pupil to accept its legitimacy—also for pupils to make impartial judgements of their *own* task performance. In terms of his development, it is important for the pupil to learn to accept objective judgements of his work and behaviour, even when they are unflattering and to be able to give out such judgements fairly and unapologetically to others. Academic work in the classroom is one context but a very limited one for learning of this kind and it would seem to be very important to provide other contexts for such learning, especially in the case of older pupils. Such other contexts may be found on the sports field, through prefects' roles and other positions of authority, in situations of adventure training of the Outward Bound type, or giving pupils responsibility for running various group activities—extra-curricular interest groups, social service activities, entertainments, cadet corps and so forth. (Note that these contexts also widen the opportunities for role-taking, the importance of which we have already mentioned.)

In order to develop this toughness fully it is helpful for pupils to work in groups where the adequate performance of each other is a matter of concern to his peers in a way that it never is under the usual conditions of individual working. It may also help for some pupils to be made responsible for organising the work of others. In this position they will have to face the possible criticism of the teachers in charge in the event of failure and, anticipating this, they will have to hand out criticism and demand that the pupils under them work up to standard. In such conditions of group work, both the democratic version and the small group leader version, pupils will have more incentive to evaluate the efforts of their peers and to communicate their evaluations. In doing this they will further internalise the universalistic standards and develop their moral "character" or toughness at the same time.

PUPIL-PUPIL RELATIONSHIPS AND MORAL EDUCATION

The relationships a pupil has with his fellow pupils will often be more important from his point of view than his relationships with teachers. We shall consider these relationships on an equal footing with pupil-teacher relationships.

A pupil who does not feel socially accepted among his peers is likely to be unhappy and insecure at school. He is unlikely, I would hypothesise, to develop true feelings of considerateness towards others though he may bend over backwards to be obliging to them in a desperate effort to earn the friendship which he lacks. In so far as sensitivity to the viewpoints of others and social skills in peer level contexts are the products of experience and practice, the isolated pupil will fall behind his age-mates in these respects too. A vicious circle is thus set up in which a low degree of acceptance among peers handicaps the pupil in developing sensitivity and other social skills and the lack of these makes him all the less acceptable to other pupils. The fact that isolates are less advanced in terms of moral judgement than peer-group leaders among school children has been documented by Kohlberg (1969). He interprets this finding in terms of the extent of role-taking opportunities which are available to the two groups of subjects but there is surely more to be found here than just that. Certainly those youngsters who are less popular have fewer opportunities for social learning and moral development, but why are some less popular in the first place? Perhaps this is a matter of accident (not being in the right place at the right time, for example) and perhaps in some cases it is because (for example) they were initially less adept at social skills, more wrapped up in inner problems (measured neuroticism correlates with low popularity, see Thorpe, 1955), or more handicapped by parental rules and restrictions.

Aside from the quantity or frequency of interaction a pupil enjoys with his fellows we must also consider the *nature* of this interaction. Competitive interaction between pupils is likely to comprise a large proportion of their activities, since not only do teachers encourage it in the classroom but pupils compete in their play as well. Competition within a group increases the amount of hostility members feel towards each other (Deutsch, 1949) and therefore would appear to be inimical to the development of concern for one another. Cooperation within the group in the context of inter-group competition tends to create a high level of cohesion within the group and motivation towards the group goal of beating the other group. This tends to tighten up informal social controls within the group and to create a clearly defined reward system in which those who contribute towards group success are rewarded and those who stand in its way are punished. The danger in this situation is that some members of the group may be incapable of helping and unable to avoid hindering their group. If motivation to the contest is very high the non-contributing member may be made a scapegoat and mercilessly punished. Under certain carefully controlled conditions this might be an effective way of teaching a thoughtless and inconsiderate child to think of his fellows and how they are affected by his actions. In general though it is a dangerous and harmful situation and one which even the resources of the most skilful teacher would be hard pressed to keep under control.

Competition may be valuable in small doses as a means of raising motivation in an apathetic class, but once they have begun to work together and find some satisfaction in the work itself it may no longer be necessary. Cooperative work may then be given to this class, not for them to compete against another class, though they may enjoy showing the results of their work to pupils outside of their own group or class. Cooperative work appears to be more effective in general than competitive in developing concern for others and also, of course, in developing the social skills of working with others, which are very important in the world of work and domestic life.

Whether cooperation occurs in the context of inter-group competition or not its effect is likely to depend upon the composition of the cooperating groups. Where the same pupils cooperate together time after time, over a whole year, they may become very considerate towards each other but this says nothing about their attitudes towards pupils outside of their small group. Where, however, the composition of groups is fluid so that pupils find themselves working in different groups from time to time, pupil's attitudes for considerateness are likely to be more widely diffused among their peers, I suggest. Where the system of formal academic grouping makes pupils' work groups homogeneous in terms of ability, background and so forth, their considerateness is likely to be limited to pupils like themselves. Thus we have two variables of pupil-pupil interaction patterns: stability versus fluidity and homogeneity versus heterogeneity. I would hypothesise that stable grouping is associated with the restriction of considerateness to those pupils with whom any individual actually associates. Homogeneous grouping restricts interaction to pupils similar to oneself and so reinforces the tendency to discriminate in favour of pupils like oneself and to restrict considerateness to them. Thus, for example, homogeneous grouping in terms of academic achievement and attitude to school tends to result in the "top" and "bottom" groups polarising in terms of achievement and attitude (Hargreaves, 1967). It also tends to result, I believe, in members of each group or class restricting their considerateness firstly to conforming members of this actual group or class and secondly to non-members who share their orientation to school. Looking at the main alternative approaches to the formal grouping of pupils into classes (though this analysis applies equally to grouping within classes) we see that streaming is the most restrictive arrangement since it is both stable and homogeneous.

One kind of group cooperation seems to have a special significance for moral education, namely the discussion group. Pupils who participate in discussion groups in school may not always increase their liking for each other, that probably depends on how far apart their opinions are to start with. They are, however, likely to increase their skills in the important area of verbal communication and the social skills of discussion and influence. They may also learn to conform to the conventional norms and customs of discussion, and debate and in this context to show more consideration for the others in the discussion group.

We have emphasised the importance of the wide teacher-pupil relationship for the development of strong concern in relationship to immediate others. The basic requirement seems to be for a progressive extension of the pupil's range of social contacts under conditions favourable to mutual acceptance. In so far as the extreme case of the wide teacher-pupil relationship is based on the stable class with unchanging pupil membership from lesson to lesson and day to day, the same teacher for almost the entire day, the scope for extending the pupil's range of social contact within such a framework is severely limited.

The teacher can set up opportunities for each pupil to work with all the other members of the class at different times in joint activities and this does represent a considerable extension of the range of social contact from the point at which the pupil first enters the school—but at this limit there is still a long way to go. After the first few years of schooling it is necessary to break through by gradual steps the hermetically sealed boundaries around the stable classroom. Occasionally pupils should be regrouped for certain activities across these boundaries, as they often are for games, and other sex-differentiated activities such as handicrafts. For some activities age-groups can be mixed, as they are in some schools for tutor group periods at the secondary level and for many lessons in some primary schools. The more that pupils of different social categories (such as age, sex, IQ and ethnic background) are mixed, the better for the extension of the range of their concern for others across these social boundaries, provided that the "mixing" involves some cooperative activities which pupils find at least moderately satisfying. So I hypothesise. The underlying assumption here is that contact under favourable conditions erases initial prejudice. For older populations there is support for this view so far as it applies to racial prejudice (Allport, 1954, Ch. 16). It seems reasonable to expect a similar process to operate for other social differences which are less visible and less solvent than this one and to expect it to work in the schools.

The context of mixing may take several forms. One form is for pupils to be regrouped across the boundaries of their classrooms for lessons in which they will work together in groups within the classroom. Another form is for groups to compete between themselves, either class against class or subgroups within the class against each other. A third context involves pupils working in their groups to provide something for other pupils to enjoy, such as a display, entertainment or refreshment (Warr, 1951). In this case there is not only the interaction of pupils working together in their cooperative task group, but also the interaction of those who are providing the contribution and those who are enjoying it. This provides additional incentive for the pupils in the role of providers and for those in the role of recipient it provides them with a view of some of their fellow pupils in a new and favourable light. At any level of mixing or heterogeneity the use of different contexts for interaction provides for different degrees of involvement and opportunity for more extensive role-taking.

There are, of course, other ways of extending pupils' social experience more widely: by sending them out on visits to see groups of people at work (newspapers, police, firemen, are some of the popular examples); by sending them out on field-work study projects; by placing them in work release situations; by bringing visiting speakers into the school; by showing them films and making them read books. There is here a sliding scale of concreteness or immediacy in the form of experience. So far as extending pupils' range of concern or their degree of insight into other people is concerned, it would seem that the learning potential in the more concrete situations involving other pupils in the same school was greatest. While the learning potential of book-stored and film-stored knowledge is very great indeed in certain areas (especially in advancing knowledge of the social and physical environment, which is also important for the MEP), when we are concerned with affecting human attitutes an ounce of concrete experience is worth a pound of second-hand, abstract experience. To make the point another way, the value of less concrete material to people depends upon how far they have extended the range of their concrete social experience and how far they have stretched their attitudes and social skills on this concrete level. The more they have achieved on the concrete level, I suggest, the more they can gain from the less concrete and more remote kinds of experience.

SOME DIRECT INFLUENCES OF THE SCHOOL'S FORMAL ORGANISATION

Here we shall discuss several features of the *organisational structure* of the school which appear to have direct implications for moral education and whose effect is not mainly mediated by the face-to-face relationships of pupil and pupil or teacher and pupil. Those aspects of the school structure which directly influence these relationships have already been discussed (Chapter Four).

Every school has a framework of *rules* which is applied to all pupils, stated partly in writing, partly through oral pronouncements. The functional significance of these rules is likely to be twofold: firstly they are important for defining normative expectations and so helping to maintain social order so that educational attainment will be possible; secondly they play an important part in moral education by structuring the social experiences of pupils and influencing the ways in which they conceptualise situations involving the possibility of moral choice. Let us explore this latter point further.

Confronted with this body of school rules, defining categories of conduct prohibited and prescribed, they learn to think in terms of such categories and concepts as they find embodied in the school rules—though not necessarily do they learn to conform to them. This understanding may be the basis for two further developments: learning to think in terms of general categories of behaviour and general, universalistic rules and, more specifically, to attach particular definitions to these categories, that is to acquire particular kinds of moral concepts.

School rules will vary in the clarity and explicitness with which they are stated and in the degree of mutual consistency among them. Clarity, explicitness and mutual consistency would seem to be necessary for pupils to learn to think in terms of general categories. The rules found in different schools will also differ in the ways in which they are justified, that is, in the higher order principles which are invoked to justify them and which are in any event implicit in them. Some will be justified in traditionalistic terms ("This school has always believed in . . ."); or in authoritarian terms ("The headmaster has decided . . ."); or in terms more consonant with our definition of moral education ("It will be best for all concerned if . . ."). It may be hypothesised that pupils will tend to be influenced to use and develop the same kinds of moral concept as the head and teachers enunciate for them in school, provided that there is a minimum degree of consistency between rhetoric and reality as perceived. Frequently, "It will be best for all if . . ." really means "It suits *me* to have it this way". Other things being equal, pupils from a school where rules are justified with authoritarian reasons will tend to use this kind of thinking themselves, more so than will pupils at another school where altruistic-utilitarian reasons are generally invoked to justify rules.

In relation to the *reward system* of the school we have suggested in an earlier chapter that this can be analysed in terms of two main variables: firstly, what area of achievement is most highly rewarded in a particular school; secondly, to what extent any single area monopolises the rewards.

The degree to which the kinds of attributes associated with the morally-educated person are rewarded in the school has, I would hypothesise, an important bearing on the effectiveness of the school for moral education. Yet a paradox is involved here because moral behaviour, as defined here, means doing the right thing *for the right reasons*. Hence a school which gave high rewards for altruistic behaviour might conceivably produce pupils who were highly altruistic in their behaviour but whose reasons were based not upon any attitude of concern for other people but merely upon the expedient desire to gain these rewards of approval, status and privileges. Such pupils would not qualify as morally educated in our present terms but such a situation might, however, set in train a sequence of developments leading to the real thing. In this the part of the teacher, counsellor or youth worker is vital, for they have the opportunity to open discussions and challenge pupils to think about the moral reasons they use tacitly to justify their behaviour.

There are other ways for an appropriate reward system to operate in a supportive way for moral education. In the first place, there is in secondary schools a great deal of academic competition on an individual basis. This is determined not within the school but by the competition for scarce university places and favoured jobs after leaving school. This competition when it is intense tends to set pupils in fierce competition with each other for these limited rewards. Though the rewards they ultimately seek may lie outside the school and outside the control of any member of the school staff, some of the earlier steps towards these goals may be helped or hindered by the actions and preferences of teachers and head, for example being selected early enough by staff as being capable enough to "deserve" the special attention necessary to compete effectively for these greater prizes outside the school. This is the basis for competition between pupils which, I suggest, may be inimical to the development of concern and considerateness towards each other. Reallocation of significant rewards within the school is likely to soften the ferocity of this competition. The object here is to get a more balanced or pluralistic reward system in the school. Sometimes this means tempering a highly academic orientation with an appreciation of achievements of an artistic, musical, athletic, handicraft or social service kind. But in some cases the one-track emphasis may be on non-academic achievement too, as for example in the ballet school.

In so far as the one-track reward system cuts off a larger proportion of pupils from the gratifications of success compared to a broader-based one, it tends to generate in more pupils feelings of failure and a sense of insecurity, alienation from school and hostility towards school and teachers (Stinchcombe, 1964). For the school this implies greater problems of discipline; for the pupils it implies unhappiness at school and failure to develop their personal resources as they might have done in a more favourable school environment. To put this point in another way, the more restricted are the areas of achievement fostered in a school, the fewer the facets of the pupils' personalities that can be nurtured thereby. Where the emphasis is on academic learning to the exclusion of other areas which engage the imagination in such important ways, some pupils will have much uncommitted energy to invest in unofficial activities and they will have great needs to engage in expressive activities of many kinds. As a matter of probability, how many of these activities stray across the border between tolerated and delinquent behaviour will be in part a function of their number and the amount of this uncommitted energy.

Then again, there are grounds for supposing that rewards attached to moral education itself may have a useful function. In those areas of moral education which involve attainment rather than attitude (basic knowledge of the physical and social environment, social skill and the conceptual ability to analyse the problem) there can be no possible objection to directly rewarding attainment in these areas. In relation to the attitude dimension, that of concern for others, we must clearly define the functions of rewards.

In the early learning of concern for others some direct reward is commonly present. This may be the gratitude of the person being helped, the perception by the empathic helper of suffering being alleviated (as in intrinsic reward), as well as the approval of the parent or teacher who learns of this behaviour. Students of animal behaviour have reported that altruism seems to characterise the behaviour of most species among themselves and therefore presumably has an instinctual basis. Among humans, however, social experience plays a powerful part in modifying instinctual drives. The altruistic drive tends to be rewarded and reinforced through social interaction whereas the instinctual drive of aggression is punished and tends to be repressed (Wright, 1971,

Ch. 6). As a result of consistent rewarding a behaviour pattern may acquire a "functional autonomy" of its own. That is, it persists in spite of the lack of continued reward, perhaps because it becomes a habit, part of the self-concept of the person or for some other reason. Those behaviour patterns (such as aggression) which are negatively sanctioned tend to become associated with guilt or shame and thereby controlled to some extent.

The school report is an important part of a school's reward system. In theory it is not a reward *per se* but an assessment of pupils. It seems appropriate to treat it as part of the reward system, though, since it is in itself a measure and expression of teacher's pleasure and displeasure; parents frequently use it as a basis for allotting rewards of their own; and within the school certain formal rewards may be contingent upon the reports, such as prizes, privileges, house points, seating in class and so forth. To both teachers and pupils the school report form, by implication at least, defines the areas of attainment and behaviour which are apparently considered important. Where schools issue blank report forms on which ninety per cent of the assessments required refer to pupils' academic performance, this will inevitably suggest to both pupils and teachers that this is ninety per cent of their job. (They may, of course, have ample reasons for wishing to define their roles in this way anyhow.) Other things being equal, it would seem likely to increase the effectiveness of the school at moral education to replace such report forms with others which include assessment by the teacher of each pupil on qualities included in our definition of the morally educated person, such as "ability to see other people's point of view", "considerateness of other people's interests", "ability to get on with other people", "competence in discussion", and so forth.

Schools vary in the kind of authority structure which they present to pupils. Along one dimension of variation there are schools which present a highly personalised authority structure and those which present a more impersonal and positional one. We have suggested in earlier discussions that this is likely to correlate with the prevalence of wide and narrow teacher-pupil relationships in the school, which in turn will be related to factors of formal structure such as the degree of specialisation among teachers. The ability to think in terms of moral principles of a general and universalistic kind is likely, I believe, to depend on the pupils being introduced, with appropriate gradualness, to a positional authority structure.

Within school authority structures of the positional kind we may further distinguish between those which are based upon ritual and tradition and those which are relatively rationalised. Schools which are highly ritualised are likely to have rules which are relatively implicit and which are justified by authoritarian or traditionalistic reasons, I hypothesise. Schools with a relatively rationalised system of authority will have rules that are more explicitly stated, relatively highly consistent among themselves and which are justified in terms of utilitarian considerations. Compared to the ritualised and traditional authority system, justifications are more often freely offered in the rationalised authority system. They will most often be based on an attempt to show how the rule is necessitated by one or more of the generally agreed values of the system, such as preventing injuries, teaching "good manners", getting pupils to pass their exams, making a viable administration and so forth.

Rules within a rationalised authority system thus are based upon these justifications or reasons in a way different from the situation in the traditionalistic and ritualised authority system. They appeal to alleged common goals and to alleged instrumental relationships between certain means (including these rules) and those goals. Thus they are (in theory) open to discussion, dispute and possibly refutation in their own terms. This is not possible within the ideology of the traditionalistic system, which rests its claims on the absolute right of those in a position of authority to impose the rules which accord with the tradition or (in the more authoritarian) which seem to them good and proper. A school council may be seen as a logical outgrowth of the rationalised authority system but inconsistent with the framework of the other one. The authorities in a rationalised authority system may or may not allow for democratic participation in the formulation of rules and decisions. This is a separate issue and is not a part of our definition *per se*. However, it is significant and noteworthy that, in propounding rules within a rationalised system and explaining the reasons behind them the authorities are, in effect, giving the rank and file members (in this case, the pupils) the opportunity to take the role of the authorities (mentally) and to understand why they deem it necessary to impose such a rule. In addition to the learning effect of being exposed to these concepts, there is the role-taking effect, expanding their moral judgement horizons through looking at things from another point of view.

The conception of the morally-educated person which is the basis of our present analysis is clearly a rationalistic one, in the sense just defined. That is, it presents a model of a person who is able to challenge an action contemplated, a rule, command or suggestion and examine its implications in terms of how it affects the interests of other people. He will not do this all the time, but will be alert for situations in which he is about to do things (or is asked to do things) which look as though they may violate the interests of other people. The child who has experienced only authority patterns of the traditionalistic or personal kinds is likely to be quite unable to think for himself in this way. He has been trained to obey those in authority without question; to regard any order given by them or rule made by them as being automatically legitimate provided it did not fall outside the traditional scope of authority. This kind of training seems commonly to characterise the early years of socialisation, since the child appears to be capable of no more than this for some time. Moral education clearly requires a transition from such authority patterns to those of a more rational kind before the conclusion of formal education.

Direct attempts to teach "moral education" may have a useful part to play. Since, however, our concept of moral education is a multi-dimensional one, it is less useful to think of a weekly "moral education" lesson than to think of contributions to moral education coming from a number of existing timetable subjects. In so far as the actual contributions that these subjects in specific schools can make fails to take care of all of the necessary components or requirements of moral education, then some new innovation on the timetable may be desirable. But modification of an established lesson would, in principle, serve just as well.

Social studies can make an important contribution to pupils' basic knowledge of the social, political and economic environment in which they live. Kohlberg (1969) suggests that the retarded development of moral judgement he finds in children from families of lower socio-economic status may be due to their families' restricted social participation. This may be compensated to some extent, he suggests, through social studies. History and literature may include discussions of the motivation of particular characters in literature and history, seen in relation to their social situations. As a form of role-taking, this may contribute to sensitivity, especially to other people from backgrounds unlike one's own. Literature, history and religious education may all involve discussions of the morality of the way certain people behaved in certain situations which have been studied. This can contribute to pupils' ability to analyse and think abstractly about moral issues and to see how different moral principles are involved. Any direct teaching of philosophy or logic might contribute in the same way. The teaching of drama, involving actual role-playing by pupils in the classroom or on the stage, is likely to improve their insight into other peoples' viewpoints. Formal discussions and debates in the classroom under a teacher's guidance may teach pupils not only communication skills and the conventional rules of debate and discussion, but the need to conform to some such conventions in order that all should have a fair hearing. Social skills may be taught directly through dancing classes, etiquette instruction (often an important subsidiary part of domestic science lessons).

These are only a few of the many ways in which moral education draws upon the direct teaching which proceeds in the school under so many different titles. There is in principle no reason why there should not be a "moral education" lesson on the timetable, except in so far as this would tend to mislead teachers into thinking that no other efforts were required outside of this lesson. This is a real danger and perhaps therefore a reason against such lessons. Such a lesson would have to cover an unusually broad array of topics (all those contained in our model of the MEP) and would require a team of teachers in all probability. It is of the greatest importance to emphasise that moral education is *not mainly* a matter of direct teaching, nor in so far as direct teaching has an important part to play can this be regarded as a *single* discipline parallel to others on the timetable such as English, science or maths.

The last factor in the school's formal organisation to be considered here for its possible contribution to moral education is the *boundary* between the school and the outside world from the viewpoint of the pupils. Here we are interested in the degree to which the school prevents its pupils from participating in the range of social experiences that is normal for people of their age in their society outside of school. At one extreme is the maximum security reformatory, followed closely by the boarding school in remote rural parts; in the broad middle group are the urban boarding school and the urban part-day part-boarding school; while at the other extreme stands the urban day school.

The moral education of youngsters may benefit in some ways from the experience of living in a very isolated boarding school. This applies not only to pupils from "bad homes", but equally to those from perfectly "good homes" too. The proposition is that when people live in an isolated group that is to a high degree self-sufficient they learn very effectively that what they do has direct and important consequences for the welfare of other members of the group. They learn that each depends for his comfort, safety and survival on the others and that offending one's companions has quick and unpleasant consequences, while cooperating with them in a successful job can create good feelings all round. Where one is confined to the company of one group, with very little opportunity to escape their attention, let alone to find solace in alternative company, the pressures to conform to the common norms of the group are strong and effective. Examples where this approach has been used with these kinds of intentions range from the short-term camps run by schools, the Boy Scouts and other organisations, through the short but more rigorous Outward Bound courses, to the Borstals, independent boarding schools and experimental residential programmes designed to rehabilitate delinquents. (Concerning the latter see the work of Homer Lane [Wills, 1964], A. S. Makarenko [1930] and August Aichorn [1935], also the therapeutic communities for drug addicts discussed in the next chapter.)

In such groups it may be hypothesised that pupils learn an increased respect for each other, greater skill in judging each others' feelings and greater facility in role-playing. The important question is whether these gains can be generalised beyond the small group of pupils who actually live together. Some account must be taken of the approach of the staff running this isolated boarding school. They may run it in an easy-going, holiday camp fashion or in a highly regimented fashion as a "total institution" (Goffman, 1961); they may set up an authority structure embodying personal authority, traditional-ritual authority or rationalised authority.

Only the last type of school would be doing moral education in the fullest sense of our present definition. The others might be included too, however, if they were only transitional phases in the schooling process, making an important contribution to some of the components of moral education, such as concern for others in the small group, sensitivity and other social skills within this small group. The hypothesis is that in the *middle* phases of schooling an isolated boarding school (*provided* that it is not run in a highly authoritarian fashion) will tend to attain higher *eventual* levels of moral education than will less isolated schools. Each one of the terms in that statement (especially those italicised) is crucial.

In the later phases of education, the requirements of moral education are quite different. At that time it is necessary to have a fair degree of integration between school and community. After all, the test of moral education lies in how people behave when let loose into the outside world and I would hypothesise that, other things being equal, young people stepping straight from an isolated school into the outside world will tend to behave less morally than those who have started to enter into these extra-school social relationships while still under the guidance of moral educators in school. Morally-educated conduct depends upon accurate knowledge of environmental conditions, sensitivity and social skill in dealing with the kinds of social relationships in which one is involved and an attitude of concern for people of all kinds—not just a narrow in-group. It is hard to see how someone coming from an isolated school can possess high levels of this knowledge or these skills, since they lack experience or practice in them.

In speaking of "isolation" of the school from the outside society, we are not just referring to geographical distance but to the whole complex matter of boundary maintenance between the school and outside society. Geographical isolation for residential schools does facilitate the maintenance of rigid boundaries between school and outside society, but this is not to say that it always implies rigid boundaries, nor that schools which are not geographically isolated from the rest of society may not in fact have rigid boundaries separating them from the outside world.

Two of the most important areas affected by school boundary are the access of pupils to the various forms of popular youth culture enjoyed by many of their contemporaries (access to radio, TV, gramophone records, comics, magazines, places of dancing, coffee bars and so forth) and pupils' access to information about and experience of the world of adult work. The monastic tradition out of which schools in Western Europe originally grew is still very much in evidence—though more so in some schools than others—not least in the assumption held by many educators that schools are by their very nature organisations whose pupil-members should be, for the duration of their attendance, cut off systematically from either contact with the youth culture or from the world of adult work. Only recently and still in a minority of schools are we becoming accustomed to the idea that the annual school musical production might be "West Side Story" instead of the perennial Gilbert and Sullivan, or that fourth- and fifth-year pupils should spend a day or two each week while at school going to work in factories, offices, or other authentic kinds of employment, or that pupils should seek out needy individuals in the outside community on whom to bestow their "social service".

The new concept that is seen here (almost endorsed by the British government report *Half Our Future*, 1963) envisions many fruitful ways of utilising the pupil's interests in the cultural world of his contemporaries and in adult work for the purposes of expanding and developing his many-sided learning. This implies partly the utilisation of the pupil's spontaneous interests in these areas but adding to his fund of knowledge about them—especially the adult work area—sometimes by sending him out on study projects or work experience, but also by bringing into the school adults with experience to share with pupils and other kinds of packaged experience in the form of films and so forth. The adults who bring this experience into the school may not only be professionals whose job is education and public relations on behalf of their industry or occupational group, but also ordinary workers who can talk about their work—ideally the parents of some of the pupils involved. Where this can be done, another part of the school-outside boundary is broken down, for a more satisfactory way is found to bring parents into the school in a less awkward and subordinate capacity than is usual and to bridge in part the gap between the generations of those who work and those who are carefully protected from the world of work—even that of their parents.

In some communities in England and Wales this integration of school and community has progressed a long way with the school serving as a focus of an integrated community life, encompassing all age levels. Cambridgeshire and Monmouthshire are two such areas where a number of these projects are found. The school runs in conjunction with a youth centre and an adult evening institute. Some of the teachers at the school also work part-time for the other two organisations. The warden of the youth centre is a half-time teacher at the school. The head of the school or his deputy is head of the evening institute. Many of the school pupils belong to the youth centre; so do ex-pupils of the school who have now left and perhaps residents of the town who attend other schools outside of the vicinity. Some of the older youth club members also attend the adult institute. All three organisations meet in the school premises, sometimes at the same times. Thus adults and teenagers are brought together more than they would be otherwise, and have a chance to develop a more sympathetic understanding of each others' interests, points of view and way of life.

So we come to the end of a complex and somewhat untidy chapter culminating in the statement of various hypotheses concerning the factors which directly affect moral development in the school. The hypotheses offered command varying degrees of support from existing research and the intuitions of experienced practitioners. What we have tried to do here is to suggest some new ideas and bring both these and many more familiar ones together within a systematic framework based on a model of the morally-educated person, an organisational model of the school and a psychological model of the developmental-learning process. This analysis is not quite finished, though, for the next chapter takes a completely different approach to some of these basic issues, concluding with its own formulation which confirms some of the basic ideas just stated, while adding important new dimensions.

CHAPTER 8 REFERENCES

August Aichorn, *Wayward Youth*, Viking Press, New York, 1935.

Gordon W. Allport, *The Nature of Prejudice*, Doubleday, Anchor, Garden City, NY, 1958.

H. H. Anderson *et al.*, *Studies of Teachers' Classroom Personalities*, 1945, 1946, cited in Brim, op. cit., 1958.

Justin Aronfreed, "The Socialization of Altruistic and Sympathetic Behavior", in J. Macaulay and L. Berkowitz (eds.), *Altruism and Helping Behavior*, Academic Press, New York, 1970.

John Bowlby, *Child Care and the Growth of Love*, Penguin, Harmondsworth, 1953.

Central Advisory Council for Education (England), *Half Our Future*, HMSO for Ministry of Education, London, 1963.

Morton Deutsch, "An Experimental Study of the Effects of Cooperation and Competition upon Group Process", *Human Relations*, II, 1949, pp. 199–231.

Robert Dreeben, "The Contribution of Schooling to the Learning of Norms", *Harvard Ed. Review*, XXXVII, Spring, 1967, pp. 211–37.

Robert Dreeben, *On What is Learned in School*, Addison Wesley, Reading, Mass., 1968.

Erving Goffman, *Asylums*, Doubleday, New York, 1961.

David H. Hargreaves, *Social Relations in a Secondary School*, Routledge and Kegan Paul, London, 1967.

Dennis L. Krebs, "Altruism—An Examination of the Concept and a Review of the Literature", *Psych. Bulletin.*, LXXIII, 1970, pp. 258–302.

Lawrence Kohlberg, "Stage and Sequence: The Cognitive-Developmental Approach to Socialization", in David A. Goslin (ed.), *Handbook of Socialization: Theory and Research*, Rand McNally, Chicago, 1969.

A. S. Makarenko, *The Road to Life*, Foreign Language Publishing House, Moscow, 1930.

G. H. Mead, *Mind, Self and Society*, Univ. of Chicago Press, Chicago, 1934.

Talcott Parsons, "The School Class as a Social System: Some of the Functions in American Society", in A. H. Halsey *et al.* (eds.), *Education, Economy and Society*, Free Press, New York, 1961, pp. 434–55.

Jean Piaget, *The Moral Judgment of the Child*, Routledge and Kegan Paul, London, 1932.

Arthur L. Stinchcombe, *Rebellion in a High School*, Quadrangle Books, Chicago, 1964.

J. G. Thorpe, "An Investigation into Some Correlates of Sociometric Status Within School Classes", *Sociometry*, XVII, Feb., 1955, pp. 49–61.

Elliott Turiel, "An Experimental Test of the Sequentiality of Developmental Stages in the Child's Moral Judgment", *J. Personality and Soc. Psych.*, III, 1966, pp. 611–18.

Edith B. Warr, *Social Experience in the Junior School*, Methuen, London, 1951.

W. David Wills, *Homer Lane: A Biography*, Allen and Unwin, London, 1964.

John Wilson, N. Williams, and B. Sugarman, *Introduction to Moral Education*, Penguin, Harmondsworth, 1967.

Derek Wright, *The Psychology of Moral Behaviour*, Penguin, Harmondsworth, 1971.

Chapter Nine

TYPES OF SCHOOLS AND LEARNING SITUATIONS

When, in the last chapter, we examined teacher-pupil relationships and their implications for moral education, we concluded that *both* the wide and narrow versions of that relationship were necessary to moral education, each contributing in different ways towards developing the various characteristics of the MEP. We argued that the wide teacher-pupil relationship is necessary for developing basic concern for others, while the narrow relationship is necessary to develop universalism in moral thinking and the toughness of character to act accordingly. In the present chapter we approach the question on a broader front, asking this time: What kind of school is most propitious for moral education? Obviously, a major element in the school is the kind of teaching which takes place there but there are other features of the school on other levels of analysis which may be considered. In this chapter then we examine other features of the school, again concluding that what moral education requires is a *combination* of two factors which appear at first glance to be opposites.

The recurrence of this duality is no mere coincidence, for it corresponds to a duality in the nature of the morally-educated person, as defined here. The MEP, we have said, is both capable of responding to other people as individuals, feeling concern for them, and also capable of holding this kind of response in abeyance when it is necessary—that is when the interests of the many absent and voiceless ones outweigh those of the one who presents himself in person. The duality in other words, is one of particularism balanced against universalism. This is the special anguish of the MEP. It is not enough to be a spontaneously compassionate person. Nor is it enough to be an emotionless "human computer" making judgements of pure universalistic justice. He must be capable of both; he must know when to give one pre-eminence of expression and when the other; and he must have the strength to do this.

TYPES OF SCHOOLS

This analysis has been a complex one. Our level of analysis has been both that of classroom interaction and that of the school as a whole; we have looked at things sometimes through the eyes of the participants, whether they be pupils, teachers or heads, and sometimes we have used the vantage-point of the outside observer with his pretence at omniscience; we have tried to view the school not just in terms of its formal structure, but also in terms of the way that a structure of relationships is created and renewed through formal and informal mechanisms working together; we have also examined the ways in which those who participate in the school (especially pupils) are changed as a result of their involvement. In the last connection our interest in learning covered a wide range of different kinds of learning and so added several more dimensions of complexity to the discussion.

There are, of course, ways to avoid such great complexity, but they all entail a stiff price. One may look at the school as a social organisation and at the psychology of learning in two separate and unrelated studies but in the end they will say nothing about learning as it takes place in the actual situation of classroom and school and how variations in the structure of the situation affect the learning process. One may select a single aspect of learning and analyse the ways in which this takes place in school situations that vary in different ways.

Another procedure is to simplify the analysis by restricting discussion to a small number of *types* of school—perhaps only two. This contrasts with the procedure we have followed in this book of defining a number of variables pertinent to the social structure of the school, to suggest what constraints they place on each other and what implications each has for learning outputs.

An especially interesting application of the second kind of typological analysis is that of the "open school" versus "closed school" put forward by Basil Bernstein (1967). He presents a twofold typology, delineating two types of school which he contrasts on a large number of variables. Whatever factors they may have in common are ignored and only those which differentiate them from each other are discussed. It is fairly clear that he is discussing extreme types. No actual school is likely to fit all his criteria for either the closed or the open school but that is not important.

What matters is that the typology should sensitise one to important aspects of schools and their functioning. Bernstein does not specify any age level or other characteristics that would delimit the kinds of schools which he is talking about. We have to assume therefore that he means his analysis to apply generally.

The *outputs* of the closed and open school are clearly different in kind, both in the cognitive and moral areas. The closed school tends to promote the notion of "one right way" in both cognitive and moral areas of learning. In the cognitive area the closed school aims to teach answers, while the open school aims to teach an understanding of general principles and methods of problem solving. This difference may be defined as one of surface structure versus deep structure in terms of linguistic theory; or in terms of concreteness versus abstraction, or tradition versus a rational orientation. In the area of moral learning the closed school aims to cultivate an acceptance of norms without question or thought, the main purpose being to produce a societal basis of common values and loyalty, while the open school aims to produce in children the habit of challenging moral judgements and the ability to discuss them rationally so that they are able to give reasons for the moral values which they hold and the norms which they accept. While the open school does not lay such heavy emphasis on producing children who all accept the same common values, it does aim to cultivate in its "graduates" the ability to work with those who hold different outlooks.

Different *pedagogical styles* are required to produce the different kinds of output and also implied is a dependence on different *learning processes*. The closed school makes heavy use of the teaching methods of formal exercises or drill, conditioning and preaching. The open school emphasises discovery and exploration methods and discussion.

The methods of *social control* typically used by teachers in the two kinds of school again differ significantly. In the closed school there is a heavy dependence on routinisation, the ritualisation of teacher-pupil relationships and a dependence on the positional definition of teacher's authority. The open school depends heavily on the personal approach to teacher's authority. There are typically different requirements for pupil *intake* into the closed and open school. The closed school requires a fairly homogeneous intake though not necessarily one in which the pupils have been very thoroughly pre-socialised. The open school, because of its lesser dependence on traditional methods of discipline does require that its pupils should have been fairly well socialised before intake.

Different approaches to the *formal organisation* of academic learning also characterise the two types of school. The allocation of pupils to teaching groups is stable in the closed school but fluid in the open school; grouping of pupils is "homogeneous" in the closed school but heterogeneous in the open school; divisions between timetabled subjects are sharp in the closed school where subjects are clearly separated from each other, while these boundaries between subjects are minimised in the open school where projects try deliberately to cut across traditional subjects and to integrate the different areas of work in terms of overarching themes or concepts.

Boundaries between the school and outside society are maintained rigidly in the case of closed schools with minimal crossing, the general exclusion of parents (except at formalised times for visiting) and exclusion of pupils' private interests and amusements. The open school by contrast allows more crossing of the boundary and attempts to utilise a variety of outside resources for learning purposes within the school.

Recent developments in the educational system have mostly taken the form of a shift towards the open school—certainly at the primary school level and to some extent at the secondary level too, mainly among those schools or those parts of schools catering for the less academically successful pupils, with the exception of science teaching where "Nuffield science" has made a considerable impact right across the ability range.

Bernstein further suggests that these two types of schools are suited respectively to two kinds of social structure in the larger society. The closed school is suited to the more traditional kind of society which depends for its social integration on common sentiments and values among its members. The more modern, complex and heterogeneous society depends on having citizens who are flexible and tolerant enough to be able to cope with a wide variety of situations, to work with others whose attitudes and values are different from their own. It therefore calls for more open schools.

One difficulty with two-fold typologies such as this is that they tend to assume or imply that the characteristics of Type A school must always be the inverse of Type B school. That is, for example, that if a certain method is used in Type A school and is important to its functioning then it will not be used in Type B. In fact it is more often the case that there is overlap and the distinction is not that A uses it and B does not but that A uses the method as its main one and B uses it as a sub-ordinate one.

A further difficulty with the Bernstein analysis concerns his hypothesis about the fit or functional compatibility between each type of society. It seems plausible when one thinks of the products of the old-fashioned ("closed") secondary school being fed into society as clerks and other kinds of low-ranking functionaries in rigid bureaucratic organisations; the changes in methods of discipline and instruction associated with the change to "open" schools seem likely to turn out pupils who are more flexible and self-disciplined, and hence better adapted to the conditions of life and work in modern society.

The main difficulty centres around the outlook of universalism and how it is learned in school. Parsons and Dreeben, as we noted in the last chapter, have argued that this is a basic necessity for the adult who is to be effective in modern society and that among the main features of the school which contribute to developing those orientations are the very formality of the social structure of the school, the plurality of teachers to whom pupils are exposed and the impersonality of the teacher-pupil relationship. These factors contribute, allegedly, to a positional view of authority which is part of the orientation of universalism. Bernstein seems to agree with this hypothesised connection between structure of school and values of pupils and he places these attributes in the closed school rather than the open one. This would seem to create a problem in the open school with its personal teacher-pupil relationships as to how he thinks universalism is to be learned by pupils. And yet Bernstein has suggested that the open school is better fitted to the requirements of modern society. In this important respect it would seem that it is not—at least as he defines it, it is not.

The resolution of this difficulty lies, I believe, in a different approach to the use of typology. Let us, instead of a typology of *schools*, use a typology of *learning situations* within schools. We are not then restricted to a forced choice between only two types of school in deciding which is more effective at moral education.

Bernstein's two types of school are each homogeneous, consisting exclusively of one or the other type of learning situation. He knows as well as anyone that in practice schools are more complex than this and comprise a variety of learning situations. He is, however, suggesting that for the purposes of discussion one can afford to simplify the situation and consider only two pure types of school. I am suggesting that this is not so; that, from the point of view of moral education, it is one of the mixed types of school, containing both open and closed learning situations which provides the optimum educational conditions for moral education. I further believe that for purposes of analysing the working of actual schools the simple two-fold typology of schools is quite inadequate and that the crucial distinctions that need to be made can only be made with a more sophisticated approach using a typology of learning situations.

Briefly stated our hypothesis is as follows. Since our definition of the morally-educated person is a multi-factor one, it is totally unlikely that any *one* type of learning situation will contain all the basic requirements for developing all of the varied components of the morally-educated person. These half-dozen components can broadly be viewed as falling into two kinds: "tender" qualities such as concern for others and sensitivity to their feelings and "tough" qualities, principally moral resolution or the ability to carry through good intentions even when difficult, especially when they involve the application of universalistic rules. This tough-tender dichotomy does not, of course, exhaust the components of the morally-educated person, but it should serve to make the point regarding the need for more than one kind of learning situation. By presenting it in this way we are understating rather than exaggerating the point. As we have argued earlier, the wide or personal teacher-pupil relationship is mainly necessary for development of the tender aspects of the MEP and the narrow or task-oriented teacher-pupil relationship is mainly necessary for development of the tough aspects. Thus these two kinds of teacher-pupil relationships represent—at least for a first approximation—two different kinds of learning situation.

TYPES OF LEARNING SITUATIONS

This open-closed distinction can be applied to two kinds of situations. A task-oriented situation in the school is defined as one in which the main priority is that a task has to be accomplished and in which the satisfactions and annoyances of the personal relationships among pupils and between them and teachers are supposed to be subordinated to the task-oriented efforts. Examples would be French, maths or woodwork lessons, athletics training and working on the preparations for a school function. Non-task situations are those where any gain in academic learning or other concrete achievement is incidental and not the main purpose of the activity. Such situations include purely recreational activities (usually informal), school rituals imposed by the teaching staff, other activities which serve or are intended to serve to strengthen social relationships among those taking part as their prime outcome and those which involve the participants in discussing and exploring their human relationships with each other and others and so learning more about themselves.

We choose the label "task-oriented learning situation" despite its clumsiness, for precise and important reasons. In the first place, we are interested in forms of learning on different levels and through various different means, of which formal academic lessons are only one. Hence we use the term "learning situation". This can be anything from a formal lesson to a brief exchange between teacher and pupil in a corridor, or a work assignment such as painting a room, in the course of which something is learned about painting, working with others, the satisfaction of doing a good job and seeing the results, and so forth. In short, any recurring situation from which people learn something qualifies as a learning situation.

In the second place, we wish to distinguish between learning situations which are structured by the requirements of a task or definite objective to be accomplished—whether it be one of formal learning or other work—and those which have no such basis. The latter include such situations as formal school rituals, informal play among pupils or discussions. Although a debate might be considered a task-oriented situation in so far as the task is to come to a decision on a pre-determined question, a discussion has a very different structure.

The feature common to all task-oriented situations—and which defines them—is that they can be seen as having an objective and all activities can be assessed in terms of how far they contribute to it. Where there is no such task or objective the activities can only be seen in terms of how they affirm and develop the relationships among those who participate. This, of course, is *one* aspect of task-oriented situations but it is the *major* aspect of non-task situations.

It should be remembered that the non-task situation is defined residually and covers a wide variety of situations. It should also be noted that very many situations in practice are a mixture. For this discussion we are concerned only with situations where there is a fairly clear predominance of one orientation or another. And we shall for now ignore the subsidiary aspect of the situation. In discussing task-oriented situations we shall ignore the fact that participants are also engaging in rituals that reinforce their relative status and so forth. Equally, in discussing situations that are mainly non-task-oriented we shall ignore any incidental instrumental gains.

Among task-oriented situations a distinction is to be made between situations in which the desired end results alone are specified, with pupils free (within broad limits) to find the most effective means they can ("open" situations) and those in which the methods are specified and prescribed in detail as well as the ends ("closed" situations). Where the task in question is one of formal academic or cognitive learning the distinction broadly becomes one between rote learning and working through standard exercises (closed) *versus* discovery methods (open). In general the closed task situation is one where the supervisor or teacher is liable to prescribe how the job must be done. He may sometimes overrule a more rational method suggested by the pupil and use the sanctions at his disposal to enforce his decision.

In non-task situations the distinction becomes one between (1) situations involving relatively routinised social relationships (closed situations such as school assembly and pupils' traditional playground games) in which interaction is highly determined by social position and (2) situations involving more personal and less determinate relationships (open) in which the participants are "getting to know each other". Midway between these extremes we find the specially important case of guided discussion groups on human relations problems. These distinctions between the open and closed versions of task-oriented and non-task oriented situations in the school can be shown in tabular form, as in Figure Two.

Fig. 2 Types of Learning Situations

TASK-ORIENTED SITUATIONS		NON-TASK SITUATIONS	
Closed	*Open*	*Closed*	*Open*
Goals and means specified. Many sanctions. Teacher as boss. e.g. drills and exercises.	Goals and broad limits to means specified. Fewer sanctions. Teacher as adviser and resource person. e.g. discovery methods.	Routinised, predictable patterns based on social positions within structure of school. e.g. assembly.	a) *partly* Guided discussions on problems in human relations. b) *fully* Person-oriented, getting to know each other and themselves. e.g. encounter group.

It should be possible to associate certain kinds of learning outcomes with each of the four types of learning situation. In the present state of our knowledge these suggestions or hypotheses can only be speculative but in principle they are all testable.

Closed, task-oriented learning situations may be exemplified by the traditional maths lesson with set examples to be worked through and solved. Non-task situations of the closed kind are mostly episodic and fleeting. School assembly is the longest in duration, the most common and the clearest example of this type. Assembly is clearly not task-oriented but is an exercise to demonstrate something about the social structure of the school as a whole—or "the school as a community" in official rhetoric. It is classified as closed because of the extreme formality and routinisation, because of how similar the basic pattern is from one occasion to another and how tightly constrained by social position is the behaviour of participants. Other closed non-task situations are mostly episodic and comprise mainly what we have earlier called the routines and rituals that establish and maintain the teacher's authority. It is the essence of closed non-task situations that they celebrate status and power differences between pupils and teachers.

What seems to be learned from continued participation in situations of these two kinds? On the whole task-oriented and non-task situations of the closed kind seem to foster very similar outcomes, so we shall discuss them together for the most part.

Closed situations are claimed to teach "discipline", an attitude in which doing as you are told by those in positions of formal authority comes naturally and also a toughness of character which is necessary to the MEP when (as often) it is hard for him to live up to his moral principles. Such situations also appear to have another effect which is more often mentioned by critics: that is to build up in the minds of those whose whole life-experience consists of situations of this kind a world-view in which the solution to specific problems always takes the form of following a set of clear-cut directions which automatically lead to success. Some of these neat problem solutions are assumed by this kind of person to be known to all "right-thinking men" (for example, the alleged efficacy of hard punishment to reduce the incidence of crime); others are only known to "the authorities" and when a problem arises in this more difficult area one can only seek out an authority and do as he says. Disagreements among authorities are most upsetting to this kind of person, for they undermine a basic part of his world-view. Such people have been described in various ways: as "dogmatists" (Rokeach, 1960), "traditionals" (Lerner, 1958), and "concrete" as opposed to "abstract" in their cognitive organisation (Harvey *et al.*, 1961). The world as they see it consists of a few certainties in the midst of great confusion and naturally they cling tenaciously to those certainties.

The kind of learning situation and the kind of personality that we are describing are both obviously much simplified and somewhat exaggerated compared to real life. We are describing (or caricaturing) the kind of learning situation that is generally found in Borstal and approved schools, the traditional elementary schools, some old-fashioned secondary schools today, more than a few independent boarding schools and most military training establishments. Boarding schools and military schools can perhaps claim some success in instilling this "discipline" into their charges, given the selective and (for the latter) voluntary intake, the preparatory socialisation in families and earlier schools of the closed type plus the fact of a working situation after graduation fairly well-matched to the closed learning situations of the schools. Borstal and approved schools generally lack all these pre-requisites for making some consistent impact on their charges and hence fail to teach them discipline or (still less) any of the effects we shall attribute to the successful open learning situations.

The effects of participation in open learning situations are varied. Open task-oriented situations tend to teach initiative, constructive thinking and responsibility, provided that the nature of what is expected is made clear and the level of expectations is appropriate. If the expectations are unclear or inappropriate all that results will be frustration and despair, a sense of failure and a feeling of resentment for those in authority who did their jobs so poorly. Especially when the task in question is one of academic learning, what is learned under favourable conditions is not just new ways of working but also ways of thinking. Rational problem-solving orientations are developed from open task-oriented situations: a logical and open-minded approach to problems in place of just repeating traditional strategies or following instructions. Also developed is the belief that one is capable of devising new solutions to problems old and new and that is a good thing to do.

Open non-task situations tend, as we have suggested in an earlier chapter, to produce effects relevant to other areas of moral education. Informal groups of people enjoying themseves together and getting to know each other better tend to become more considerate of each other. Closed situations, by definition, are rigidly structured in ways that tend to determine behaviour on the basis of social role regardless of individual differences and hence tend to prevent those participating from getting to know each other as individuals. That is why closed situations (whether task or non-task) are less prone to develop sympathetic identification between participants. That is also why in closed situations it is less difficult for participants to make universalistic judgements and act accordingly. In a situation where one sees the other participants as the faceless occupants of their roles it is easier to evaluate their work and conduct objectively, to communicate unfavourable evaluations to them and impose negative sanctions when appropriate. Similarly it is easier to reject their claims for favouritism (particularistic treatment) or suggestions of collaboration for mutual gain by defrauding a relatively anonymous collection of others (perhaps a large organisation) and to live up to the universalistic moral rule of considering the interests of all those affected by one's action as contemplated.

Now this shift from concern and consideration for one's fellow-members in a small group to concern and consideration for a much wider universe of people, most of them anonymous and unknown to one, is a vital shift from an early and important (but still primitive) phase of moral development to a later and more advanced one. Thus, although we have rejected the thoroughly closed type of school for the purposes of moral education, it is clear that the closed learning situation has a crucial part to play. It is needed for both the moral toughness it tends to develop and for the pattern of universalism. The "discipline" cultivated in closed situations is a close relative of the moral toughness required by the MEP. However, he needs to deploy this quality in a much more discriminating and rational way than the typical product of a completely closed education. In both cases, that of universalism and that of discipline, the problem is: *how the closed learning situations conducive to learning universalism and moral toughness can be integrated with the open learning situations essential for learning rational thinking and responsible attitudes*. Some light can be thrown on this difficult question by a consideration of moral education in a very different setting from the schools which have been our main basis of discussion.

THE THERAPEUTIC COMMUNITY

We may learn much that can be fruitfully applied to the analysis of the school from the therapeutic communities which have grown up in the USA, serving mainly drug addicts who wish to make a radical break with the addict's way of life. Recently two similar groups have begun operating in England. The pioneer organisation is known as "Synanon" and operates on the west coast of the USA. Various former Synanon members (ex-drug addicts who have learned to change their way of life) have left to start similar organisations. Recently started in Britain are two pioneer organisations on the same model, Phoenix House in London and Alpha House in Portsmouth.

Having lived and worked in several of these organisations and studied their workings at first hand, I can outline their main features from our present point of view. We shall take it as read that we have here a significant rate of success—far more than any comparable agency of resocialisation—and concern ourselves with the question of what sort of social organisation can make this possible. (For a summary of the success data as well as an extended analysis of the implications of this kind of therapeutic community for schools, see Sugarman, 1970.)

This kind of therapeutic community operates a full-time residential treatment programme lasting from eighteen months to two years or longer, with residents being free to come and go on their own only in the last phase of this time period. It is a strict and totalitarian structure: there are numerous rules which are strictly enforced—there are no areas of privacy—all residents work, the newest and those who are not conforming doing the most menial tasks, while more senior residents who have demonstrated some maturity occupy positions of authority. As well as the strictness of social control, though, there is a noticeable warmth between residents, an effort to show concern and friendliness for each other and a sense of common purpose in becoming mature enough to live without drugs. It is this latter side to these therapeutic communities which, tough as they are, distinguishes them sharply from military schools (see Dornbusch, 1955) or other total institutions (Goffman, 1961).

From the time when he is interviewed for possible admission, the newcomer hears it stated that *he* is personally responsible for what he has done and cannot blame it all on parents, society or other culprits. He must accept this—or at least *say* that he does. He also hears and must accept that he is addicted because he is stupid and immature—a baby in terms of emotional and character development. Therefore they will treat him like a child at first: he must obey all the many rules of the house and all the decisions of the senior members without question. He may not leave the house, write letters, make phone calls, have visitors; he must perform the tasks assigned to him which at first will be the most menial household cleaning chores.

Although the new entrant is at first treated like a child and simply told he must accept the rules without question, he will soon find that other residents explain the reasons behind the rules. These explanations are given at various times—either in formal meetings or informal conversations. This is a strict group but it is a *rationalised* authority system—not an arbitrary or traditional one. For all residents three rules are fundamental: no drugs; no physical violence; no shirking of responsibility. There is great stress on the need for pride in one's work and in doing a really good job—even though one may have no previous experience at that kind of work. All residents have some definite position within the work structure which is organised along classically bureaucratic lines at least in two separate respects. Separate departments take care of different areas of work; each department is hierarchical in structure and those who occupy positions on each level are required to obey fully and promptly the orders of those placed above them. During work time the boss is boss and must be respected and obeyed (closed situation); in the encounter group all are equal and anything may be said (open situation, to that extent). During work time the main focus of interaction among residents is task-oriented, limited in scope and impersonal. All the work done is necessary for the welfare and comfort of this group of people living together. There is no "busy work" or "occupational therapy". This means that anyone doing a poor job is making his peers suffer and he will have this brought home to him. It is essentially a very closed task-orientated situation.

It is emphasised to the newer members by the senior ones that they have only achieved changes themselves by virtue of the help they have received from fellow-members. Mutual help and concern for each other is a prime group value, constantly reiterated and embodied in many specific norms and expectations that require it to be demonstrated. From constant practice and verbalisation, the genuine feeling of concern for one's fellows—generally lacking in addicts—is nourished and grows. This is, of course, a prime component in moral education. The fact that it is also manifested by fellow-members of the group is important since it provides highly-valued gratifications in this difficult environment.

The one form of mutual concern and help that is supremely important in these therapeutic communities is in the area of sorting out one's personality problems and helping fellow-residents with theirs. Talking about these matters takes place informally at all times and also at set times in the formal context of the encounter group. These informal talks may be classified as open situations, while the encounter groups have to be considered partly open and partly closed.

Encounter groups are convened several times a week at fixed times and for special crises that may require them. Residents are assigned to groups of about ten members, who sit in a circle. One senior resident at least will be included. Hostilities and grievances may now be aired and in any verbal form whatsoever, for the taboo on bad language that applies the rest of the time is lifted for encounter groups. Those who are attacked verbally may respond in kind. After they have "got their feelings out", a searching examination of the reasons for the problem will be conducted by the group, normally leading to one or more of those present (often including the complainant) being indicted for immature behaviour which caused the problem. Forceful demands will be made for them to change their behaviour in specific ways, which they usually promise that they will do, in front of the whole group.

The encounter group is considered "open" in so far as the *content* of sessions—what is discussed, by whom, how participants respond—is highly unpredictable and determined by the personal needs of the participants. The activities of the group are oriented towards helping members to cope with their personal problems better and to know each other as persons better. The onus is basically on those who have grievances or are bothered about something to bring out their feelings about it, which will spark off other people's feelings in the group. However, the group is also "closed" in important respects, in so far as there are very strict rules which permit only one person to speak at a time, no one to move from their seat, no threats to be uttered, one person to have the floor at a time after which other group members demand a calm analysis of the issue that has been raised. For any breach of these procedural rules severe sanctions are imposed.

I believe that the success of this kind of therapeutic community is due in large part to the combination of closed learning situations (most obviously in the work area) and open learning situations (most obviously in the informal conversations which occupy so much of residents' "free time"). The encounter groups, which form a crucial part of the resocialising programme, again demonstrate this vital juxtaposition of open and closed learning situations together.

The kinds of learning that take place in this kind of therapeutic community cover several of the key dimensions of moral education: learning concern for others and an awareness of how the consequences of one's own conduct affect others (and oneself); learning greater sensitivity and other social skills in one's social interaction with fellow-members of the group; learning to apply universalistic standards impartially to others, regardless of one's personal, particularistic feelings, whether by playing authority roles or by learning (as all residents are expected to learn) to show "responsible concern" for fellow-members—that is, to do what will help them in the long run even though they do not like it at the time, for example reprimanding them for inconsiderate behaviour in such a way as to embarrass them publicly and so make them more likely to remember another time.

PHASES OF MORAL DEVELOPMENT

What we are arguing here is that the resocialising of drug addicts and delinquents in the therapeutic community has a direct relevance for moral education in the average school, inasmuch as both are social organisations through which moral education is taking place. In the average school it takes place alongside many other activities, which are generally given far more prominence and attention. Whereas moral education is the *exclusive focus* of the therapeutic community, it generally takes a poor *second* place in most schools to academic learning for formal examinations or even a *third* place behind the goals of formalised academic learning and keeping an orderly custodial institution. Because of this we can see the processes of moral education operating with much greater clarity in the therapeutic community than in the schools. In so far as we wish to look at schools, from the point of view of their contribution to moral education, this analysis of the therapeutic community is highly pertinent.

We have claimed that the provision of *both* open and closed learning situations including some situations combining both features in this kind of therapeutic community is crucial to its effectiveness in moral education and we are suggesting that the same proposition applies to schools. Neither the "open school" nor the "closed school" is the answer—even in the context of a simplified theoretical discussion. We have not yet taken account of the time factor—of the problem of phasing the two types of learning situation relative to each other—and this we must now do.

In our therapeutic community the typical resident's stay may be divided into two phases. The earlier phase is mainly a closed one, with open situations very much in second place; the later phase still has closed situations, though their presence is diminished relative to the initial phase, while open situations become far more important. To oversimplify, we could label these phases as "mainly closed" and "mainly open". Between phase one and phase two the resident finds that he is less closely supervised; he is responsible for supervising others more; instead of being told what to do and exactly how to do it, he is just told what results are wanted and left to find the best way for himself, knowing that he must face the consequences if he either bungles the job or arranges the work of his subordinates in a way that contravenes the rules or principles of the community. Phase two is obviously closer to the stage of being an autonomous adult. By the same token it is riskier than phase one and presupposes successful learning of certain things in the earlier phase—the basic principles and rules of the group, appropriate social skills, impulse control and some measure of self-confidence. Through a person's period of residence the exploration of his behaviour and personality is a continuing concern, though the emphasis in phase one is mainly on behaviour while in phase two concern with psycho-dynamics and the internalisation of basic principles becomes greater.

The process of normal child development, that which is not interrupted by serious deviant behaviour (such as drug addiction) and prolonged, full-time efforts at resocialisation, presents a rather different and more complex picture. In earliest childhood—say as a first approximation, the first year of life—the child's situation cannot very well be specified in terms of these concepts. It is one where the parents indulge and protect the child from physical hazards and virtually all social expectations. Interaction between parent and child revolves around feeding and cleaning, interspersed with very limited (and hence predictable) play activities between them. As the child's motor abilities develop and permit a greater variety of movement, a wider range of play activities becomes possible, though still within the bounds of parental-cultural stereotypes, and more precautions are needed to save the child from crawling or walking into dangers or creating them by knocking objects down on top of himself. These precautions tend to make the child's initial social situation somewhat closed: he can only use implements and objects passed by parents as being safe playthings. But, given these playthings, he can use them in almost any way desired—to this extent the situation is open. In his relationship with parents the emphasis is on creating a feeling of security, i.e. closedness. But, as we say, the "open" and "closed" categories are not well-suited to describing this stage of development.

In infant and junior schools of the old-fashioned type we find that learning situations fall mainly into the closed variety, both task-oriented situations and, with the rituals of classroom and assembly, other situations too. Within this kind of school there is a high degree of consistency between the patterns of relationship between pupil and teacher throughout the school.

In the most "progressive" kind of infant school we find task-oriented situations of a predominantly open kind. Discovery methods and projects are the means through which pupils acquire a great part of their learning. There may be some teaching in the closed fashion, with set exercises and drill to be performed, but these will be restricted to the minimum and some attempt made to make pupils appreciate the relevance of the knowledge so taught. Even in the progressive infant school there will be closed learning situations on the non-task side, in aspects of teacher-pupil relationships which in any school probably must be routinised. The larger the school, the greater the need for routine and ritual in the relationships between teachers and pupils, if teachers are to keep the upper hand.

On the move to a secondary school many things may change for the pupils. They will find themselves in a much more fluid working situation, changing their companions several times a day. This fluidity means more frequent changes of classroom in the course of the day in a large school where many others are doing the same and hence implies a considerable problem of social control, which necessitates a more *formal* system of rules and controls.

The formality in the social organisation of the secondary school will be more familiar to pupils from traditional primary schools than it is to those from progressive ones and the former will be more prepared to comply. But even to them, such a high degree of formalisation and impersonality will be strange. In some secondary schools attempts have been made to modify the official structure in an effort to bridge this gap between primary and secondary schools by ensuring that the social organisation of at least the first year of the secondary school resembles that of the primary school, with a degree of stability in the composition of working groups and the assignment of form teachers who teach their form for a significant number of lessons and have some pastoral responsibility for them. With their feet on this small island of familiar ground the new pupils have a better chance of coming to terms with the unfamiliar features of the social organisation of the school at large.

In the average secondary school task-oriented situations are considerably more closed on average than they are in the progressive primary school and marginally more or less than they are in the traditional primary school. There is considerable variation within secondary schools from one subject to another, for example from the open situation of Nuffield science methods to the closed situation of technical drawing or PE.

In most secondary schools there are some teachers who strive to create wide personal relationships with their pupils and take an interest in their moral development whether they do this in class, informally out of class, or through organised extra-curricular activities. In some schools this is the norm in the sense that many teachers do it, and it can be regarded as a significant element in the learning environment of the average pupil.

In a few schools there are attempts to organise formally open learning situations in the human relations area and incorporate them in the timetable—whether this is in the form of officially designated "human relations" lessons and discussion periods, or as part of established subjects such as English, domestic science or social studies. In these cases the aim is to encourage pupils to discuss problems that concern them, with the teacher playing the role of group leader, rather than that of preacher or someone trying to sell a preconceived answer (Glasser, 1969).

This non-directiveness is necessary to make the situation open —otherwise it is just another closed non-task situation. The overwhelming emphasis in secondary schools is on situations of the task-oriented (mainly academic) and closed type. Any change is significant, therefore, which tends to increase the extent of either open situations or non-task situations (or task situations of a non-academic nature).

We may argue, further, that such changes are not only "significant" but also likely to improve the effectiveness of moral education in the secondary school that introduces such changes. The introduction of more open situations, firstly, may be argued to represent an improvement in that a school presenting overwhelmingly closed task situations cannot gain much involvement from teenagers and so cannot influence them much. Nor can it prepare them to act morally in a world where many of the situations they will find themselves in will be open ones—and this is precisely the nature of the world we live in today, a world of change and open situations, in which traditional procedures cannot be depended upon for ever and hence new ones have to be found and applied by flexible people. Secondly, the introduction of more open non-task situations may be argued to be a step forward in so far as it means open situations for exploring human relations matters. This is something that most teenagers want to do, provided they can do it with teachers whom they trust. It is, equally, something that is necessary for the morally-educated person, who must have insight into the personalities of his fellows as well as his own and work through some of the problems or "hang-ups" that get in the way of behaving like a morally-educated person even when one wants to.

Though it would be absurdly optimistic for us to attempt to construct a precise model of the ideal phasing of open and closed learning situations for moral education in schools, our analysis does suggest certain points. It suggests that the *final phase* of schooling must contain a significant proportion of open situations; that this must nevertheless be accompanied by some clearly closed situations or by some which combine open and closed features, in the sort of way that the encounter groups in the therapeutic community do; that the earliest phase of schooling succeeds well with open task-oriented methods, even if they are accompanied by more closed non-task situations; but that some closed task-oriented situations probably should be introduced into schools from the middle years. Cautiously, we might suggest on the basis of these propositions and the discussion preceding them that, if we divide schooling into three phases, a distribution between open and closed situations such as that shown in Figure Three might be expected to give the best results for moral education.

We have not tackled the question of how the balance between task and non-task situations should be varied. We show them each occupying equal amounts of time in all three phases, for the sake of simplicity. This question is obviously one to be tabled for future discussion, as is the question of how many phases we need to consider.

Future research attempting to assess the effects of different kinds of school on pupils relevant to moral education cannot be considered satisfactory if it merely compares schools designated as "open" and "closed" with each other, or if it compares resocialisation programmes based on so-called "traditional" methods with others based on "progressive" methods. In the light of our present discussion, one would expect differences in some specific area of learning (though our available methods of measurement may not be capable of registering all of them) but in overall success at producing morally-educated people one would not expect very much difference, since we would expect *both* to be very ineffective. Even given the greatest dedication on the part of teachers this gloomy prophecy must stand, for we believe that even the most dedicated efforts of individuals are doomed to be robbed of full success unless they can be exerted in a favourable environment. And in moral education it seems very clear that this necessary environment is defined by a certain combination of at least two major factors at each of several phases of the pupil's career in school.

Fig. 3 Hypothesised balance of open/closed situations for most effective moral education

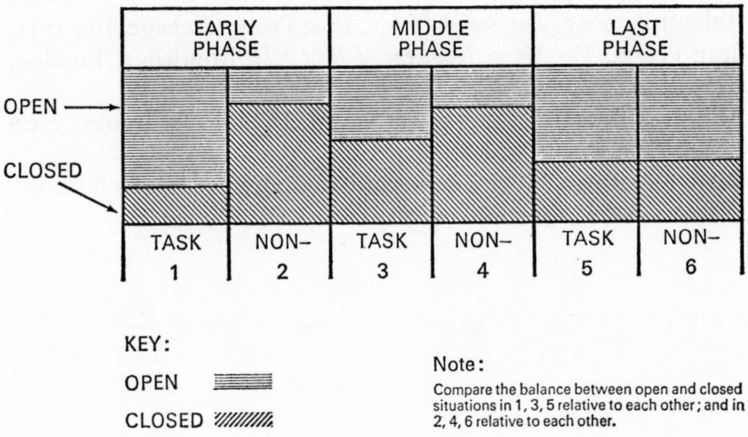

EARLY PHASE
MIDDLE PHASE
LAST PHASE
OPEN
CLOSED
TASK 1
NON– 2
TASK 3
NON– 4
TASK 5
NON– 6

KEY:
OPEN
CLOSED

Note:
Compare the balance between open and closed situations in 1, 3, 5 relative to each other; and in 2, 4, 6 relative to each other.

CHAPTER 9 REFERENCES

Basil Bernstein, "Open Schools, Open Society", *New Society*, September 14, 1967.

John A. Clausen, "Drug Addiction", in R. K. Merton and R. A. Nisbet (eds.), *Contemporary Social Problems*, Harcourt, Brace and World, New York, 1961.

Sanford Dornbusch, "Socialization in a Coast Guard Academy", *Social Forces*, XXXIII, May, 1955, pp. 316–21.

Robert Dreeben, *On What is Learned in School*, Addison-Wesley, Reading, Mass., 1968.

William Glasser, *Schools Without Failure*, Harper and Row, New York, 1969.

Erving Goffman, *Asylums*, Doubleday, Garden City, NY, 1961.

O. J. Harvey, D. E. Hunt and H. M. Schroder, *Conceptual Systems and Personality Organization*, John Wiley, New York, 1961.

Daniel Lerner, *The Passing of Traditional Society*, Free Press, Glencoe, Ill., 1958.

Talcott Parsons, *The Social System*, Free Press, Glencoe, Ill., 1951.

Jean Piaget, *The Moral Judgment of the Child*, Routledge, London, 1932.

Milton Rokeach, *The Open and Closed Mind*, Basic Books, New York, 1960.

Barry Sugarman, "The Therapeutic Community and the School", *Interaction*, I, 1970, pp. 77–96.

Chapter Ten

CONCLUSIONS

At the end of this long and sometimes difficult analysis of the school in relation to moral development, in which we have tried to derive some clear and testable hypotheses that are integrated within a coherent approach, we must, firstly, remind ourselves of several points. We are *not* assuming that the school is the most important influence—that it accounts for more of the variance in levels of moral development than do other influences, such as mass media, peer groups, youth culture, neighbourhood, church, youth organisations, siblings and parents. On aggregate it seems likely that the school makes less difference than do parents, though possibly more than do some of the other factors just mentioned. The framework of this analysis is set by the assumptions that the school plays *some* significant part in the process of moral development or moral education and that it is possible to identify some of the features of the school which specifically contribute to this process.

Now, if some variations in a school can make it more effective, it follows that the inverse can make it *less* effective. And if some schools can make a net positive contribution to moral development, others can have a net negative effect—either on specific aspects of moral development, or even on all of them. In our analysis of structural variations, suggesting consequences, we always presented our hypotheses in terms of "more effective" and "less effective". At some stage, of course, "less effective" crosses the zero point and becomes "detrimental". So, although we have mostly tended to look on the bright side, focusing on features of schools that seem likely to contribute to moral education, there is no escaping the fact that many schools in actual fact are harming their pupils from a moral development standpoint and undoubtedly in other ways too.

At any period of time, I assume, the range of variation actually found in schools is only a fraction of the possible range. If we can assume that variation on some of these features is important for moral education, then what we are saying is that schools could be organised so as to be more effective in moral education. The introduction of such changes would simultaneously mean that the range of variation among schools would increase and that the proportion of the variance in moral development for which the school can account also increases. In short, whatever the importance of the school for moral education right now, this is no measure of its potential importance.

Research on schools in operation now can only measure the difference between these schools overall or between particular segments of them and the measured effects they have on pupils. When we can demonstrate what are some of the specific features which are conducive to moral education and then build them into schools in much stronger forms than they are presently found, we may hope to raise the effectiveness of the schools and their relative importance in the whole process of moral development. Until then our position is the modest one that schools make *some* difference; that the precise sources of these effects need to be located and that the first stage in this business consists of formulating testable hypotheses tied into a limited body of theoretical assumptions. This has been our aim in the preceding chapters.

POLARITIES IN THE EDUCATIONAL SYSTEM

Through two independent lines of argument, we have come to a similar and most important conclusion. The conclusion is that the key to moral education lies in no single factor but in a balance between *two* major factors which are not only radically different but *opposite* in their characteristics. In the first argument we labelled the two factors as the "wide" teacher-pupil relationship and the "narrow" one; in the second argument we called them "open" and "closed" learning situations.

Yet this is not some dialectical process of opposites interacting to yield a product unlike either. The process of causation is more straightforward than this. What makes it complex is that the product in which we are interested—the morally-educated person (MEP)—is comprised of some six components (concern for others, social skills, universalistic thinking, etc.) each with its own prerequisites and each of these sets of prerequisites comprises several factors, some of which are very different from each other.

For an example of how *two* components of the MEP have contrasting requirements, we may recall that the development of a basic concern for other people requires a wide and intimate relationship, while the development of moral "character" or toughness requires narrow and more remote relationships (often of a task-oriented character).

For an example of how *one* component of the MEP may have multiple prerequisites, of which two are contrasting in nature, we may take the example of learning control over impulses, which requires two factors in the home: love-oriented methods *and* consistent rules. Neither factor alone is any use: love without consistent rules tends to produce children who are either spoiled or confused or both; rules without love produce children who obey only when they are watched.

Then again, learning to think and act in universalistic modes would seem to require ideally more than just narrow teacher-pupil relationships—though these are the major *single* requirement here. The ideal combination, I suggest, involves *both* narrow and wide aspects together. The most effective way of teaching children to think and behave in terms of universalistic standards is probably not by means of a socialising agent who behaves like the stereotype "narrow" teacher but by means of one who has established a relationship with the child which is, at least in part, highly personal. When the child sees that this person who patently likes and cares about him nevertheless gives him a low mark for a bad performance on a test, a punishment for his bad behaviour or fails to choose him for his football team because there are better players available, then he is likely to understand the seriousness of the universalistic principles of fairness and merit. If they are important enough to require a particularistic loyalty which is valued by both parties to be set aside, then they are truly important. This measure of the importance of universalistic rules and principles does not operate where there is a purely narrow and impersonal relationship. This hypothesis is supported most strongly by our therapeutic community analysis.

In both these cases (learning impulse control and learning universalism) we see a similar process of causation, one that resembles the operation of a pair of scissors. When the two blades work together as scissors they cut; but when the blades are separated, each by itself is useless.

This picture of moral education in terms of polarities may be oversimplified in some respects but it is very necessary to emphasise the polarity picture since prevailing conceptions about moral education all assume that some *single* factor is the key. They differ as to whether that key factor is "discipline", "love", "security", "freedom", or whatever but they agree on one point—that one factor represents, not the whole story, but the key. And here we disagree. On the same level of oversimplification, we say that the key to moral education lies in combinations of contrasting factors —open and closed learning situations, wide and narrow teacher-pupil relationships, and (in the home) love-oriented controls and moderate, consistent restrictiveness.

To go beyond this level of radical simplification and return to the kind of analysis which we have followed throughout this book, this picture of polarities must be set in the context of five major components of the morally educated person, each with its prerequisites in terms of certain kinds of relationships with parents, early friends, teachers, and peers in school and certain kinds of school structure. This last factor (the school) is relevant to our problem in two major ways: firstly, as a constraining context, affecting teacher-pupil and pupil-pupil relationships and affecting the probability that they will take one form rather than another and, secondly, as a direct influence on pupils through such aspects of its structure as the nature of its rules, sanctions and reward systems.

The school as a social institution occupies a bridging position between the family, where the child is treated in a wide and personal fashion, and the wider society where he will soon be treated as a worker and a citizen, that is, in a narrow and impersonal fashion. At the same time the child finds himself more often the object of universalistic evaluations on his performance and conduct; finds that he is expected to learn to apply the same evaluation standards to himself and others. Viewing modern society as one based to an unprecedented degree on universalistic standards, socialisation for adulthood has to include learning to assign priority to universalistic standards over particularistic ones in many situations. The school, we believe, plays an important part in this learning of universalism. In so far as the young do internalise the moral obligation of being "fair" and "just" they will react twice as strongly when they find they are treated unfairly in school, outside school, or in later adult life.

The situation of the child in school may be considered as a polarity between the child's needs for nurturance (originally supplied entirely by the family) and his need to equip himself for survival in the adult world. Two closely connected polarities are those between "narrow" and "wide" teachers and between the claims to authority which they make based (respectively) on "positional" and "personal" grounds. The "wide" and "personal" are linked more to the nurturance function and the "narrow" and "positional" more to the function of preparing for adult life.

A further polarity that is built into the structure of the school as we know it and which was noted in our opening chapter, is that between the ideals and norms of conduct which many heads and prominent teachers embrace—ideals of humane concern for other people and dedication to the truth—and the realities of the world in which most pupils will have to live—where occupational success often seems to require a callous disregard for the interests of others. The conflict here may also be expressed in terms of the question of whether it is the school's main function to prepare its pupils to be morally-educated people or to be successful in the world as it is. Of course, some of the qualities of the MEP are also conducive to secular success, qualities such as social skills, knowledge, impulse control and moral toughness. But the conflict arises over the characteristically moral qualities of universalism and concern for others.

RAMIFICATIONS

To the extent that schools operate as if their function is to produce morally-educated people, they will (to that extent) set in train several consequences. They will affect the relationships between children and their parents in those homes where the moral standards to which the parents adhere differ in character or in stringency from those (of the MEP) promulgated in the school. They will affect the relationship children have with their parents and teachers in that universalistic moral principles are supposed to bind the adult as well as the young. It is not common for parents and virtually unheard of for teachers to permit open criticism of their own behaviour by their children/pupils. Where they obviously use their power position to prevent evaluation of their own behaviour in terms of the supposedly universalistic principles they are teaching (even within a framework of rules that requires a respectful manner of criticism) the overt preaching is reduced to blatant hypocrisy and harm is probably done to the child's moral development. Where, however, the socialising agent, whether parent or teacher, lives up to the full meaning of the universalistic principles and permits responsible criticism of his own conduct in terms of those standards, a qualitatively different and more mature relationship will develop.

To take the extent that moral education is done effectively, there should be some cumulative net effect on society. For a start, there are now so many more people behaving in a morally-educated fashion and perhaps influencing others. We do not underestimate the inertia of social systems in tending to neutralise many sources of possible change. To some people the example of these MEPs demonstrating concern for them is welcome and induces them to act with more concern themselves. To other people, though, it is not welcome, for they do not want to become involved in closer relationships with others, so they will provide themselves with appropriate beliefs to neutralise the uncomfortable effects on themselves of this MEP's example of concerned behaviour—it is not "true" altruism . . . he will claim repayment later . . . people should keep themselves to themselves, and so forth. The MEP who occupies a position of influence or power, whether it is at work, in voluntary associations or in government, can make his influence felt far more widely than is possible just as a private individual. He can secure the adoption of policies which encourage people to help others even when it does not benefit themselves directly. These policies can encourage responsible altruistic behaviour by making it less costly to the individual (e.g. by making reward systems less competitive, by making people feel less insecure about their positions, and so forth); by providing models of altruistic behaviour with official approval and by positively rewarding such behaviour for an interim period until an autonomous motivation can take over.

Moral education is and always has been a dangerous profession, as the careers of Socrates and Jesus indicate. These two emphasised different approaches—the one featuring rationality in making decisions and the other featuring love and concern for one's fellow men—but both displayed a total commitment to their respective values. This insistence on following their principles, regardless of their unpopularity with powerful interest groups, led them to their deaths.

It seems to be a general characteristic of all societies that there is a clear gap between the ideals preached and the way people behave in everyday life, hence the moral educator becomes a serious thorn in the side of other citizens when he challenges them to change their behaviour. Ideologues who preach the ideals and values are not necessarily perceived as a threat by the citizenry. Nor even are preachers who thunder about the guilt of the congregation. The effect of either is readily neutralised by people thinking "he's right, we should behave differently—but we are what we are and cannot do better". The person who is really felt to be a threat is the one who takes the stance that people should try harder and who takes it upon himself to confront people with their shortcomings and to ask what efforts they are making to improve. This is the viewpoint and stance of the missionary—whether he wears the uniform of a church, political party or that of no organised body. This is the stance of the more advanced members of the therapeutic communities we discussed in the last chapter; it is the stance of some teachers and heads of schools—usually in a milder form.

In so far as schools and other agencies of moral education are successful, they will produce pupils who challenge the people with whom they come into contact. A proper concern for other people will sometimes necessitate challenging those who trample on the rights of their fellows (litterers, queue-jumpers, cheats, etc.); those who act in ways which are harmful to themselves (heavy smokers or drinkers, people engaging in blatant self-deception, etc.) as well as those who step on one's own toes and violate what one considers as one's own rights. As a pupil such a person may challenge his teachers, including those who do not subscribe to this view of moral education and therefore do not react at all favourably—sometimes with great hostility. As a son or daughter; as a friend; as an employee and in other roles this person will treat parents, friends, bosses, colleagues and others in a way with which they are not always familiar—a way that many of them find threatening and interpret as hostile when it is not intended this way at all.

Those who engage in moral education as defined in this book open a Pandora's box of unpredictable consequences for themselves and for others. To many these consequences are more than they bargained for and they soon panic and abandon their efforts. They are not prepared to enter into more mature relationships with their pupils or children, accepting challenges on their own conduct as well as giving them out. So they attempt to return to more traditional and authoritarian relationships in which they can hide behind positional concepts of authority and avoid person-to-person involvement.

Some of these faint-hearted pseudo-moral educators only tried this approach because of the patent failure of the traditional attempts to keep children under teachers' control. More traditional approaches have aimed to train children in conformity to adults and comprehensive inhibition of impulses. Such approaches have been relatively "successful" only with a minority of children where their homes were structured appropriately for such results and where parents also lent concurrent support to the teacher's efforts at discipline. And even in these "successful" cases the common side-effects of timidity, neurosis, and rigidity give us cause to question the wisdom of this approach.

BEING A MORALLY-EDUCATED PERSON

There is another reason, though, for preferring the definition of the MEP presented in this book and this approach to moral education. Apart from the doubtful future of the traditional approach and its high cost in terms of side-effects, there is a strong reason in terms of *principle* for trying to educate in terms of moral principles, applied by the individual for himself. It is precisely this —that the MEP decides *for himself*, applying his standards or moral principles in his *own* way. Even if he comes to the same conclusion as everyone else, he has made up his *own* mind. This we cannot say (in the same sense) of the person who is conforming to a specific rule even though he has internalised it and made it his own to that extent. The MEP is "his own man" and he feels it to a degree uncommon in modern complex society. To this extent his alienation is curbed and, despite the conflicts and the compromises that he will probably have to make in order to survive in a world full of people who cannot accept the terms of the MEP, he is likely to feel a greater sense of integrity or wholeness as an individual than most of those who operate on more primitive levels of moral development.

Romantic opponents of this view point to the fancied contentment of the "simple folk" who live apparently uncomplicated lives in the context of a long-unchanged traditional way of life—Wordsworthian shepherds, South Seas fishermen, stolid farmers and blacksmiths. But these worlds to which they appeal are fast disappearing because they cannot survive contact with larger civilisations. Only a very few groups, such as the Amish and Hutterites in the USA, have shown a capacity to survive sustained contact. There is no longer a choice. We have to live in a complex society of competing norms and loyalties, in which decisions need to be made by everyone as to which alternative he will take. In speaking of moral development we are speaking of making decisions on the basis of more complete or less complete considerations of the implications of the decisions, including as a central focus the perspectives of the other people who may be affected. Is not a more complete consideration more morally desirable? If you were one of those peripherally affected you would surely think so.

One apparent exception to the trend for simpler societies to disappear is the recent trend, small but significant, for small groups of young, upper middle-class drop-outs from US society to form communes, often in rural areas, where they live in a technologically primitive and socially "permissive" style of life. To choose such a way of life, after acquaintance with other ways is, however, very different from being born into such a society and knowing no others. In other words, it would be rash indeed to assume that these once-sophisticated drop-outs thought the same way about moral decisions as the shepherds, fishermen, farmers and blacksmiths. And even if it transpired that the drop-outs had indeed deliberately "regressed" to a less sophisticated mode of moral thinking, apparently similar to the born rustics, the big difference remains that they are voluntarily renouncing a more sophisticated outlook, which they have experienced and still have available to them, whereas the born rustics know only the simpler forms. In short the drop-out communards *choose* that way of life out of various alternatives that are open to them and hence are affirming their *individual* values and identities in a way that would not be true of the inhabitants of the simple and segregated society who know only that one society and that identity, defining it as their destiny to live that way and to be constrained to conform to the norms of that community.

Again, while the picture of the "noble savages" dealing simply and honourably with the uncomplicated moral issues thrown up in their simple society may be attractive (and may or may not be an accurate representation of what actually happens or happened in such societies), the picture of the rustic immigrant in a complex society blundering uncomprehendingly from one misfortune to the next is very unattractive. So is the similar picture of the rustic folk trying to cope with changes in their own society induced by contact with a more complex and powerful society, using the same concepts and modes of thinking which served them adequately when their society was still simple.

RESISTANCE TO CHANGE

We have occupied ourselves in this book with analysing the part played by the school in moral development and the part that *might* be played by the school if it were structured in certain ways. Earlier we have suggested that the potential contribution of the school is far greater than its actual, present contribution. Whether its full potential will ever be fulfilled is doubtful. There are three main reasons for this pessimistic conclusion. Firstly, there are all the difficulties of establishing by dependable research exactly what changes should be made. We have suggested many lines of investigation here, none of them easy to pursue. Secondly, if this knowledge should be established, it is doubtful that there would be a public mandate or even a legislative mandate to the educational profession, authorising them to implement policies designed to produce more MEPs. Kohlberg (1969) has estimated that only twenty-five per cent of adults in the USA attain his stage six of moral development, which corresponds roughly to our MEP and certainly is not a higher standard. If the general adult population is mostly at stage four on Kohlberg's scale ("doing one's duty"), this presumably is what they would want their children to be too. Whereas many of them are happy for their children to exceed their academic performance, since this is related to career success, I do not believe they would have the same attitude to moral education. But this is yet another question for research. In fact, though, there is not a very high degree of support for *any* form of moral education in secondary schools. When presented as "moral training" around fifty per cent of a national random sample in Britain ranked it as the first or second most important function for the school (National Opinion Poll, 1969).

The third difficulty is that, even given the knowledge and the permission to proceed full steam ahead with moral education, there is a tremendous inertia in the educational system resisting any major change. Comprehensivisation would be a trivial change compared to the kinds of changes that teachers might have to make in their manner of work if the revolution in moral education ever came about.

We have to consider the possibility that schools may not be the appropriate organisation to have the function of moral education anyway—nor the church, the government, the Boy Scouts, mass media, or any other institution that presently exists. What would this new institution be and how would it work? That is much too big a question to attempt to answer properly here, but one possibility is that this new institution might look *in part* like a therapeutic community. Another possibility is that it might be modelled on the "work-release" idea.

There might be an agency that assumed responsibility for all young people from the age of (say) fourteen up to school leaving age. They would assist each youngster to plan his programme of self-development, taking account of his future goals, present interests and needs as seen by the professional guidance staff. Available to them would be classroom courses, based on methods similar to the best of those seen at present. Also available would be "apprenticeship" situations in which they would work under the direct supervision of an adult worker, housewife, or retired person, who had been licensed as basically competent to take on such a responsibility and as a person of good moral character. He or she might have several young people at a time, who would assist in his or her work and enjoy a wide relationship for the duration of the apprenticeship.

Learning the work itself would not be the main function of the apprenticeship but rather it would be learning to understand a segment of the "grown-up world", to work responsibly and to begin to learn to be an adult, rather in the way that children used to when they could work alongside their own parents or as the medieval apprentice or squire in a knightly household would have done under good conditions. The length of the apprenticeship would be variable. It might be sandwiched between periods of classroom work or the two might run concurrently, part-time. One youngster might be apprenticed to several different mentors in succession or stay with one. Residential "schools" resembling our therapeutic community, though less strict, would be provided for some. Each youngster's adviser would visit him every so often to review his progress with him and with his mentor.

In order that the possibilities of learning from peers should not be lost in this scheme, youngsters could be assigned to mentors in small groups of (say) four or five initially compatible learners; local recreation centres could provide for sports, hobbies, dances, camping and other social activities. There will also be peer interaction in the classroom, where group learning methods will probably be heavily emphasised, and in the residential schools.

Teachers would need considerable retraining to serve as advisers (a role not unlike the teaching practice supervisor in some ways), recreation leaders, organisers of mentors, or even as classroom teachers in the new regime. Recruitment, evaluation, selection and orientation of members would be a vast undertaking. It would be important, for example, to make sure that they did not exploit their apprentices by using them just as menial helpers, kept at a great distance.

"It could never work," I hear many readers say scornfully. But how well does the existing system work? And, even if it is sheer fantasy, such intellectual exercises have an important part to play in helping us to understand the present situation.

THE PRESENT CRISIS

Many qualified observers have concluded that the school, especially the secondary school, is an institution which operates in such a way that many pupils learn to hate school, to expect regular punishment which they provoke out of frustration, and do not even learn to read or write with minimal competence. Meanwhile another sizeable proportion of pupils learns to fear making a mistake, to be passive, to conform to what teachers seem to want in conduct and in answering questions. In between is a group for whom school is merely a nuisance they cope with without getting into too much trouble and without learning very much of what the school aims to teach them (see Silberman, 1971; Henry, 1971;

Jackson, 1968; Hargreaves, 1967; Partridge, 1966; Central Advisory Council on Education [England]; Reimer, 1971; Waller, 1932).

The first group, who hate school, are the pupils whom teachers recognise as their failures; the second group they see as their successes but various observers have pointed out how great a side-effect the school generally has in stunting the creativity and originality of these pupils by teaching them to reproduce standard answers to set questions; by rewarding only for such responses and by refusing to entertain other questions that occur to pupils themselves. As pupils are being intellectually stultified they are simultaneously being retarded in moral development (Getzels and Jackson, 1962).

It is not hard to see how the most basic features of the school tend to make this inevitable: the crowding of thirty active youngsters into one room in the charge of just one adult; the fact that the adult is expected by his or her superiors to keep that room quiet, to keep them engaged in activities which frequently have no interest for them, and to show at some future date that they have learned certain designated skills and facts. Add to these problems the fact that the day is divided arbitrarily into time periods usually of forty minutes within which activities must repeatedly be started and stopped, so that teachers can change groups.

Under this pressure the teacher tends to routinise and ritualise the activities of the class. Some do this to the minimum degree necessary to create a framework of order for what we have called "progressive" teaching; others do this to a far greater degree, so that it pervades the entire lesson, as they struggle to maintain the shaky discipline of the "traditional" approach. The traditional teacher and the pseudo-progressives operate their classroom by the survival principle that so long as they can threaten the self-regard of pupils (by sarcasm, ridicule, "making an example of them", calling on them to answer questions they do not know, or by whatever means they do this) they can keep some degree of control.

Here lies a great paradox. The school cannot contribute in any way to moral education unless a certain level of social control is maintained. Yet the principal methods for maintaining this control, once they go beyond a very modest limit, become dysfunctional for moral education because they undermine one of the basic elements—thinking for oneself, applying universalistic concepts. Only teachers who are strongly committed to the "progressive" approach and to encouraging pupils to raise questions that are not always preprogrammed by the teacher can hope to overcome the effects of classroom routinisation, especially the passivity and stultification it creates. But there are, so far, few of these teachers; they are spread very thinly and handicapped by various other features common to school organisation.

In short, the changes that are likely to be necessary in schools so that they will stop hindering moral education—let alone increasing their positive contribution—are bound to be radical. So it is perhaps a moot point whether it may be more helpful to think in terms of reforming the school as we know it, or to think in terms of designing a basically new structure—for example, perhaps along the lines of the "apprenticeship" programme. True there are bound to be many serious problems with such a new approach but so will there be in trying to change radically the structure and functioning of the schools as we know them.

Radical change in education has to mean a radical change in the teacher's role definition, job performance and attitude. Radical changes have taken place before in British education—such changes as the Arnold reforms in independent boarding schools, the growth of progressive schools, or the changes in infant schools in England since before the Second World War. In each of these examples, though, there were special factors which facilitated change and which would probably not apply to more widespread change throughout the system. The recent changes in the infant schools were created by many teachers and teaching-heads who were uniquely child-oriented among their profession (that, presumably, is why they chose infant teaching). They were allowed to make the changes they wanted because there were no side-effects that bothered parents or administrators and because their pupils were still quite a long way from any competitive exams. As soon as the first exams at age ten loom up at the end of the junior school, a pressure develops to train and drill pupils specifically for these exams.

Well, it will be hard to make the kind of changes necessary to do a good job of moral education but if it can happen anywhere, it can happen in Britain. For here the head has more autonomy than in the USA, France or Russia; here there is a tradition of concern among educators with moral education, albeit viewed in a more limited way (Musgrove, 1965); there are some elements in the schools which seem to be making a positive contribution to moral education, so that strengthening these features rather than introducing completely new features can take the process of change a significant way; and the absence of strong local control by the public makes it possible for the schools to move ahead of public opinion, provided they avoid specific areas of sensitivity. There have been signs in recent years of a sudden interest by educators in moral education.

So, I believe, there will be changes in schools in a direction favourable to moral education, especially in Britain and even in the USA. I cling on to this residual optimism for several reasons, besides the fact that temperamentally I find it easier to keep going if I look on the optimistic side. There is a concern among educators to provide an educational experience that is meaningful to their pupils in terms of the problems of becoming an adult and many are aware to some degree of the shortcomings of schools at present. Some see this only in terms of the breakdown of discipline but others see the problem as much wider than this. The traditional place of religion in the British schools has come under doubt and question, leading many educators to be dissatisfied with the old but not knowing what to put in its place. Unlike most American educators, their British colleagues see a definite need for a moral-cum-religious element in the school.

The changes in the British infant schools, which in retrospect look so radical and important, took place over a long period of time and without much benefit of theorists to point the way. The changes we have had under discussion here are, in some respects, more complex and perhaps less likely to happen in the optimum way if just left to the unguided instincts of morally-educated teachers striving to do a better job of education for their pupils. So I hope that this book will be some help in this process and that it will lead to better minds and greater resources than I command being directed to the problems raised here.

In the end, though, moral education stands or falls on the quality of the efforts of the many teachers who earn neither glory nor wealth from their exertions. Sometimes, tragically, they do not even receive the approval from their superiors to which they are surely entitled. Usually, though, they at least get some kind of appreciation from their pupils and invariably the satisfaction of knowing that they are doing what they believe they should be doing. Why do they persist in such strenuous efforts in return for such unspectacular rewards? Why? Because they are themselves morally-educated people.

CHAPTER 10 REFERENCES

Central Advisory Council for Education (England), *Half Our Future*, H.M.S.O, London, 1963.

Jacob W. Getzels and P. W. Jackson, *Creativity and Intelligence*, John Wiley, New York, 1962.

David H. Hargreaves, *Social Relations in Secondary School*, Routledge and Kegan Paul, London, 1967.

Jules Henry, *Jules Henry on Education*, Vintage Books, New York, 1971.

Philip W. Jackson, *Life in Classrooms*, Holt, Rinehart and Winston, New York, 1968.

Lawrence Kohlberg, "Stages and Sequence: The Developmental Approach to Socialization", in D. Goslin (ed.), *Handbook of Socialization Theory and Research*, Rand McNally, Chicago, 1969.

Peter W. Musgrave, *The Sociology of Education*, Methuen, London, 1965.

National Opinion Poll, *Moral and Religious Education: What People Want*, 1969.

John Partridge, *Middle School*, Gollancz, London, 1966.

Everett Reimer, *School is Dead*, Penguin, Harmondsworth, 1971.

Charles E. Silberman, *Crisis in the Classroom*, Random House, New York, 1970.

Willard Waller, *The Sociology of Teaching*, John Wiley, New York, 1932.

Appendix One

THE SCHOOL'S EFFECTS ON PUPILS: A RESEARCH SURVEY

Chapter One of this book ended with a brief reference to some of the research on the effects of inter-school differences on pupils. We concluded there that there seems to be a *prima facie* case for believing that differences between schools can lead to differences in the development of their pupils—differences in the form of probabilities or tendencies only. The evidence from research to date would suggest only that the school *can* make a difference—not that it always does, nor that any difference due to school is large relative to differences resulting from other factors, such as home background. Nor would the state of evidence to date enable us to say with any confidence what specific effects are most often associated with specific school differences.

There has been very little replication of research in this area, so that mostly we have just a single study focusing on a particular set of outcomes and a particular difference between schools. We shall now review the more important studies in this field and some of the methodological problems which are encountered. We may begin with the advantages and disadvantages of prospective (follow-up), retrospective and concurrent or cross-sectional research designs. In many of the studies we shall consider, pupil characteristics are measured concurrently (while they are still attending school); in others they are measured later, some years after pupils have left school.

There are two main problems with concurrent measurement of the variables hypothesised to be *effects* of the school. One is that effects by definition arise later than the factor causing or influencing them and by concurrent measurement one has no way of checking that the supposed effect does in fact occur later. Also it is very difficult with concurrent measurement or cross-sectional study, to separate the differential effects of the school from differences in their populations at the time of intake. The second problem with cross-sectional studies is that one does not know how lasting the effect will be and how dependent it is upon continued reinforcement in school. While this does make a considerable difference to the significance of the findings, even temporary differences are not without interest—especially from the viewpoint of social control in the school.

Retrospective studies involve collecting data long after the school days of the subjects are over. They have the advantage, that information about the dependent variables—the subsequent attitudes, careers or other attributes of the subjects—is more accurate and that one is not dealing with very short-lived effects. There is the disadvantage however, that most information about school conditions when subjects were at school is based on their memories and highly inaccurate due to forgetting and systematic distortion. There is usually very little possibility of objectively verifying what school conditions were like in the past.

The advantages and disadvantages of the cross-sectional and retrospective studies are virtually the mirror-image of each other. Both have the advantage of cheapness and simplicity of administration over the design which is altogether more satisfactory from a scientific point of view, the panel study or longitudinal follow-up design, which involves repeated surveys of the same population while they are still at school (perhaps several times) and then several years later. Few studies have met the requirements of this more demanding design. Apart from considerations of cost, there are also problems of losing subjects from the original sample due to death, migration and loss of patience. In spite of these problems, however, there are good examples of studies using this design. See for example, Chamberlain (1942), McDill and Coleman (1963), Barker-Lunn (1970).

HAS THE SCHOOL ANY EFFECT?

The first two studies we look at are concurrent or cross-sectional in design. At this stage we ask the question in its most simple form: Have we any reasons to suppose that the school can make a difference? Certainly, it is conceded that the major factors which influence children's development lie in the home. That is not in dispute. The question is: given the home background that children have does it make any difference what sort of school they attend? The answer, I shall contend, is that it *may* make a difference, that some schools influence the development of their pupils differently from others.

The two studies we consider now offer some support for this position with respect to two different dependent variables or effects—official juvenile delinquency and altruism measured on attitude questionnaires.

A study of twenty secondary boys' schools in East London (Power *et al.*, 1967) showed that the proportions of boys convicted in the courts varied considerably between schools, four schools having under three per cent and four having over ten per cent. More significantly, they analysed all convictions over a six-year period in terms of the boy's school and neighbourhood of residence. They found that within any school there was little difference in delinquency rates of boys from different districts but substantial differences between boys from similar districts in different schools. In other words, although delinquency rates vary between districts and between schools, the statistical effect of school is greater than that of district. This does not *prove* that schools differ in their ability to prevent or encourage delinquency, but it lends considerable support to this view.

A second study revealing some inter-school differences was concerned with the attitude of altruism as measured by pupils' responses to a questionnaire (Sugarman, 1973). This study, conducted in five comprehensive schools in the rural Midlands was not focused mainly in inter-school difference, as there were too few schools willing to cooperate and the five used were the only ones volunteering. Hence it is impossible to relate the difference observed to any *specific* features of the schools. All we can say is that when the altruism scores of older and younger pupils were compared and the effects of home background (correlated with altruism in the direction of the more intellectually rich backgrounds tending to have more altruistic children) held constant, there were clear differences among these schools. In two schools altruism scores tended to *rise* with the age of pupils; in two schools they seemed to stay at about the same level; while in one school they *declined* with age. Thus the first two schools seem to have the effect of increasing altruistic attitudes and the last one seems to have the effect of decreasing it.

Neither of these studies attempted to specify what features of these schools might explain their different patterns of delinquency and altruism. Other studies have attempted to establish such connections between *specific* features of the school and *specific* outcomes in various areas.

THE EFFECTS OF DIFFERENT STRUCTURES OF ABILITY GROUPING FOR PUPILS

There have been many attempts to determine the effects of different policies for grouping pupils of differing levels of apparent ability or academic learning. Goldberg's (1966) study in US primary schools cast "serious doubt on the effects of ability grouping *per se* in raising the academic attainment of pupils" and suggested that "the pattern of broadest spread appeared to be most consistently associated with greatest academic gains for all pupils" (3–81). The author notes that this conclusion seems to hold in the *absence* of specific plans for adapting the content and methods of teaching to suit each ability level of pupils. Barker-Lunn's (1970) study in British junior schools found some slight overall superiority of streamed pupils on conventional attainment measures but Svensonn's (1962) study in Swedish secondary schools found "no clear-cut differences in achievements between homogeneous and heterogeneous groups" (p. 127). In a critical review of a number of experimental studies of this kind completed before 1961 Ekstrom (1961) again called attention to the importance of teaching methods along with grouping practices, claiming that in studies "that specifically provided for differention of teaching methods and materials, and made an effort to push bright, homogeneous classes, results tended to favour the homogeneous groups" (p. 223).

There is sometimes a confusion in discussions of this question as to whether one is talking about grouping in terms of imputed ability *between* different *classrooms* in the same school, *within* the classroom, or *between* different *schools*. The studies cited in the previous paragraph all refer, so far as I can ascertain, to grouping as between different classrooms—"streaming" versus "non-streaming" in the jargon of the British educationalists. Another important sector of the issue is that concerning grouping as between schools—the "comprehensive" versus "selective" school issue as we know it in Britain. There is strong evidence that the achievement of Negro children in the USA is affected by the composition of the school's intake—the more favourable the socio-economic background of their fellow pupils and the higher their aspirations, the better the achievement of the Negro pupils (Coleman, 1966). This confirms an earlier study by Rogoff (1961) who had shown that the kind of community in which schools were located affected pupils' achievements and aspirations to attend college, on top of the familiar influences of home and IQ, large suburban schools being the most highly favoured and the least favoured being small towns and large city schools.

Comparisons between comprehensive and secondary modern schools on several non-academic criteria are made in the Newsom Report (Central Advisory Council for Education, 1963). Comprehensive pupils truanted less than secondary modern ones, were rated more cooperative over school uniform by their heads, belonged to more school societies (boys only) but were considered less cooperative about discipline by their heads. The last finding, depending as it does on a non-objective rating, may be misleading. It could be, for example, that comprehensive heads set higher standards than secondary modern heads since they have the example of more highly striving pupils before them and hence may have been over-severe in rating their pupils.

Miller (1961) compared the values and social attitudes of pupils with matched IQs from three grammar schools and three secondary moderns with other pupils of similar ability in three comprehensive schools. He found that high ability comprehensive pupils had a higher regard for practical subjects than did grammar school pupils and that low ability comprehensive pupils had a higher regard for academic subjects than did secondary modern pupils. This he calls "narrowing the cultural gap". He found that the amount of agreement between high and low ability comprehensive pupils on the social standing of various occupations was higher than that between grammar school pupils (who upgraded white-collar jobs) and secondary modern pupils (who upgraded manual jobs). This he calls "a tendency for greater social unity". He found, thirdly, that the "quality of leisure interests" (assessed in terms of the proportions of "active" relative to "passive" ones) among average and low ability pupils was higher in the comprehensive schools than in the secondary moderns, while among high ability pupils the comprehensive average was as high as the grammar school. This he calls "raising the cultural level".

The author of this study himself notes one complication in interpreting his results, namely that his comprehensive schools were on the whole newer and characterised by greater enthusiasm among their staff than the segregated schools. This means that the "effects" he finds are due to several factors in unknown proportions: the comprehensiveness of intake, newness of facilities and enthusiasm of staff. All these factors are, however, attributes of the schools proper and this is our main concern for now.

THE EFFECTS OF SCHOOL "ATMOSPHERE" OR "CLIMATE"

Other studies have fallen back on the concept of the "atmosphere" of the school rather than on a single aspect of formal structure. D. E. M. Gardner (1966), in a study of ten-year-old children, distinguished between "sit-still-and-listen" schools and "move-and-talk-and-play" schools. Children from the latter type of schools were clearly superior in listening and remembering, neatness and skill, ingenuity, free drawing and painting, English and interests. They *tended* to be ahead in several other areas, including reading and moral judgements. Children from the "sit-still" schools were clearly ahead in only arithmetic and there was no significant difference in moral conduct.

Several secondary modern schools thought by "experts" to have different atmospheres were studied by W. J. A. Vaughan (1961). He compared four using an academic approach with "restrictive stereotyped teaching" and an "authoritarian" climate and four using a "broad", "developmental" approach, "flexible" teaching methods and a "permissive or democratic" climate. The second group of schools was found to be more effective in developing the following qualities in its boys: emotional stability and independence, ability to assume personal responsibility, ability for self-expression, maturity, knowledge of social structure and its functioning, ability and willingness to participate in discussion of civic affairs, ability to choose an occupation "wisely" and tolerance (p. 262).

Pupils from thirty "progressive" high schools in the USA were followed up into their colleges, where their performance in several areas were compared with those of students from other high schools (Chamberlain, *et al.*, 1942). The graduates of progressive schools excelled in their academic records, were more often judged to be systematic and objective in their thinking, to have intellectual curiosity and drive, and considered more resourceful in meeting new situations. Moreover, they had more non-academic honours awarded to them and did not differ from the control group in adjustment to their peers. They participated more in all organised student groups *except* religious and social service activities.

"School atmosphere" as a concept with which to investigate differences in the effect of different schools on their pupils is not very satisfactory. Its main appeal is that it seems to correspond to the common-sense perceptions of lay observers that there are differences between schools in the way they strike one. There is sometimes an appreciable amount of inter-observer agreement about this—though not always—and some successful attempts have been made to measure differences in atmosphere as perceived by participants. Halpin and Croft used teachers' perceptions to compare (US) elementary schools (Halpin, 1966, Ch. 4). Walberg (1969) has used pupils' perceptions to compare classroom atmospheres across and within schools; Pace and Stern have used undergraduates' perceptions to compare colleges and universities (Stern, 1962); and Revans (1965) has shown that pupils' perceptions of their teachers tend to correlate with teachers' perceptions of their heads and other authority figures.

THE EFFECTS OF TEACHERS' ATTITUDES OR STYLE OF THINKING

In so far as there is any agreement about the sources of the observed differences, it centres on the notion that there is some pervasive quality about personal relations, especially teacher-pupil relations. Certainly, one can reduce many of the hypotheses about school "climate" or "atmosphere" to others about teachers' attitudes to pupils. One can then, in principle, measure these attitudes of teachers independently and see empirically if this is the factor that varies between schools and correlates with the observed effect. "Atmosphere" may mean more than this though. It can include a wide variety of factors, such as the kind of school rules that exist, the provision for pastoral care, the emphasis on different forms of achievement, the degree of mutual support among staff and many things besides. In fact we might define the purpose of this whole book as an attempt to unravel some of the strands that make up this complex fabric of "school atmosphere".

If it is to be reduced to any *single* factor, "teacher's attitude" or "style of teaching" is probably the best. The studies we shall now review do not compare schools but individual teachers with different approaches—often in the same schools. Although the unit of analysis is shifted, the results of this research can be applied to inter-school comparisons equally, in so far as different schools differentially recruit their teachers and expose them to pressures to work in one way rather than another.

A variety of research findings support the common-sense view that differences between teachers are at least among the most important variables affecting the development of pupils. This is especially true in the area of attitude development, more so than in the areas of cognitive learning (Stern, 1963). An early study by Anderson (reported in Gage, 1963, p. 477, and in Brim, 1958, p. 51) focused on two teachers in the kindergarten and the first year of primary school. One of them was more dominating, in the sense of restricting the spontaneous behaviour of pupils, compared to the other. Pupils of the two teachers were carefully observed in the classroom and it is reported that those in the class of the more dominating teacher were seen more often whispering, playing with foreign objects and refusing to carry out requests or orders from the teacher. At the end of the year when this class was succeeded by another group of pupils the new pupils of the dominating teacher were seen to fall soon into the same pattern of behaviour, while those who moved on to the class of the less dominating soon changed their ways of behaving.

A more extensive study, based on ninety teachers of kindergarten and first-grade pupils by Harvey and his associates (1968) has on the whole supported these findings and added some further detail. They found that the more resourceful were the teachers, the less dictatorial and the less punitive (as judged by observers in the classroom), the more their pupils tended to show the following characteristics (again as judged by observers): cooperativeness, involvement, activity, achievement, abstract thought and development and helpfulness.

These teacher studies (both Anderson and Harvey) represent a more sophisticated methodology than any of those previously cited here. In both cases we have an experimental design, that is, although each *individual* pupil is not assigned to one teacher or the other by random methods, pupils are assigned to a class by methods that are random or nearly so and each class is assigned to a teacher by similar methods. The great advantage of this design over the cross-sectional one is that cause and effect can be more confidently identified and when we find a differential effect we can be more confident that it is a result of the difference in the independent variable (in this case the teaching style). The next study we look at is also cast in the experimental mould.

The teachers of older children (thirteen to fourteen years) were studied by Flanders (1964) who also found clear-cut differences in pupil's behaviour and attitudes. Like the Harvey study, this one too was based on observers' measurements of teachers' style and method for the independent variable and both used a quasi-experimental design. Flanders used thirty-one teachers who were classified by the classroom observers into those who used more "direct" or "indirect" styles of teaching. Direct teaching involves heavy teacher domination, while indirect teaching allows for expanded pupil participation in the classroom exchange. The more indirect teachers got better academic achievement from their pupils; their pupils had more favourable attitudes to teacher, class and learning in general; and they had less trouble with discipline. (See Chapter Six of the book for a fuller discussion.)

THE EFFECTS DUE TO TEACHERS COMPARED TO OTHER FACTORS

Other studies have measured the effect of both teacher-related variables and others at the same time and hence were able to estimate the relative importance of these different variables. Goldberg and others (1966), in a large-scale study of ability grouping systems in primary schools, came to the conclusion that the effects on academic learning of the different patterns of ability grouping which they examined were inconsistent and far less important than the effect of differences between teachers. Even IQ differences between pupils made less difference to their attainment than differences between teachers. In their research on cheating and other forms of dishonesty Hartshorne and May (1930) found similarly that differences between classrooms (i.e. between teachers) made more difference to honesty than most of the other variables they examined.

Outcomes of both academic learning and attitude development are included in a study of streamed and unstreamed primary schools by the NFER (Barker-Lunn, 1970). This study looks not only at different kinds of outcomes but also looks specifically at two classes of independent variables associated with the school: the formal structure of the school (streaming versus non-streaming) and teacher attitudes to the job. This research found that *neither* variable made any substantial difference to academic learning (English, reading, arithmetic, number concept, verbal reasoning and non-verbal reasoning). Turning to attitudes towards school and towards self, the survey finds that for above-average ability pupils *neither* school organisation nor teachers' attitudes make much difference. For average and below-average ability pupils, however, *both* of these factors have a significant effect on pupils' attitudes and the way they change over a year. The most significant attitude changes are found in the case of pupils of these ability levels who are taught by teachers favouring non-streaming in non-streamed schools. These pupils tend to see their teachers as more approving of them, to assess their own academic competence more favourably, to be more highly motivated to do well in school and to have favourable attitudes to the other members of their class. Pupils of all ability levels in streamed schools (nearly all taught by teachers favourable to streaming) only increase their scores on two of eight attitude scales. One reason for this was the tendency for pupils of different ability levels to change their attitudes in opposite directions, those of high ability increasing their scores and others decreasing them, thus tending to cancel out in the aggregate.

School organisation and teacher attitudes operate together to affect the development of pupils' attitudes. Attendance at a formally non-streamed school has different consequences for the child compared to the streamed alternative if (but only if) his teachers there have attitudes compatible with the philosophy of non-streamed education. This study suggests, though not explicitly stating it, that the "non-streamed" teacher cannot operate as such in the streamed school. If this is so, the appropriate conclusion about the relative status of these two kinds of variables would seem to be that formal structure and teacher attitudes have roughly equal status as influences on the educational process and its impact on the child. One cannot say that teacher attitude is the more important, since a streamed formal structure obliterates any effects of "non-streamed" teachers. Nor can one say that formal structure is, in general, the more important, since the effect of a non-streamed structure depends in large part on teachers' attitudes. The form of data used and presented in this study does not permit any more precise conclusion on the relative weights of these influences such as one might make on the basis of a two-way analysis of variance.

EXPERIMENTAL DESIGNS

There are serious weaknesses in all these studies if we want to infer from them that differences between the schools caused the observed differences between their pupils in the same sense that the experimental biologist would infer that differences in soil content affect the growth of seeds planted in it. The researcher interested in schools cannot normally allocate his children randomly to different schools (as the biologist can his plants) and so cannot be sure that the schools have similar inputs or "raw material" (see Campbell and Stanley, 1963).

This is the classical experimental procedure. One modification that is often necessary for research using human subjects in ongoing organisations is that subjects cannot be *individually* assigned to different "treatment" groups but must be taken in groups dictated by the structure of the organisation. Thus, in schools it is commonly necessary to assign each of several pre-existing classes of pupils to different teaching methods. A further modification of the classical experimental model is for the researcher to capitalise on a change of methods or the operation of different methods side-by-side, not initiated for the benefit of his research but for the organisation's (or rather, its administrators') own good reasons. Though lacking the classical control over *who* is exposed to the different treatments and *when*, he can still plan his data collection so as to measure whom he wishes, when he wishes. The Flanders and Harvey studies were conducted in fairly close conformity to the classical experimental model (with the modification of *group* assignment to different treatment conditions) and the Chamberlain, Barker Lunn, Goldberg, Gardiner and Vaughan studies represent the "opportunistic" or "naturalistic experiment" designs.

Where studies are based on comparing two groups of pupils who happen to be in different classes and even more when they happen to attend different schools, there are always legitimate worries about the initial similarity of those pupils before exposure to the different treatments. It is possible to measure incoming pupils and test for differences but this depends *firstly* on knowing all the possible relevant variables to measure and *secondly* on being able to measure them. What makes this weakness all the more serious is that differences among schools in their pupil intakes arise not only as random biases but are systematically generated. Certain schools acquire good and bad reputations; the more ambitious and sophisticated parents learn of them and scheme in order to get their children admitted to the supposedly "better" schools. So even if initially that reputation was entirely unjustified it would operate as a self-fulfilling prophecy and the more concentration of children whose parents were both more ambitious than others and more effective manipulators of the system would produce a body of pupils likely to score relatively highly on any tests related to academic achievement, middle-class values, social skills and many related areas.

One way in which researchers have tried to avoid such fallacious findings is to test pupils on admission as well as later (on the same variables) and to take *differences* between the two scores rather than just the later scores. This procedure, superior though it is, still does not preclude the possibility that pupils who were similar at one point of time may still have different profiles of development. For example, although they were similar in academic attainment at the initial time of measurement, it might happen that in between the first and last testing pupils (for example) began to have homework assigned. If some pupils were more able to do their homework conscientiously (whether because their parents supervised them, or because they had more room at home or for whatever reason) and this did not correlate with initial attainment scores, a spurious school effect might easily be attributed.

Another approach to overcoming this problem is by focusing not on the *average* scores in different schools but on the *spread* or *distribution* of these scores. Thus, Coleman (1961, pp. 74–6) studying the values of pupils in nine US high schools, found a narrowing in the spread of scores between first-year pupils and those in their last year. Thus in each school "seniors" are more like each other than "freshmen", though the values for which this operates in the different schools are not always the same. This he attributes to the effect of the pupils' peer groups' social norms. Comparing schools with different normative systems or climates, Coleman ascribes their differences mainly to differences in intake rather than to any difference in the social structure of the schools.

Another version of the same approach was used in a small study in one London school conducted by James Savage and Barry Sugarman. In this study we focused not on value convergence but—because we looked at different values—at polarisation. The values under investigation were those of "future orientation" and we were interested in how the difference between high and low streams would change over time. The school was an all-boys' secondary modern. In each year from the first to the fourth a high and low stream were given attitude questionnaires to fill in. An equivalent high (but not top) stream in each year was chosen to represent the same ability level; so was a low (but not bottom) one. The subjects were asked to respond "agree" or "disagree" to a series of statements designed to tap the attitude or value dimension of "future-orientation" as defined in Chapter Five.

The results showed that in the first year the high stream boys started school with rather higher scores (more future-oriented) than the lower stream boys but this difference was small compared to the difference between fourth-year boys. In the fourth year the future orientation scores of the low stream boys was similar to that of the third-, second- and first-year (low stream) boys, whereas among the high stream boys each year showed a higher average score than the previous one. Now since the high stream represents the pupils who are performing well in terms of the requirements of the school and the low stream represents those performing much less well, we may say that future orientation is not only a factor associated with success in school (see Chapter Five) but it is also a factor that is *increased by successful adaptation* to school. That is, it is both required for success in school (as represented by the difference between scores of high and low streams in the first year) and it is cultivated by the school in those pupils who are in tune to its requirements (as represented by the increase in that difference year by year).

The same polarisation effect was *not* found with respect to the value of altruism also measured by questionnaire. This must mean that altruism is not emphasised in the school to anywhere near the same extent as future orientation is. This research obviously needs replication but its findings so far as they go are both clear and important in their implications.

RETROSPECTIVE STUDIES

The retrospective study classifies the school experiences of the people studied on the basis of their reports after their schooling is over—often many years afterwards. Such an approach has some advantages but also some serious drawbacks. The main drawback is its dependence on the highly unreliable and bias-prone memories of respondents and the fact that no other sources of information about the schools are usually available due to the passage of time. In the kinds of study which we have been reviewing at least the investigator can visit the schools; can make his own observations and examine documents; and can interview, test and observe aspects of the school and educational process the effects of which he is trying to assess. Counter-balancing these serious disadvantages, the retrospective study has the advantage of providing data pertinent to the question of the *long-term* consequences of schooling. All the studies reviewed so far have focused on very short-term consequences, several years at the most but typically only a few months. In principle these concurrent or prospective studies can be extended to follow-up periods of much greater length but the cost is very great. The retrospective study has the merit of relative cheapness compared to the long-term follow-up study.

Almond and Verba (1963) in a retrospective study surveyed adults in five nations to get information on political attitudes and behaviour, as well as experiences in earlier life, in order to explain differences in "civic competence" or the subjective feeling of being able to participate effectively in the process of affecting governmental decisions and being interested in so doing.

Adults who were high on civic competence tended to be those who reported that they had had some influence in family decisions when they were teenagers, who had some freedom in school to discuss unfair treatment and to take part in discussions or debates, who at work considered that they were consulted and felt themselves free to protest decisions they disliked. The general picture is one in which people grow up learning about the sharing of power and the possibility of individual influence from concrete experiences in family, school and work. Their attitudes to politics and the role of the citizen tend to be generalised from these earlier, more parochial but more meaningful experiences, in so far as they are broadly consistent.

Where there are clear inconsistencies some interesting consequences seem to follow. This can be seen in considering the two areas of power-sharing in formal organisations—school and work. We shall look at the data for the UK (Table 27, p. 367). Respondents who report participation in both situations produce 77 per cent with high civic competence scores; those participating in neither produce 57 per cent. Those participating in work although they had not previously in school fall exactly mid way (67 per cent but those who reported participation in school followed by non-participation at work produced the lowest level of civic competence of all (34 per cent). The effects of school and work are not simply additive. Apparently, being introduced in school to authority relationships in which one has some rights of protest and discussion creates an expectation that such rights belong to one in other areas too and finding that such rights are denied when one moves on to the world of work tends to create a feeling of disillusionment and impotence which is generalised also to the area of politics and citizenship.

CONCLUSION

It is acutely frustrating to all who are concerned with education, whether as parents, practitioners, or planners, that we have no better knowledge of the probable effects on pupils of different methods of running schools. Our review of some research findings has referred to some of the practical and methodological difficulties involved in attempts to build up this kind of knowledge.* A less obvious difficulty is that our understanding of the basic social dynamics of the school is so inadequate. We are not sure whether to regard it as a social institution with a prevailing "atmosphere" which determines its effects; as a bureaucratic organisation which programmes a set of educational experiences

* Some valuable further discussion of the methodological problems entailed in this sort of enterprise can be found in Barton, 1959, a detailed critique of Phillip Jacobs' study, *Changing Values in College,* Harper, New York, 1957.

by careful administration; as a quasi-tribal group with its own rituals and loyalties; as an immensely complex web of individual relationships between teachers and pupils; or as all of these at once. Until we have a clearer idea about how to view the school and the many-sided processes of learning taking place there, we shall continue to be crippled in our ability to even formulate fruitful hypotheses to be put to empirical test. This belief underlies the whole of this book, which presents no major new findings but does, I believe, present some important new perspectives on these issues and the basis for a viable view of the school and how it affects its pupils.

APPENDIX I REFERENCES

Gabriel A. Almond and Sidney Verba, *The Civic Culture*, Princeton University Press, Princeton, NJ, 1963.

Joan C. Barker-Lunn, *Streaming in the Primary School*, National Federation for Education Research, Slough, 1970.

Allen H. Barton, *Studying the Effects of College Education*, Edward W. Hazen Foundation, New Haven, 1959.

Orville G. Brim, Jr., *Sociology and the Field of Education*, Russell Sage Foundation, New York, 1958.

Donald T. Campbell and J. C. Stanley, "Experimental and Quasi-Experimental Designs for Research", in N. L. Gage (1963), op. cit.

Central Advisory Council for Education (England), *Half Our Future*, H.M.S.O., London, 1963, pp. 232–3.

Dean Chamberlain *et al.*, *Did They Succeed in College?*, Harper, New York, 1942. Summarised in N. L. Gage (ed.), *Handbook of Research on Teaching*, Rand McNally, Chicago, 1963, pp. 471–2.

James S. Coleman, *The Adolescent Society*, The Free Press, New York, 1961.

James S. Coleman, *Equality of Educational Opportunity*, US Dept. of Health, Education and Welfare, 1966.

Ruth B. Ekstrom, "Experimental Studies of Homogeneous Grouping: A Critical Review", *School Review*, LXIX, Summer, 1961, pp. 216–26.

Ned A. Flanders, "Some Relationships among Teacher Influence, Pupil Attitudes and Achievement", in Bruce J. Biddle and W. J.

Ellena (eds.), *Contemporary Research on Teacher Effectiveness*, Holt, Rinehart and Winston, New York, 1964.

N. L. Gage (ed.), *Handbook of Research in Teaching*, Rand McNally, Chicago, 1963.

D. E. M. Gardner, *Experiment and Tradition in Primary Schools*, Methuen, London, 1966.

Miriam L. Goldberg, *et al.*, *The Effects of Ability Grouping*, Teacher's College Press, New York, 1966.

Andrew W. Halpin, *Theory and Research in Administration*, Macmillan, London, 1966, Ch. 4.

Hugh Hartshorne and M. A. May, *Studies in Deceit*, Macmillan, New York, 1930.

O. J. Harvey *et al.*, "Teachers' beliefs, classroom atmosphere and student behavior", *American Journal of Educational Research*, V, 1968, pp. 151–66.

E. L. McDill and J. S. Coleman, "High School Social Status, College Plans and Interest in Academic Achievement: A Panel Analysis", *American Sociological Review*, XXVII, Dec., 1963, pp. 905–18.

T. W. G. Miller, *Values in the Comprehensive School*, Oliver and Boyd, London, 1961.

M. J. Power *et al.*, "Delinquent Schools?", *New Society*, Oct. 19, 1967.

R. V. Revans, "Involvement in School", *New Society*, Aug. 26, 1965.

Natalie Rogoff, "Local Social Structure and Educational Selection", in A. H. Halsey *et al.* (eds.), *Education, Economy and Society*, Free Press, Glencoe, Ill., 1961, pp. 242–51.

George G. Stern, "Measuring Non-cognitive Variables in Research on Teaching" in N. L. Gage (1963), op. cit., pp. 398–447.

George G. Stern, "Environments for Learning", in N. Stanford (ed.), *The American College*, John Wiley, New York, 1962, pp. 690–730.

Barry Sugarman, "Altruistic Attitudes in School", *Journal of Moral Ed.*, II, Feb., 1973, pp. 145–57.

Nils-Eric Svenson, *Ability Grouping and Scholastic Achievement*, Stockholm Studies in Educational Psychology 5; Amquist and Wiksell, 1962.

W. J. A. Vaughan, "A Study of Different Psychological Climates in Secondary Modern Schools", unpub. Ph.D. Thesis, London University, 1961.

Herbert J. Walberg, "Social Environment as a Mediator of Classroom Learning", *J. Ed. Psych.*, LX, 1969, pp. 443–8.

Appendix Two

SOCIOLOGICAL STUDIES OF SCHOOLS: A REVIEW OF LITERATURE

Between the publication of Willard Waller's *The Sociology of Teaching* (1932) and the recent spate of studies of schools there is a gap of nearly thirty years. We may classify these publications into four categories: studies of single schools, several schools of one type, single classrooms, and several types of school.

Studies of single schools include Fichter's (1958) study of a Catholic elementary school in the USA; Gordon's study of a suburban high school in the USA (1957); Hollingshead's study of social class divisions among *Elmtown's Youth* (1949), which contains some valuable material on the communal high school; the study by Hargreaves (1967) of a secondary modern school in Salford, Lancashire; that by Lacey (1966) of a grammar school in the same town; Brown's unpublished thesis (1955) describing a grammar school in London's East End; and Wylie's (1957) study of a French provincial village and its local school, forerunner of a whole series of studies by anthropologists of schools in different cultures and their interdependence with the local community (see, for example, King, Singleton, Warren, Walcott).

All of these studies have in common an attempt to collect some "objective" data (usually in the form of questionnaire responses by pupils) which they present in partial support of their interpretations. Two further studies of real value depend completely on observational data presented without quantification: Brian Jackson's (1964) description of a primary school and Partridge's (1966) account of one secondary modern school based on his experiences as a *bona fide* member of staff—by contrast with the "participant observer" roles of many of the authors previously cited, who had some quasi-staff position although their colleagues knew that their main role was that of researcher.

Studies of *several schools of one type* vary more widely in their perspectives, since the larger field they have undertaken necessitates even more drastic selectivity in the analysis than we find in the studies just cited. Coleman's (1961) widely-known study of ten Midwestern high schools is noted for his ambitious use of quantified data to support his dramatic thesis concerning the power of the peer group and the impotence of the teachers in affecting the aspirations and academic achievement of pupils; Blyth (1965) offers a "sociological description" of English state primary schools and Taylor (1963) does a similar job for the secondary modern schools; the ILEA report on *London Comprehensive Schools*, 1966 gives some useful descriptions of formal organisation, its varieties and rationales; Skidelsky's study of *English Progressive Schools* (1969) focuses on the educational ideologies of three such schools with briefer references to several others; accounts of the independent boarding school are provided by Bamford (1967) (mainly historical and dealing with the Victorian reforms), by Lambert and his associates (1969) (contemporary data gathered by extensive observation, interviewing and use of questionnaires) and by Wilson (1962) (mainly impressionistic); Bereday, Brickman and Read (1960) provide a useful account of *The Changing Soviet School*, virtually the only contribution from the whole field of comparative education that gives us any information about what goes on within the four walls of the schools (aside from studies of syllabus content and age structure of school populations).

All the British government reports on education, which were numerous and weighty in the ten years 1959–69, contribute little to our knowledge of how the school works as a social organisation. The Plowden Report, *Children and their Primary Schools* (1966) gives only two chapters out of thirty-two to the discussion of "The Child in the School Community" and "How Primary Schools are Organized"; the Newsom Report, *Half our Future* (1963), shows the same lack of interest in these matters; and the Crowther Report, 15–18 (published in 1959), shows only a little more interest in problems of social organisation in its discussion of new forms of provisions that might in future be made for further education and of changes in sixth-form education.

Studies on the smallest possible scale, those of *the single classroom* have recently become voguish and have even given rise to the coy title of "the microsociology of the school". A number of the studies already cited include classroom observation among their methods of data collection (Lacey, for example) but here we shall restrict mention to those based exclusively on research in one classroom. Jules Henry (1965) pioneered this approach; Smith and Geoffrey (1968) made a year-long study which they conducted as a shared enterprise involving both the class-teacher and full-time researcher-observer; Philip Jackson (1968) developed equally meticulous methods using a high degree of quantification of observations. Flanders (1964) must be mentioned too for his important research on teaching styles and the resulting effects on teacher-pupil interaction patterns and pupil behaviour. Unlike the previously cited works, he has collected data in a number of classrooms, arranged his study design in quasi-experimental form and used his data to test hypotheses as opposed to mere description. We refer to this work in detail in Chapter Six.

Finally, in this review, we come to studies dealing with *several types of school* and those operating at a high level of generality that do not specify type. Sexton's analysis of *The American School* (1966) discusses some matters of key sociological importance, such as power in the school system, communication problems among staff and the standardisation of the education process; Dreeben (1968) tries to show how some of the typical features of the social structure of schools provide experimental situations from which pupils can learn certain important values and social skills that they could not learn from the family; Riesman and his associates in *The Lonely Crowd* (1950), in their wide-ranging interpretation of changes in the American social structure and national character, have a little to say about what the change implies for the role of teacher and the pattern of schooling; and, operating on the same broad historical canvas, Margaret Mead (1961) depicts three contrasted images of the school—the elite academy, the traditional, small rural school and the inner-city school serving a host of immigrants. An impressively wide-ranging and perceptive account of what goes on within the four walls of a variety of different kinds of schools in different countries is by the journalist Martin Mayer (1961). One may wish that more journalists had his insight and interest in the school. Indeed, one may wish that more social scientists did.

APPENDIX 2 REFERENCES

T. W. Bamford, *The Rise of the Public Schools*, Nelson, London, 1967.

George Z. Bereday, W. W. Brickman and G. H. Read (eds.), *The Changing Soviet School*, Constable, London, 1960.

W. A. L. Blyth, *English Primary Education, A Sociological Description*, 2 vols., Routledge and Kegan Paul, London, 1965.

Morven S. Brown, "A Sociological Study of a Grammar School in a Working-class Community", unpub. Ph.D. Thesis, London University, 1950.

Central Advisory Council for Education, *Children and Their Primary Schools* (Plowden), H.M.S.O., London, 1966.

Central Advisory Council for Education, 15–18 (Crowther), H.M.S.O., London, 1959.

Central Advisory Council for Education, *Half Our Future*, (Newsom), H.M.S.O., London, 1963.

James S. Coleman, *The Adolescent Society*, Free Press, New York, 1961.

Robert Dreeben, *On What is Learned in School*, Addison Wesley, Reading, Mass., 1968.

Joseph H. Fichter, *Parochial School*, Notre Dame, University of Notre Dame Press, 1958.

C. Wayne Gordon, *The Social System of a High School*, Free Press, Glencoe, Ill., 1957.

David H. Hargreaves, *Social Relations in a Secondary School*, Routledge and Kegan Paul, London, 1967.

Jules Henry, *Culture Against Man*, Random House, New York, 1965.

August B. Hollingshead, *Elmtown's Youth*, John Wiley, New York, 1949.

ILEA, *London Comprehensive Schools*, 1966, ILEA, London, 1967.

Brian Jackson, *Streaming: An Education System in Miniature*, Routledge and Kegan Paul, London, 1964, Ch. 4.

Philip Jackson, *Life in Classrooms*, Holt, Rinehart and Winston, New York, 1968.

A. Richard King, *The School at Mopass: A Problem of Identity*, Holt, Rinehart and Winston, New York, 1967.

Colin Lacey, "Some Sociological Concomitants of Academic Streaming in Grammar School", *B.J.S.*, XVII, Sept., 1966.

Royston Lambert *et al.*, *New Wine in Old Bottles?*, Occasional papers in *Social Admin.*, no. 28, Bell, London, 1969.
Martin Mayer, *The Schools*, Harper, New York, 1961.
Margaret Mead, "The School in American Culture", in A. H. Halsey *et al.*, (eds.), *Education, Economy and Society*, Free Press, New York, 1961, pp. 36–41.
John Partridge, *Middle School*, Gollancz, London, 1966.
David Riesman *et al.*, *The Lonely Crowd*, Doubleday, Garden City, NY, 1950.
Patricia Sexton, *The American School*, Prentice Hall, Englewood Cliffs, NJ, 1966.
Robert Skidelsky, *English Progressive Schools*, Penguin, Harmondsworth, 1969.
John Singleton, *Nichu: A Japanese School*, Holt, Rinehart and Winston, New York, 1967.
Louis Smith and W. Geoffrey, *The Complexities of an Urban Classroom*, Holt, Rinehart and Winston, New York, 1968.
William Taylor, *The Secondary Modern School*, Faber, London, 1963.
Willard Waller, *The Sociology of Teaching*, John Wiley, New York, 1932.
Richard A. Warren, *Education in Rebhausen: A German Village*, Holt, Rinehart and Winston, New York, 1967.
John Wilson, *Public Schools and Private Practice*, Allen and Unwin, London, 1962.
Harry F. Wolcott, *A Kwakiutl Village and School*, Holt, Rinehart and Winston, New York, 1967.
Lawrence Wylie, *Village in the Vaucluse*, Harvard University Press, Cambridge, Mass., 1957.

Index